A Road Map to War

A ROAD MAP TO WAR

Territorial Dimensions
of International Conflict

Edited by
Paul F. Diehl

Vanderbilt University Press
Nashville and London

First edition 1999
99 00 01 02 03   5 4 3 2 1

This publication is made from paper that meets
the minimum requirements of ANSI/NISO Z39.48 (R 1997)
Permanence of Paper for Printed Library Materials (∞)

Library of Congress Cataloging-in-Publication Data

A road map to war : territorial dimensions of international
conflict / edited by Paul F. Diehl. -- 1st ed.
    p. cm.
  Includes bibliographical references and index.
  ISBN 0-8265-1311-5 (cloth : alk. paper)
  ISBN 0-8265-1329-8 (pbk. : alk. paper)
    1. International relations. 2. World politics--1945- 3. Boundary
disputes. 4. Partition, Territorial. I. Diehl, Paul F. (Paul
Francis)
  JZ1242 .R63 1998
  320.1'2--dc21
                                        98-40129
                                        CIP

Manufactured in the United States of America

CONTENTS

Part IV. Territory and the Resolution of Conflict

Part V. The Future of Territorial Conflict

ACKNOWLEDGMENTS

This project was completed with the generous support of many individuals and organizations. The idea for a collection of writings on territorial conflict was first suggested to me by Glenn Palmer. Through his support and that of Stuart Bremer, a special issue on territorial conflict appeared in the journal *Conflict Management and Peace Science* in 1996. Five of the articles from that special issue are reprinted, some in revised form, in this book. I owe special thanks to the Peace Science Society (International) for granting me permission to reprint those articles. John Vasquez and Gary Goertz were most helpful, in that each of them reviewed several articles in this compilation, and their suggestions resulted in significant improvements. Vanderbilt University Press and its editor Charles Backus nurtured and improved the project, and I benefited from the suggestions of two anonymous reviewers whose ideas helped broaden and deepen the collection. Finally, Phyllis Koerner was instrumental in preparing yet another manuscript of mine, with good humor and efficiency amid rushed deadlines and sometimes mystifying computer formats.

INTRODUCTION

Territory and International Conflict: An Overview

Paul F. Diehl

Territory has always been considered a central part of international relations theory, in particular the study of international conflict. Early geopolitical writings, such as those of Alfred Mahan, Nicholas Spykman, or Halford Mackinder, put geographical concerns at the center of theories of international security. More recently, territorial components of international conflict models have assumed a less prominent and less deterministic role. Scholars have commonly used geographical contiguity to define a population of "politically relevant" dyads in which some meaningful possibility of militarized conflict is said to exist; generally, though, geography plays little or no role in the explanations of the initiation or escalation of that conflict. Other models use geographical distance as a limiting or discounting factor in estimations of a state's military capability, employing the principle of the "loss-of-strength gradient" (Boulding 1962; Lemke 1995). Finally, geographical contiguity is said to act as a facilitating condition for the spread or diffusion of conflict (Siverson and Starr 1991). Again, however, territorial concerns do not play a central role in national choices for war.

The decline of territorial concerns in international conflict research roughly parallels the historical decline of colonialism and the age of empire building from the acquisition of *terra nullis*. As the twentieth century draws to a close, states are no longer seeking to gain new territories from colonialism—indeed, most dependent territories have been relinquished—and few, if any, unclaimed, inhabitable parts of the world remain. Although territory, on the face of it, would seem less important to international relations now than in the past, a closer inspection reveals the continuing salience of geographical concerns in international conflict decisions. According to Holsti (1991), territory remains the prime issue of war between states, even in the contemporary era. Furthermore, the end of the cold war represents a renewal of territorial concerns in international relations, for ethnic and nationalist conflicts, many which are intimately and inexorably tied to territorial claims, have returned to the forefront. The war in the former Yugoslavia and the continuing dispute between Israel and Syria over the Golan Heights demonstrate that territorial concerns are central to contemporary and future international conflict behavior (see chapter 9 by Andrew Kirby and chapter 10 by Saul B. Cohen in this volume).

This book is designed to restore territorial concerns to a more central location in models of international conflict. Geography should not occupy a unicausal, deterministic position, as was common in early geopolitical writings, but neither should it be treated only as a "facilitating condition" (Diehl 1991) or a case-selection device in models of international conflict. Rather, territorial concerns belong as one of several important factors that directly affect how, when, and where states decide to use military force in pursuit of national objectives. In this sense, this collection is a continuation of recent work by Goertz and Diehl (1992b), Kacowicz (1994), Vasquez (1995), and Huth (1996) that looks at how territorial concerns condition interstate conflict behavior.

Thus the contributors' purpose is to explore the role of territory in the conceptualization, initiation, escalation, recurrence, resolution, and future of militarized interstate conflict. Although this body of work by no means represents the final or definitive word on the territorial dimensions of conflict, we hope that our results both clarify the important role that territory has in international conflict behavior and stimulate further research that more precisely specifies the general relationships reported here.

CONCEPTIONS OF TERRITORIAL IMPORTANCE

As is evident in the empirical sections, conflicts over territory are more likely to involve military force and escalate to war than are disputes

over other issues. Yet we know that not all territorial conflicts become militarized, and some are easily resolved. In fact, approximately
three-quarters of all territorial changes are completed without violence (Goertz and Diehl 1992b). This raises the questions of what it is
about territory that makes states willing to fight over it and why it is
that one territory is considered more valuable than another.

Various authors have sought to define the elements of territorial
importance. Generally, and under a variety of labels, two dimensions
of territory make it valuable to the sovereign who controls it. The first
dimension is what I have referred to elsewhere as the "intrinsic" importance of territory (Goertz and Diehl 1992b), or what elsewhere is
referred to as its tangible or "concrete" value (see chapter 1 by David
Newman in this volume).

This intrinsic importance of territory, in turn, has several aspects.
One is the natural resource base: the availability and control of minerals, energy sources, and water. In earlier times, primacy was placed
on the accessibility of the ocean, because trade and military power
were determined largely by naval capability. Although access to port
facilities is still important, greater emphasis is now placed on mineral
and other resources in a territory. Most prominently, oil reserves are
cited as elements that make otherwise barren territories, such as
Kuwait, valuable. Still other territories have economic value in that
they provide markets for the sovereign. Much of the colonial expansion in the nineteenth century was predicated on such a mercantilist
strategy. A final economic value is the utility that territory may have
for agricultural production or for other purposes, such as the expansion of tax collection in order to strengthen the state.

A second aspect of intrinsic importance is the strategic value that
the territory provides a state. Many of the early geostrategic conceptions of territory emphasized this aspect. For example, control over
the "Heartland" (Mackinder 1919), a central section of the Eurasian
landmass, was thought to be essential for security; indeed, global
domination might result for whoever controlled it. Now, the size and
configuration of territorial holdings may be critical in assuring the national security of a state (see chapter 3 by John Vanzo in this volume).

Finally, sovereignty over a territory signifies control over the population within those borders. This can be a tremendous benefit if the
population is large and the working-age citizens are educated and

highly skilled. Such a population can assist in economic development by permitting advanced economies of scale as well as offering the prospect for a mass army with a minimum of economic dislocation. Territory can also provide additional space for a growing population, a value that is sometimes exploited for propaganda purposes, as evidenced by Nazi Germany's quest for Lebensraum.

The value of a territory is not confined to its intrinsic elements. Indeed, mounting evidence suggests that another dimension of territorial importance may have a greater influence on a state's willingness to fight over territory: "relational" (Goertz and Diehl 1992b), intangible, or symbolic importance (see chapter 1). Unlike intrinsic importance, with respect to relational importance, a territorial characteristic may be considered vital to one disputant but largely insignificant to its rival.

The concept of relational importance has several features. One is the ethnic composition of the populace that occupies the territory. States may attach a high value to territory where people of a common national background reside. Somewhat related to ethnic considerations are the linguistic and religious ties between the population in a state and those in the disputed territory. In either case, states may be willing to fight in order unite or reunite "common" peoples, even though the intrinsic value of the affected territory may be quite limited; the war between Ethiopia and Somalia over the Ogaden is indicative of such a motivation.

Beyond ethnic, religious, or linguistic commonality, territories may be considered valuable because of an intangible historical value attributed to them by some states. The Israeli annexation of some territory occupied in the 1967 war was rooted in its historical claim that the areas were part of the ancient Jewish homeland. Similarly, some Syrians regard Lebanon as part of "Greater Syria."

As an illustration of how territorial value is conceptualized, chapter 1 by David Newman examines the changes in the concrete and symbolic values attached to territory in the Arab-Israeli conflict through the course of its history. From a principally Israeli perspective, Newman shows that the disputed territories of the West Bank, Golan Heights, and Jerusalem have some significant intrinsic value: for example, to expand agricultural cultivation and to ensure access for freshwater supplies. Territory is also a strategic asset for Israel, and this has provided the rationale for continued occupation of the so-called security zone in southern Lebanon. Finally, Newman discusses the concrete value of disputed territory as "demographic container." Yet territorial ambitions in the Middle East have always been driven at least as much by the intangible characteristics of the disputed territory as by its concrete value. Thus, Newman illustrates the religious and historical values that are part of territorial claims in the region. He concludes with an analysis of the implications of five major phases of territorial change in the area. Both concrete and symbolic aspects of territorial importance have played a major role in those configurations and will likely condition the politics and prospects for violence in the Arab-Israeli relationship for years to come.

THE ORIGINS OF TERRITORIAL CONFLICT

One of the key issues of international conflict research is how such conflict begins. For our purposes, we are especially concerned with the role of territory in the origins of militarized conflict. States regularly have disputes of all varieties, including trade and human rights, with other states. Similarly, states often have territorial claims against their neighbors. Such claims may stem from a range of different disagreements over territorial sovereignty.

The distinction between territorial disputes and other disputes is not straightforward: it encounters at least four problems. First, at one level, one may regard almost all disputes between states as having a territorial component. Most obvious are conflicts over the delineation of an international border or a given piece of territory, as occurred between Argentina and Chile over the Beagle Channel. More problematic are cases involving disputes over resources—for example, Iraq's complaints against Kuwait—when control over those resources is tied to control over the territory in which they are located. Even more difficult to distinguish are ethnic or religious conflicts when such differences are intimately tied to specific territories—in Jerusalem or in Kashmir, for instance. Definitions must distinguish between those disputes that are primarily over territory and those that merely have a territorial component.

Much of how one views different kinds of territorial disputes is determined by the breadth of one's definition of the phenomena. Broad definitions of territorial disputes, such as that by Huth (1996), naturally lead to identifying multiple types. Others analysts focus exclusively on one type of territorial dispute: the delineation of an international border. Indeed, an obvious distinction among territorial disputes is the difference between border/boundary disputes and other kinds of disputes. The former include both serious and minor differences over the exact location of a dividing line between states; this is what Friedrich Kratochwil, Paul Rohrlich, and Harpreet Mahajan (1985) refer to as a "positional" dispute. The latter include disputes over dependent or colonial properties, competing claims to large tracts of territory, or politically/economically strategic areas—for example, Walvis Bay in Namibia—that are not necessarily centered on national border areas. Although such distinctions may be useful in classification, differentiating disputes on these kinds of dimensions has primarily served a descriptive, rather than a theoretical, function.

Stephen Kocs (1995) makes the distinction between previously resolved and never-resolved disputes. Previously resolved disputes are something of a misnomer, in that the disputes may be ongoing, but some legal entity—a treaty or some other agreement—has at one time established a boundary location or territorial ownership. Even when territorial claims are ongoing and competing, not all of them involve the threat of militarized action or the actual escalation of the conflict beyond the militarized threshold. One key concern is to determine when such claims lead to militarized action and then they remain more benign.

In chapter 2, Paul Huth looks at the role of territorial claims since 1950 in the origins of enduring rivalries. He adopts a broad, yet precise, definition: "a territorial dispute involves either a disagreement between states over where their common homeland or colonial borders should be fixed, or, more fundamentally, the dispute entails one country contesting the right of another country even to exercise sovereignty over some or all of its homeland or colonial territory" (Huth 1996, 19). Although the number of ongoing claims over territory in this period is large, not all of the claims have resulted in militarized disputes or the development of long-standing rivalries. The rivalry element is particularly important, in that enduring rivalries represent the most serious threats to international peace and security (Goertz and Diehl 1992a). Huth uses a modified realist model, which includes both domestic and international political factors, to explain how states become involved in enduring rivalries over territory. Importantly, he notes that the relative strength of the challenger does not have much of an effect and that states also do not frequently challenge allies or extant treaty commitments by resorting to militarized action. Rather, domestic concerns, especially ethnic and linguistic ties between one's own population and the people in the disputed territory, are significantly associated with the recurrence of militarized conflict. Such findings are of special policy concern, given the renewal of nationalism and ethnic conflict in the post–cold war era.

Chapter 3 by John Vanzo considers whether states are motivated by security concerns in seeking territorial alterations, many of which would necessitate the use of military force to modify their borders. From his analysis comes a basis for ascertaining some of the security concerns that underlie state attempts to change their borders. Using geographical information systems (GIS) analysis, he presents what may be the first empirical test of Lewis Richardson's proposition that states pursue a goal of geographical "compactness"—borders of nearly round or rectangular shape, with short borders spread evenly around a central region, thereby making it easier to defend—through territorial expansion. This proposition suggests that some territorial disputes have their origins in the expansionist desires of states that wish to reconfigure their borders to enhance national security. Vanzo looks at the historical development of Israeli and German borders to see whether changes in those borders reflect a strategy of compactness; competing explanations are also tested. His results find strong support for the compactness strategies, and he notes that compactness is also a concern when victors in a war impose settlements on losing states.

THE DYNAMICS OF TERRITORIAL CONFLICT

Not only are territorial concerns significant in generating militarized conflict, they also play a role in the dynamics of conflict behavior between the disputants. Given militarized conflict, the presence of central territorial issues in the dispute has a significant impact on the behavior of the disputants. In his "steps-to-war" model, Vasquez (1993, 1995) has argued that the absence of a boundary dispute between two rivals all but ensures that the conflict will not escalate to war. In the study of international conflict in general, evidence is also increasing that the presence of territorial issues in a dispute significantly increases the hostility levels and prospects for escalation. The two chapters in this section present empirical evidence of the impact that territorial disputes—vis- à-vis other types of disputes—have on militarized conflict behavior.

Paul Hensel looks at more than 2,000 militarized disputes since 1816 and assesses the behavior of states when territorial issues are involved. He finds that territory-based disputes are generally more severe and more likely than other disputes to prompt violent responses from the target of the initial militarized action (whereas many other disputes end quickly when the target states do not respond with military actions and/or launch diplomatic initiatives). This finding should not, however, imply that territorial conflicts are easily resolved. Indeed, he finds that territorial conflict is more likely to recur and to do so in a shorter period of time than are disputes over nonterritorial issues. In effect, Hensel implies that territorial conflict is more likely to evolve into an enduring rivalry (and Huth pinpoints when this occurs). These findings confirm the danger of territory-based conflict and are consistent with John Vasquez's (1993, 1995) formulations.

Paul Senese extends the preceding analyses of the territorial dimensions of dispute behavior: he examines the same militarized disputes as did Hensel, but his analysis also has several unique elements. First, many of the contributors to this book analyze the impact that territorial issues have on state behavior, but Senese also considers geographical contiguity, an important element of many writings on geopolitics and conflict. In addition, he focuses on the escalation of conflict, effectively considering how territorial issues and geographical proximity affect the bargaining behavior of states in militarized disputes. He confirms Hensel's findings that territorial disputes are more severe overall than are other conflicts, and he also notes that geographical contiguity contributes to greater severity (because it may be easier to project military force close to home). Yet he finds no strong evidence that geographical concerns lead to the escalation of disputes; that is, geography is an important influencing on the probability that militarized conflict will arise and may even affect the severity of the initial actions in the conflict, but other processes—involving, for example, democratic regimes—determine whether states will choose a progressively more hostile series of actions during a dispute.

The research reported thus far in this volume illustrates that territory is an important component in the development of militarized conflict, increases its severity, and promotes its recurrence. Yet territorial concerns apparently do not have much of an impact on the escalation of conflict once that conflict has begun.

TERRITORY AND THE RESOLUTION OF CONFLICT

The next three chapters in this compendium consider the role that territory can play in the termination or resolution of militarized conflict. This consideration is rarely given much attention in the scholarly literature, yet one of the keys to understanding the recurrence of conflict, especially enduring rivalries, is to know how the cycle of conflict can be broken. Among the key concerns is whether states can actually agree to resolve their territorial disputes peacefully, most commonly through international treaties and agreements. Given such an agreement, additional central considerations are whether those agreements will hold and whether future disputes are actually handled through constructive and peaceful channels. This section of the book looks at the viability of territorial-settlement treaties—when states choose legal mechanisms to resolve their territorial disputes— and at how states may construct those agreements so that they are perceived as fair by the parties involved.

In his survey of alliances, Douglas Gibler discovers that a significant portion of peaceful alliances contained territorial-settlement agreements; that is, the agreements resolved long-standing territorial claims between states. Critically, he reports that alliances of this variety were not followed by war. In effect, the territorial-settlement treaties removed one of the contentious issues between states and ushered in an era of peaceful relations (again consistent with the argument made by Vasquez 1993, 1995). Thus, territorial settlement treaties may be one key to ending war and rivalries between states.

If territorial settlement treaties can indeed resolve the most serious conflict between states, what happens when disagreements arise over the provisions of those agreements? Do mechanisms other than treaties, such as appeals to third-party legal mechanisms, exist for achieving peaceful resolution of territorial conflicts? On one hand, there is reason to expect that states may be reluctant to place an issue as important as territory—to some degree, the great propensity for violence in territorial disputes is indicative of the importance that states attach to territory—in the hands of third parties. Legal solutions run the risk of being zero-sum and run contrary to the expectations of realpolitik views, which argue that states will resort to self-help mechanisms, rather than supranational ones, in addressing key security issues.

Beth Simmons explores the conditions associated with various legal aspects of territorial dispute resolution. She first models when states will consent to an agreement that mandates binding arbitration in the case of border disputes. Surprisingly, this willingness to arbitrate is largely the result of a failure to ratify a boundary treaty; that is, states that have domestic difficulty in approving territorial agreements may bind themselves to arbitration partly in order to insulate the dispute-resolution process from the domestic political arena. This, of course, begs the question about the conditions under which states will reject boundary treaties that would have settled their territorial disputes. (Note that such cases of failed treaty ratifications do not appear in Gibler's analysis, which includes only fully operational agreements). Simmons thus looks at the factors that affect ratification failure. Surprisingly, nondemocratic states have more difficulty with ratification than do their democratic counterparts, although she has a compelling explanation for the surprising finding that domestic political factors are more influential in authoritarian states than in nonauthoritarian ones. In addition, states closer to equality in capabilities are more likely to have difficulties in ratification; in asymmetrical pairs of states, the weaker side may have no choice but to ratify, whereas the stronger state may be expected to sign only an agreement that is clearly favorable to its interests and that is, therefore, easily ratified.

Lastly, Simmons investigates when the treaty commitment to arbitration is manifested in actual arbitration rulings on territorial disputes. She finds that general multilateral treaty commitments to arbitrate are not necessarily successful in promoting legal resolution of territorial conflict. Rather specific and ad hoc commitments seem to promote actual arbitration; this is likely because the commitment to arbitrate is directly tied to the territorial dispute in question.

In addition to alliances or arbitration, multiple ways of securing the settlement of a territorial dispute exist. Yet a formal agreement or an apparently binding arbitration decision is not an automatic guarantee that conflict will not recur (Goertz and Diehl 1992b). What is necessary is that the settlement continue to be acceptable to all parties, to be regarded as fair. The greater the degree of perceived fairness, the more likely it is that the settlement will endure: some territorial conflicts may appear to be settled, but in the long run a settlement agreement provides only an interregnum in militarized conflict. Thus, more than just the process of territorial settlement—the subject of the previous two chapters—concern for the content of those settlements must be adequate.

The concept of fairness is difficult to define operationally, and it may vary substantially depending on whose perspective is adopted. Nevertheless, Steven Brams and Jeffrey Togman utilize the "Adjusted Winner" (AW) model, which examines the resolution of conflict from the perspective of the multiple issues that often characterize conflict and at the differing values often attributed to those issues by the disputants. From the AW perspective, the authors explore whether the Camp David Accords, perhaps among the most significant peace agreements since 1945, could be judged "fair," especially when they are not necessarily regarded as such by many observers. This examination is of particular interest here in that many of the key issues surrounding the Arab-Israeli peace process have a territorial component, among them the disputes over the Sinai, Jerusalem, and a Palestinian state. Yet territorial disputes are also linked to other conflictual issues that must be resolved in a broader "package," and therefore it may be misleading to concentrate only on the territorial element in a multi-faceted dispute. Perhaps surprisingly, the Camp David Accords meet the standard of fairness posited by Brams and Togman, with both Israel and Egypt attaining the satisfaction of at least two-thirds of their main interests. Indeed, this fairness may help explain why the signatories have had relatively peaceful relations in the last twenty-plus years, after several decades of war. The AW method suggested by Brams and Togman may be the mechanism with which to resolve territorial conflicts and promote long-term conflict resolution, especially when territorial concerns are arrayed and interwoven with other issues in a complex pattern.

THE FUTURE OF TERRITORIAL CONFLICT

So far, all of the chapters in this book—with the possible exception of Newman's analysis of the Middle East conflict—have focused on interstate territorial conflict. Yet, because of the virtual complete mapping of the earth and the demarcation of most international boundaries, some portion of previous territorial conflict is unlikely to recur. Furthermore, with the end of the cold war, much of international conflict in general has shifted to nationalist or ethnic-based conflict, in which internal conflict concerns at minimum coexist equally with interstate elements, if they do not dominate threats to peace and security in the world. Although the contributors to this work do not dismiss such trends, they do hold a common viewpoint that interstate territorial conflict is a critical, core, international political interaction. Nevertheless, this compilation would be remiss if it did not examine what future territorial conflict may look like and whether a state-centered view of the phenomenon is appropriate.

Andrew Kirby addresses the issue of whether the trend toward globalization and an integrated world economy will necessarily diminish the importance of the territorial state. With the development of such regional trading blocs as the European Union (EU) and the North American Free Trade Agreement (NAFTA), one may argue that traditional security concerns between neighbors have been be superseded by economic concerns or even eliminated through functionalist processes that diminish hostilities between states. Although globalization may alter some forms of territorial conflict, Kirby argues that there is good reason to expect more pronounced tension between neighboring states that attempt to maintain political and ideological integrity as their economies become less autonomous and distinct. A brief case study of Mexico and the United States allows him to illustrate these new kinds of border conflicts.

Finally, Saul Cohen explores the prospects for war and peace as a consequence of the geopolitical changes occasioned by the end of the cold war. He argues that such changes mean that international conflict will remain, sometimes in very intense fashions. Yet he expects such conflict to be more geographically contained and of shorter duration. Among the changes and implications he discusses are the emergence of geopolitical regions and the proliferation of new states—a paradoxical consequence of the weakening of the state in the international system.

The general conclusions of the two chapters in this final section of the book suggest that the configurations of future territorial conflicts may differ from those of earlier eras. Nevertheless, it is clear

that territorial conflict will remain a cornerstone of international relations and that states will continue to occupy a prominent place in
those configurations.

REFERENCES

Boulding, Kenneth E. 1962. *Conflict and Defense: A General Theory*. New
York: Harper and Row.
Diehl, Paul F. 1991. "Geography and War: A Review and Assessment of the
Empirical Literature." *International Interactions* 17: 11–27.
Goertz, Gary, and Paul F. Diehl. 1992a. "The Empirical Importance of Endur-
ing Rivalries." *International Interactions* 18: 151–163.
———. 1992b. *Territorial Changes and International Conflict*. London: Rout-
ledge.
Holsti, Kalevi J. 1991. *Peace and War: Armed Conflicts and International
Order, 1648–1989*. Cambridge, U.K.: Cambridge University Press.
Huth, Paul K. 1996. *Standing Your Ground: Territorial Disputes and Interna-
tional Conflict*. Ann Arbor: University of Michigan Press.
Kacowicz, Arie. 1994. *Peaceful Territorial Change*. Columbia: University of
South Carolina Press.
Kocs, Stephen. 1995. "Territorial Disputes and Interstate War, 1945–1987."
Journal of Politics 57: 159–175.
Kratochwil, Friedrich, Paul Rohrlich, and Harpreet Mahajan. 1985. *Peace and
Disputed Sovereignty: Reflections on Conflict over Territory*. Lan-
ham, Md.: University Press of America.
Lemke, Douglas. 1995. "The Tyranny of Distance: Redefining Relevant
Dyads." *International Interactions* 21: 23–38.
Mackinder, Halford. 1919. *Democratic Ideals and Reality*. New York: Henry
Holt.
Siverson, Randolph, and Harvey Starr. 1991. *The Diffusion of War: A Study of
Opportunity and Willingness*. Ann Arbor: University of Michigan
Press.
Vasquez, John. 1993. *The War Puzzle*. Cambridge, U.K., and New York: Cam-
bridge University Press.
———. 1995. "Why Do Neighbors Fight?: Proximity, Interaction, and Territo-
riality." *Journal of Peace Research* 32: 277–293.

PART I

Conceptions of Territorial Importance

1

Real Spaces, Symbolic Spaces: Interrelated Notions of Territory in the Arab-Israeli Conflict

David Newman

The study of territorial conflict is usually associated with the concrete manifestations of territory as either a strategic or economic resource. Positional disputes concerning the location and course of international boundaries, particularly as they relate to the control of strategic areas, the presence of valuable natural resources, minerals, or water, and/or the presence of ethnonational minorities that promote irredentist policies, are the common causes of territorial conflict (Goertz and Diehl 1992; Coakley 1993). Territorial disputes are generally seen as constituting one of the major reasons for war between states (Holsti 1991; Vasquez 1993; Kocs 1995; Huth 1996; Senese 1996).

Recent discussions of conflict and territorial change focus on the role of territory as an important component in the formation of social, spatial, and national identities. Geographers have begun to investigate the links between notions of geographical compartmentalization and the extent to which this creates the spatial frame for the emergence of national identities (Hooson 1994; Knight 1994). The impact of globalization has suggested that the links between fixed notions of territory and national identity formation need to be rethought, along the lines of shared spaces and multi-identities, in which boundaries are not just territorial containers but also a reflection of the multidimensional constructions of group and national identities (Billig 1995; Taylor

3

1995, 1997; Paasi 1996; Newman and Paasi 1997). These studies focus on the symbolic aspects of territory and the way in which metaphysical and historic manifestations of territory contribute to the formation of group and national identities and feelings of territorial belonging (Schnell 1993, 1994; Paasi 1995, 1996).

National identity formation is itself a function of the attachment to territory displayed by the national group, for whom the fixed territories of the state act as spatial containers but are also subject to change (Johnston 1995; Taylor 1995, 1996). Such territorial attachment is often the result of a long historic process of territorial socialization (Duchacek 1970; Gottmann 1973; Sack 1986). Landscapes are imbued with symbolic and mythical characteristics as part of this socialization process. These, in turn, are transformed into concrete meaning through the formation of state territories, the demarcation of land boundaries, and the exercise of effective control throughout the bounded territory. Homeland territories are imbued with greater importance than territories belonging to the "other." These territories become exclusive, the rights to which are defended against alternative claimants. Claims to sovereignty based on historical priority or duration have been evoked throughout human history as a means of justifying territorial expansion or obtaining recognition by the international community (Burghardt 1973; Murphy 1990, 1996). Conflict and competition over the rights to territory can result in warfare, bringing about changes in the territorial configurations and boundaries.

At the concrete level, territorial control and management are reorganized in such a way as to maximize the potential benefits of newly acquired territories and, gradually, as a new base map from which to commence the next stage of territorial change—be it through warfare or conflict resolution. At each stage of this changing territorial configuration the participants in the conflict redefine the nature of both the concrete control of, and the symbolic attachment to, territory. The state attempts to translate its de jure sovereignty into de facto territorial control, at the same time manipulating the agents of socialization in an effort to focus on those elements and myths that are most compatible with the new spatial realities.

The concrete and symbolic manifestations of territory constitute a single system in which each feeds into, and reinforces, the other. Proponents of one will often use the arguments of the other as a means of strengthening their case for a specific form of territorial policy.

With rare exceptions, groups that desire to retain control over territory for symbolic and historic reasons use some form of strategic and/or resource discourse as a means of backing up their claim by recourse to concrete arguments that are meaningful to a larger sector of the national population. While the symbolic aspects of territorial attachment, discussed below, often provide the basis for territorial rhetoric, conflict and conflict resolution are more focused on these empirical and concrete aspects of territory. These elements have universal meaning and can be understood, and combated, by other participants in a conflict and by third-party negotiators, unlike symbolic and metaphysical characteristics of territory, which remain within the exclusive domain of a single participant in the conflict. Conversely, groups that desire to control territory for strategic reasons may also draw support from groups for which the symbolic dimension is the key factor in the territorial claim. This form of instrumental coalition helps create a wider political lobby but, at the same time, makes it more difficult to undertake conflict resolution if, and when, the tangible obstacles are overcome.

In this chapter I examine both the concrete and the symbolic implications of territorial change within the Arab-Israel context. Each of these elements has been used to justify specific territorial claims at different stages in the Arab-Israel conflict during the past hundred years. Five key periods of territorial change are identified, each of which has resulted in changed orientations concerning both the concrete (resource, strategic, demographic) and the symbolic (attachment, identity, mythical landscapes) toward the territory in question.

CONCRETE MANIFESTATIONS OF TERRITORY

The concrete manifestation of territory in the Arab-Israel conflict is threefold, focusing on territory as an economic resource, a strategic asset, and a demographic container. These provide the background to competing territorial claims, often resulting in conflict.

Territory as an Economic Resource

First and foremost, territory is an economic resource, to be used for agricultural cultivation, hillside terracing, and/or the construction of urban neighborhoods. It constitutes the space within which national life takes place and develops. As the population grows, so the finite territory becomes transformed into an increasingly scarce resource. One possible outcome is for additional territorial claims to be made on neighboring territories, particularly if that territory is relatively sparsely settled or if it contains populations with similar cultural/national characteristics. This, in the past, has been the basis for policies of lebensraum and the justification of territorial expansion at the expense of neighboring territories.

The competition for land between Arabs and Jews is particularly fierce because of the small piece of real estate in question. The areal extent of Israel is no more than 20,000 square kilometers, to which the Occupied Territories—the whole of the West Bank, the Gaza Strip, and the Golan Heights—add approximately 5,000 square kilometers. In terms of its economic value, land does not play the same role for Jewish and Arab communities. Despite the "return to the land" practiced by the early Zionist pioneer settlers, Jewish Israel is an urban society, within which land is being taken over by metropolitan sprawl and exurbanization. Land that, for forty years, was preserved for agricultural use is now being covered by strips of concrete, settlements, and commercial and industrial developments. For much of the Arab population, land remains a basic agricultural resource, on which crops are grown and cultivated. Territorial attachment is often based on tradition, rather than on land deeds and land titles. This is particularly the case with respect to the Bedouin communities in the Negev region, which now compete for land with the state (Falah 1983; Meir 1997). The "greening of the land" and the "blooming of the desert" is not just part of the Zionist "return to the land and agricultural roots" but is also a means through which land is brought under control. The designation and enclosure of land for agricultural cultivation or as pasturelands, like the planting or uprooting of trees and orchards, are seen by both sides as a political act that either strengthens or weakens the attachment to, and control of, a piece of land by either one of the conflict participants and that can result in violence (Cohen 1993).

Thus the conflict over territory as land is about not only sovereignty but also ownership. The expansion of land purchase and ownership prior to the establishment of the State of Israel was viewed as a means by which legitimate claims to future sovereignty would be justified (Kimmerling 1983; Kellerman 1994). This was expressed through the collective purchase of land by the Jewish National Fund on behalf of the people as a whole and through the transfer of this land to state control immediately subsequent to the setting up of the state. Within the pre-1967 boundaries, the state claims ownership of more than 90 percent of the land and, until recently, has rejected any moves toward land privatization because of the political implications inherent in selling land to so-called undesirable elements. Jewish settlers on the West Bank have attempted to purchase land from Palestinian landowners as a means of enhancing the nature of their control, while, in turn, Palestinian landowners or agents who sell land have been threatened and, on some occasions, murdered by their compatriots for "selling out" this most important of national symbols.

Legalistic notions of sovereignty and ownership do not necessarily ensure effective territorial control under conditions of conflict. Sovereignty over an empty area may result in its being claimed by "others." Marginal and frontier regions will often be settled, against all economic logic, as a means of demonstrating a physical presence within a region. For Israel, settlement policy has always constituted an important means through which territory is managed and controlled and justifications for territorial claims are made (Kimmerling 1983; Kellerman 1994). The presence of civilians and the cultivation of land create a stronger basis for territorial claims than does the existence of military garrisons and fortifications (Hasson and Gosenfeld 1980; Newman 1989). The settlement map of the 1940s was a major factor in the desire of the fledgling Israeli army to retain control over those areas. The settling of the border zones and other strategic sites in the period immediately following the state's establishment in 1948, the colonization of West Bank, and the "outpost" project of the late 1970s in the Galilee region all indicate the continued importance of settlement as a means of establishing and expanding the effective territorial control practiced by the state under conditions of ethnoterritorial conflict.

It is also important to note that de jure concepts of sovereignty are not absolute. Israel is recognized as the sovereign within its post-1948–1949 boundaries, mainly because the international community has chosen to recognize Israel's control of these regions and despite the fact that this territory is significantly larger than that which was voted on in the 1947 United Nations partition proposal (see below).

The international community does not recognize Israel's claim to sovereign rights in any part of the post-1967 Occupied Territories. Internally, however, Israel sees itself as the sovereign entity in East Jerusalem and in the Golan Heights by virtue of the laws it has passed extending civilian rule to these areas. The reversibility or irreversibility of de facto annexation in a number of territorial contexts has been questioned by Ian Lustick (1993), and these questions have been extended to the perceived and unilateral de jure annexation of East Jerusalem and the Golan Heights by the Israeli government (Yishai 1985; Lustick 1997). The point to make is that the relationship between ownership and sovereignty constitutes a vicious circle. Extended presence, land purchase, settlement expansion and cultivation, and demographic majorities all strengthen the claims to sovereignty, which in turn provides the internal justification for extending effective control even farther, through concrete actions.

Territory as a strategic asset

The second concrete manifestation of territory is its role as a strategic resource. Traditional military doctrine holds that the key upland sites and transportation arteries must remain under the control of the state if it is to retain strategic superiority. The notion of security has always been part of an internal Israeli discourse that carries the weight of consensus among much of Israel's Jewish population (Newman 1997b). Retaining control of territory is, for many, the most tangible means by which security is achieved. Creating a cordon sanitaire, well away from the major (Israeli) population centers; controlling the strategic high ground, such as in the Golan Heights; and maintaining strong and defensible boundaries—these are the traditional territorial concepts of security. The assertion that territory is strategically important is not in question within Israel. The debate focuses on the question of just which territories and how much area needs to be controlled as a means of enhancing the strategic posture of the country. Certain areas, such as the Golan Heights, carry a greater consensus among army generals concerning their strategic importance, as compared with the West Bank and the Gaza Strip, over which views are divided. The fact that the pre-1967 "green line" boundary runs parallel to the upland slopes was always seen as constituting a strategic threat to the Israeli towns in the coastal plain, whereas most Israeli proposals for the ultimate territorial configuration of separate Israeli and Palestinian entities on the West Bank have insisted that Israel retain control of the Jordan Valley in the west as a means of ensuring defensible and secure boundaries (Allon 1976; Newman 1995a). This continued to play a major role in the post-Oslo territorial discourse, when the precise territorial configurations of Palestinian statehood/entity that appeared, for a time, to be an inevitable outcome of the Oslo peace process were the subject of much debate concerning those areas which should be retained by Israel for security purposes (Heller 1997; Inbar and Sandler 1997).

Despite Israel's military superiority, especially in times of war, the long-term territorial doctrine has not always proved to be an asset. Immediately after the Six Day War of June 1967 it was decided to maintain a frontline defensive position along the Suez Canal rather than to withdraw to the strategic passes in the center of the Sinai Peninsula. This "Bar Lev" line became the focus for an ongoing war of attrition, in which many lives were lost, and it was easily overrun by Egyptian forces during the October 1973 Yom Kippur War. During the same war, the settlement network on the Golan Heights proved to be an obstacle, rather than a support, in the way of the regional defense system in the face of the Syrian army invasion. The Israeli army had to devote valuable time and resources to evacuating these settlements before it could face the immediate military threat.

The territorial security doctrine has also come undone in South Lebanon. Israel has maintained direct control over a security zone parallel to its own boundary as a means of removing the direct threat to its border settlements. But this has not prevented the firing of rockets from areas beyond the security zone into Israel. Moreover, the number of Israeli military fatalities that have occurred as a result of military operations inside Lebanon, of retaliations for rocket attacks, and of the prevention of guerrilla activities inside the security zone itself is far greater than the number of civilian casualties that have resulted from the rocket attacks, such that for some the zone has become known as one of insecurity, rather than security (Norton and Schwedler 1993; Eisenberg 1997). Since the stated objectives of the Hizbolla fighters is to remove Israel from Lebanon, as contrasted with the prior intentions of the Palestinian occupants of Southern Lebanon during the 1970s to inflict damage within Israel, it is questionable whether continued control of this security zone serves any long-term strategic objective. It also explains the grassroots movement among many Israeli citizens, especially parents of soldiers serving their tour of duty in South Lebanon, to persuade the government to unilaterally withdraw from this region.

But traditional notions of security, worldwide, are being modified. Modern warfare technologies have meant that the strategic role of territories has changed significantly. The introduction of ballistic missiles has brought the boundary into the heart of the Israeli cities. The Gulf War brought a new component into the security discourse, namely the fact that no one is safe from missiles, even in the heart of the country. In his book on *The New Middle East* Shimon Peres, former Israeli prime minister and architect of the Oslo Agreements, argues that in an age of ballistic missiles which can fly over distances of hundreds of kilometers, paying scant regard to the land boundaries and antimissile systems on the way, microterritories no longer have a major role to play in the modern era of warfare and security doctrine (Peres 1994).

This new reality led to the outward flow of people from the cities, especially Tel Aviv, during the Gulf War and to the subsequent creation of a new army command—the *oref,* or hinterland command—as a means of dealing with the different security threats facing the population centers during a potential future conflagration. Prior to this, the army commands were focused exclusively on the border regions and frontier zones. In the wake of the Gulf War the Israeli government attempted to use this changed security perspective to promote population decentralization, away from the center of the country and into the peripheral regions, in much the same way as the Barlow Report in Great Britain during World War II attempted to use the strategic concerns of overcentralization as an argument for population dispersal away from the southeast region and the growing metropolis of London.

Despite the impact of the ballistic missiles, territory is still perceived as the ensurer of a more secure country. The farther the boundary from the place of residence and the stronger the armed forces lined up along that boundary, the greater the sense of security each side feels. Within Israel, it is the security discourse that continues to be the discourse of "consensus," one which can be conjured up after every terrorist attack or Syrian army exercise, as a means of creating internal national unity in the face of perceived external and existential threat (Falah and Newman 1995; Newman 1997b). This discourse has not changed significantly, even since the signing of peace treaties with both Egypt and Jordan, despite the fact that the security boundary of Israel has been pushed away from its borders (see discussion below).

Territory as a demographic container

The third concrete manifestation of territory is its role as a container of people, within which national identities are formed and through which the state attempts to transform de jure sovereignty into de facto control. The dual dimensions of the Arab-Israel conflict concern the struggle for territorial control and demographic superiority. The Arab-Jewish ratio within the territory controlled by Israel has always been of major significance in justifying claims to sovereignty (Romann 1989). These ratios have changed through time and space. Jewish immigration into pre-state Palestine and post-state Israel, along with the outflow of Palestinian refugees, has created Jewish demographic superiority within the boundaries of the State of Israel. While natural growth rates tend to favor the more rapid growth of the Arab-Palestinian population, short-term hiccups occur as a result of sudden mass Jewish immigration, as occurred in the years following the establishment of the state, after the Six Day War and with the mass immigration from the former Soviet republics in the early 1990s.

The different territorial configurations give rise to different demographic ratios. Within the pre-1967 boundaries, Israeli Jews account for approximately 81 percent of the population. This changes to only 65 percent when the Occupied Territories are included, and it is often cited as the major reason for nonannexation of these territories by the right-wing Israeli governments of the early 1980s. Scale reduction also changes the picture, as the Palestinian-Arab citizens of Israel are concentrated into three regions inside Israel, within each of which they constitute a local majority. This is particularly the case in the upland regions of the Galilee, within which the Arab-Jewish ratio is, in some cases, 80:20 in favor of the Arab inhabitants of the region. Successive Israeli governments have attempted to change these ratios by encouraging Jewish settlement policies in these regions, but they have not succeeded in substantially altering the demographic ratio in favor of the Jewish population (Yiftachel 1991, 1992).

At the most microterritorial scale, there are also a number of "mixed" Jewish-Arab towns in Israel. The past forty years have witnessed an increased tendency for residential segregation and separation in these towns. Arab residents have tended to remain in the older, poorer parts, while the Jews have moved into new neighborhoods and, more recently, into exurban communities as they have experienced upward socioeconomic mobility (Gonen 1995; Falah 1996a). Individual settlements remain segregated and monoethnic, such that a single geographical region may be best characterized as constituting a dual space in which Arabs and Jews rarely visit the villages and know little about the language or customs of the "other." Any interaction that does take place tends to be limited to economic transactions.

Thus territory acts as a container within which peoples are controlled through zoning and land-development policies. At the local level, territory becomes the focus of conflict between competing groups, a competition that is exacerbated in situations of ethnic and national conflict. The power to allocate scarce resources, such as land parcels, zoning permits, and developmental resources, is a tool used by the state to ensure its own hegemonic control. This, in turn, increases the frustration and political exclusion felt by the minority populations and results in a strengthening of their own sociospatial and national identities as separate from the identities of other groups that reside in the same locale.

TERRITORIAL SYMBOLISM

While the concrete manifestation of territory, either as an economic resource or as a strategic asset, can be quantified by each side in the conflict, this is not the case with the symbolic dimension. For both peoples, the territory of Israel/Palestine is part of an ancestral homeland, filled with sites, locations, and myths that form an integral part of national identity formation. As territory becomes the focus of competing claims, the conflict participants imbue specific sites with historic and religious importance, often through the use of historical and archaeological narratives, as a means of proving priority (which group can trace its roots in the territory back farther), duration (which group can demonstrate continuous residence over a longer and uninterrupted period of time), and exclusivity to the territory in question (Burghardt 1973).

Territory as historic and religious homeland

Attachment to territory is based on the identification of symbols and signs in the landscape, as well as on the creation of territorial histories and myths that reflect the singular importance of one piece of territory over any other. Simply being present is often not sufficient when making competing claims for territory. Within the frame of national consciousness, all of us are subject to strong processes of territorial socialization, the aim of which is to emphasize the importance of our territory as a key element in our personal and group identity, "the acquisition of identity with a political area" (Duchacek 1970; Paasi 1995, 1996). Territorial indoctrination constitutes a nationalist focus within the socialization process, through the use of maps, flags, symbols, and territorial semantics, all of which enable us to become more acquainted with "our" territory and to elevate it in importance in comparison with other, more distant, territories. Yi-Fu Tuan (1991) stresses the importance of textbooks, words, and narratives as part of the socialization process through which territories are created.

The emotional and symbolic man-territory relationship is normally centered on that territory within which the ethnic or national group is located. Histories are composed of events and incidents that took place in certain locations and that can be visited as part of the socialization process. Anthony Smith (1981) notes that, in the absence of a territorial base, Diaspora ethnic communities retained ancestral memories of homeland that were associated with formative events of the group. As a means of maintaining the national bond, territory becomes a central element of the socialization process, through which members of the group retain a loyalty to a distant territory. In the process of geographical detachment, however, the territorial concept is removed from the concrete to the metaphysical realm and from one that has relatively clear boundaries to one that is unbounded and abstract.

A powerful element in the socialization process is the use of religion and religious experience as a means of cementing the bond between a group and its territory. This form of reverential relationship between people and their perceived terrestrial home has been termed *geopiety* (Wright 1947; Tuan 1976). This assumes a sense of belonging to, and ownership of, homeland as an exclusive right emanating from a divine, or other supernatural, claim to territory.

Judaism as a religion has a clear territorial focus, centering on the "Land of Israel" (Davies 1974; Hoffman 1986; Sicker 1992; Newman 1997a). The concept of an ancient homeland was maintained through a process of territorial socialization that penetrated many facets of religious and cultural behavior. This socialization drew both directly and indirectly on the spiritual roots for territorial attachment to be found in scriptural sources and interpreted through both prayer and precept. The symbolic and metaphysical attachment to the specific piece of territory was formalized in the Declaration of Independence of the State of Israel:

Eretz Israel was the birthplace of the Jewish people. Here their spiritual, religious and political identity was shaped . . . after being forcibly exiled from the land, the people kept faith with it throughout their dispersion and never ceased to pray and hope for their return to it and for the restoration in it of their political rights.

(Preamble to the *Declaration of Independence*, State of Israel, May 1948)

Contextually, this has been the case with the processes of territorial socialization undergone by Israeli schoolchildren (Bar Gal 1993) as well as by generations of pre-state Jewish residents of the Diaspora (Newman 1997a). Maps focus on past periods in which there were Jewish kingdoms in this region, and sites are renamed according to historic Jewish places or modern Israeli events, while children are taken on hikes and field trips so they can come to know their country and, it is expected, to develop a strong feeling of exclusive attachment to this homeland.

Territory as an exclusive entity

The formation of national identity around a specific piece of territory reflects the exclusive attachment to, and control of, these spaces. By defining the "self" nationality contained within the territorial boundaries, the "other" is constructed and often excluded (Taylor 1994; Johnston 1995). Other national groups are, at the best, perceived as alien residents or second-class citizens, and, in some cases, they may be forced out of the territory through policies of so-called ethnic cleansing. This is particularly the case in situations of ethnoterritorial conflict, such as has been evidenced in the former Yugoslavia and Bosnia or in the partition of Cyprus, as well as in the new rhetoric of exclusion that has been emerging as part of the contemporary debate concerning European integration (Stolcke 1995) and that, at the microlevel, is often used as an excuse for creating new spaces of exclusion in favor of the dominant ethnopolitical group and at the expense of ethnic and national minorities (Sibley 1995; Dragadze 1996).

In laying claim to a specific piece of territory, history and myth are interwoven to demonstrate a unique attachment to the territory in question by a particular group. Claims for territorial exclusivity are based on both arguments of priority and duration (see discussion above) (Burghardt 1973), to which purpose questionable pseudoscientific evidence may be used, both as a means of proving the exclusive historical attachment and in order to contest any alternative, competing, territorial claims.

Contextually, the symbolic attachment to the biblical Land of Israel is an exclusive one. The land in question is perceived as being divinely promised to a specific group/nation, while all other groups have, at best, the rights of alien residents. As long as the other groups do not endanger the security or stability of the political entity they can remain within the area. The concept of a binational, democratic, entity in which all population groups have equal rights to own land, obtain power, and/or share equally in all resources is unacceptable from the perspective of territorial exclusivity. Both Israelis and Palestinians strongly reject the option of a single binational state. Either they are opposed to any form of conflict resolution or they prefer some form of territorial separation between the two peoples and the creation of ethnoterritorial, homogeneous entities. But they refuse to consider the notion of shared spaces.

The exclusive attachment to territory is reflected in the naming and renaming of places and locations in accordance with the historic and religious sites associated with the dominant political group. Not only did the outflow of Palestinian refugees bring about a change in the Jewish-Arab demographic ratios, it also brought about the replacement of an Arab-Palestinian landscape with a Jewish-Israeli landscape (Reichman 1990; Morris 1993; Falah 1996b). The names of abandoned villages disappeared from the map and were replaced with alternative Hebrew names, while new Israeli settlements were named after incidents and people from ancient Jewish or modern Israeli history (Cohen and Kliot 1981, 1992). Israeli settlements throughout the West Bank have taken on biblical names associated with the specific sites as a means of expressing the Jewish priority in these places and the exclusive nature of the territorial attachment. Modern Israeli and Palestinian maps of Israel/Palestine possess the same outer borders, but the semantic content of the maps is completely different. The means by which new landscapes are created to replace or obliterate former landscapes is a good example of the way in which metaphysical and symbolic attachment to territory is translated into concrete realities on the ground.

Symbolic and metaphysical attachment to territory, defined as intangible or relational values by others, can often be the most critical forms of attachment in determining actual policy decisions with respect to territorial claims. Gary Goertz and Paul F. Diehl (1992) argue that territorial changes with high relational importance are the most likely to involve violence, as indeed is the case with respect to the West Bank ("the historic and religious heartland of the ancient Land of Israel") or Jerusalem ("the eternal capital of the Jewish people, never again to be divided"). This is consistent with the logic outlined by John A. Vasquez (1983) and James D. Fearon (1995), which indicates that conflict is more likely when issues are less tangible or divisible or, in other words, when territories are perceived as belonging exclusively to one group of people and when all other groups are seen as usurpers. Contextually, Jerusalem is often perceived as constituting an "indivisible" good (Albin 1991), which is much more difficult, if at all possible, to negotiate. This contrasts with Michael Dumper's argument (1997) that it is possible to redivide Jerusalem, based on his analysis of the physical infrastructural networks (roads, pipelines, and the like), rather than the symbolic and intangible elements. While divisible aspects may open up the basis for compromise and territorial division, symbolic and religious attachment to land does not allow for compromise, in which case the conflict becomes more protracted and violent.

CHANGING TERRITORIAL CONFIGURATIONS

The political map of Israel/Palestine has been one of the most fluid cartographic representations of the twentieth century. Boundaries, as the ultimate territorial demarcators of sovereign territory, have not, as such, been fully determined. Despite the common perceptual images of state territory, based on a map of post-1948 Israel stretching from the Mediterranean Sea in the west to the Jordan River in the east (with or without a separate West Bank territory) and from the Lebanese boundary in the north to the Egyptian boundary in the south, this configuration does not, as yet, represent the spatial domain of sovereignty.

Five key phases in the process of territorial formation can be identified, each of which has both concrete and symbolic significance for the conflict participants. These range chronologically from the dissolution of the Ottoman Empire in the early part of the century, through to the peace agreements between Israel and some of its neighbors during the past two decades. The boundaries, as drawn up in 1948–1949, were no more than armistice lines. Israel's first internationally recognized boundary did not come about until the early 1980s, when the Camp David Accords with Egypt were implemented. This was followed by much of the Israel-Jordan boundary in 1994. The remaining boundaries, with Lebanon and Syria in the north and with a Palestinian entity/state, must still be determined as part of the ongoing and future processes of conflict resolution. The ensuing discussion develops Lustick's (1993) ideas concerning the nature of state shaping as a continuous process, one that consists of both expansion and contraction of state territory. His argument (pp. 8—9) that, unless the borders of the state are accepted as immutable, different groups within the state will align their own perceptions of the proper (desired) border in light of the implications of different borders (the concrete manifestations of territory) or different principles of inclusion and exclusion (symbolic manifestations of the configurations of state territory) are of particular relevance to the discussion of the Arab-Israel conflict.

From Empire to Mandate

The dissolution of the Ottoman Empire following World War I heralded the creation of new political territories in the Middle East. In 1920 the League of Nations granted the right of government in the

conquered territories to Great Britain and France. The granting of the
Mandates resulted in the creation of new state territories. The area
under French administration was eventually divided into two state
entities, Lebanon and Syria, while the area of Palestine under British
administration was also divided into two separate territorial entities,
with the creation of the State of Transjordan in 1921.

The superimposition of new state boundaries was not supported by
Syria or the Zionist movement, respectively, each of which argued
that the actions taken by France and Great Britain amounted to an illegal form of territorial partition. Within the Zionist movement, a
new faction was formed espousing the territorial wholeness of Palestine on both sides of the Jordan River. This faction later broke away
from the Zionist movement and set up an alternative Revisionist
Zionist Movement, whose chief slogan was the territorial cry: "The
River Jordan has two banks: this one is ours, so too is the other." This
formed the basis for the post-state Herut Party of Menachem Begin,
who came to power in 1977. By then this irredentist political party
had renounced their claims to both sides of the Jordan, but they continued to pursue a territorial policy aimed at retaining Israeli sovereignty over the whole of Western Palestine including the West Bank,
which had been conquered in the Six Day War. It also forms the political basis for the current right-wing administration of Benjamin Netanyahu, which is opposed to further withdrawal from the West Bank
as part of the Israel-Palestine process of conflict resolution.

At the symbolic level, both Syria and some Israeli leaders continued to argue for a return to the historic territories, a Greater Syria and
a Greater Israel, respectively. At the concrete level, territory became
the focus of conflict, with both Arabs and Jews attempting to purchase
land and demonstrate their effective control through the cultivation
of land, the establishment of settlements, and the expansion of an
ethno-exclusive domain. In response to the ensuing interethnic violence, the British administrators attempted (albeit without success) to
take the territorial sting out of the conflict by slowing down the
process of purchasing and settling land.

Notions of territorial partition

If the 1921 partition of Palestine was difficult for many of the Zionist
leaders of the time to swallow, then any notions of further partition-

ing Western Palestine was anathema, both to the Jewish and Palestinian populations of the region, each of which perceived the whole of this territory as constituting a future independent Jewish or Arab state. The developing conflict between Arabs and Jews in Palestine during the 1920s and 1930s resulted in a number of proposals for territorial partition of the area into Jewish and Arab states. The partition discourse comprised two main phases. The first consisted of the initial partition proposals in the 1930s, during which period the idea was raised for the first time and gradually became a legitimate part of the territorial discourse. The second phase took place in the 1940s, between the end of World War II and the eventual establishment of the State of Israel in 1948.

At both the symbolic and concrete level, the notion of partition caused much heated debate within the Zionist movement (Haim 1978; Galnoor 1991; Katz 1994). Some groups strongly opposed any form of partition, arguing that the British government had already implemented one partition in 1921, with the creation of the State of Transjordan. Other groups within the Zionist movement were prepared to accept the notion of partition, however begrudgingly, if only because it would ensure some form of concrete territorial and political gain. Holding out for a single, undivided territory might, in their view, result in the continuation of the Mandate. As such, in the short term they preferred a smaller state to no state at all. The latter position won the day, thus legitimizing the notion of territorial partition and pragmatism within the Zionist movement.

Unlike their Jewish counterparts, the Arabs took little part in the territorial discourse. They rejected the notion of partition, arguing that the whole area was an Arab territory, in which the Jewish population constituted a demographic minority, the vast majority of which had arrived in Palestine only during the previous fifty years. Arab leaders did object to some of the specific aspects of the Peel proposal for partition, as drawn up by the British Royal Commission in 1936, most notably the inclusion of the heavily Arab populated Galilee region in the Jewish state, but they did not engage in a public debate or negotiation concerning the practical implementation of any form of territorial partition.

All partition proposals, ranging from the British commissions of the 1930s to the United Nations proposal of 1947, attempted to achieve as high a degree of ethnoterritorial homogeneity and separation as possible.

The notion of a binational democracy within a shared territory was as unacceptable to both Jews and Arabs in the 1940s as it is now. The mutual feelings of fear and distrust felt by each group for the "other," the desire for spatial exclusivity and ethnic homogeneity, spurred on by a continued refusal for more than forty years even to recognize the legitimacy of the existence and the aspirations of the "other," has meant that the most democratic solution to the problem, namely a binational state in which all are equals, has always been the least desired solution on the part of both population groups.

Territory and sovereignty: Establishing a state

It is often forgotten that the territorial configuration of the State of Israel, following the signing of the armistice agreements in 1949, was significantly different from that proposed by the United Nations Special Commission on Palestine and approved by the U.N. General Assembly. The U.N. Partition Proposal gave more territory to the Arab sovereign entity, including many of the Arab population centers, such as Ramla, Lydda, Tayibe, and most of the Galilee region, all of which were incorporated into Israel after the 1948—1949 War of Independence and the subsequent Rhodes Armistice agreements of 1949. The demarcation of the boundaries of the new state closely followed, with some minor amendments, the lines that had been reached as a result of the War of Independence. These lines, rather than those approved by the United Nations, formed the basis of the eventual boundaries of the state.

The U.N. vote on partition authorized the implementation of three significant territorial changes: the establishment of Jewish and Arab states and the internationalization of Jerusalem. In reality, only the Jewish state was established. The West Bank, rather than becoming the core territory of a separate Arab-Palestinian state, remained under Jordanian administration, while Jerusalem was physically divided between Israel and the West Bank–Jordan.

Concrete and symbolic notions of territory coincided in the Israel decision to capture the Negev Desert rather than the upland region, later to become known as the West Bank. The notion of settling the undeveloped desert, of making the desert green, became a symbolic cornerstone for the development policy undertaken by the new state. Israeli Prime Minister David Ben Gurion argued that it was essential for the new state to control a large area that was relatively unpopulated and undeveloped and that would serve as the essential reservoir of territory required for future population absorption and economic development. The mountainous interior of the region, by contrast, was densely populated by Palestinians. No land was available in the upland regions for agricultural expansion, specifically not the extensive forms of cultivation practiced by the Jewish settlements in the lowlands and the plains.

The establishment of a sovereign state had a number of concrete manifestations. In the first place, significant demographic changes took place: an outflow of approximately 600,000 Palestinian refugees and an inflow of a similar number of Jewish refugees/migrants from post-Holocaust Europe and from North Africa, Iraq, and the Yemen. Abandoned lands were transferred to Israeli administration (Golan 1995), and the state took direct control of more than 90 percent of the land within its sovereign domain. Settlement planning took on a regional dimension, as contrasted with the site-specific focus of the British Mandate period. During this period settlements were also perceived as filling a security-defensive role, so they were established in border regions and in other areas of strategic priority. Settlements were viewed as contributing directly to the defensive posture of the state, for military and civilian functions were closely interlinked (Newman 1989).

At the symbolic level, attachment to land became an important part of the socialization process for citizens of the new state. For those newcomers who did not yet feel a strong tie to the new homeland, this attachment had to be created. Schools placed great emphasis on practical geography, field trips, archaeology, and visits to historic sites as a means of inculcating territorial values within the confines of those boundaries that existed in reality. The term for these studies was *Moledet*, literally translated as "homeland studies," later to be used as the name for one of the most extreme right-wing political parties in Israel, which opposes any form of territorial concession or withdrawal and advocates the transfer of Arab-Palestinian residents out of Israel to neighboring countries.

Territorial expansion: The Six Day War

In the fifty-year period since the establishment of the State of Israel, two additional major phases of territorial reconfiguration have taken place: expansion, as a result of the Six Day War; and contraction, which has begun as a result of the peace agreements between Israel and some of its neighbors.

After the Six Day War, Israel occupied the whole of the West Bank and Gaza Strip territories, as well as the Sinai Peninsula. The results of the Six Day War removed the perceived security threats emanating from Jordanian control over the West Bank and Syrian control over the Golan Heights. The new territories provided an expanded security cordon sanitaire for Israel while tripling the length of the land boundaries that had to be patrolled and defended. The capture of the Sinai Peninsula provided Israel with its most significant security advantage, both as a security buffer and as an area in which to establish army bases and airfields and to undertake army maneuvers.

Significant demographic implications also resulted from the territorial expansion. Israel directly controlled, and was responsible for, some 800,000 Palestinian residents (now approaching 2 million) of the West Bank and Gaza Strip, as well as approximately 20,000 Druze inhabitants of the Golan Heights (Israel, Central Bureau of Statistics, 1995). As in 1948, war had resulted in a new wave of refugees. Many of the Palestinian refugees from the West Bank were second-time refugees, having been forced to move some twenty years previously. In the Golan Heights, approximately 100,000 residents departed, leaving behind only two Druze communities that opted to stay and to retain contact with the Druze communities of Israel (Harris 1978).

Unlike the territory within the 1949 boundaries, the territories captured in 1967 do not constitute part of the sovereign area of the state. Under international law, occupied territories are subject to the Hague and Geneva Conventions. For its part, Israel views East Jerusalem and the Golan Heights as constituting part of the sovereign entity by virtue of the decisions taken by the Israeli Parliament (the Knesset) to annex these territories in 1967 and 1982, respectively. As the sovereign, Israel applies civilian, rather than military, law to these areas, while continuing to control those parts of the West Bank that have not been transferred to the Palestinian Authority through the agency of the military administration. As far as the international community is concerned, the decisions taken by the Knesset do not constitute the necessary de jure justifications for asserting sovereignty over territory captured as a result of warfare.

During the first ten years of Israeli control of the West Bank and Gaza Strip, territorial policies, as epitomized by the Allon Plan (Allon 1976; Harris 1978), focused on the concrete, rather than symbolic, desire to control land. This plan, drawn up in the immediate aftermath of the Six Day War, was central to Israeli government policy in the West Bank for the next decade. Settlement policy focused on the perceived need to ensure "defensible boundaries" in the Jordan Valley while leaving much of the interior, densely populated Palestinian areas to be part of a future autonomous area linked to Jordan (Horowitz 1975). Territory was perceived as a tangible asset that could be negotiated for other gains, such as mutual recognition and a peace agreement. As a container of demography, the Six Day War had a negative outcome, for it transformed Israel into a controller of another people, the results of which were only too plain to see from the late 1980s onward.

But it is at the symbolic level that the Six Day War had its greatest long-term spatial effect on Israeli territorial discourse. The conquest of the "historic heartland" of the Land of Israel gave rise to the birth of a territorial ideology that emphasized the "return" to and "liberation" of the promised land. The Greater Land of Israel movement was established as a pressure group aimed at ensuring that Israel would not withdraw from any of these historic lands, while in the mid-1970s the Gush Emunim religious-nationalist movement became a powerful extraparliamentary political force whose objective was to ensure that the whole of the Land of Israel, as divinely promised to the Jewish people, would remain forever under Jewish/Israeli control and sovereignty. The West Bank was now referred to by the historic name of Judea and Samaria, the territories were "liberated" rather than "occupied," and the many Israeli settlements established in the West Bank by these movements were given biblical and historic names, attesting to the Jewish attachment to these areas. Land was now to be kept because of its historical and religious symbolism, rather than because of any inherent economic or strategic considerations. Indeed, the establishment of Israeli settlements throughout the region defied demographic logic. The creation of concrete settlement facts on the ground resulted in continued control, and hence territorial sharing with, rather than separation from, a rapidly growing Palestinian population (Newman 1996b).

Territorial contraction: The Peace Agreements

Territorial change has again taken place as a result of conflict resolution between Israel and its neighbors. Commencing with the implementation of the Camp David Accords between Israel and Egypt in the early 1980s, the gradual implementation of the Oslo Agreements between Israel and the Palestinian Authority, and the peace agreement between Israel and Jordan in 1995, the political map of the region has once again undergone internal reconfiguration.

Unlike previous territorial modifications, the current changes are taking place as part of a process of conflict resolution, rather than as a result of armed conflict or some form of unilateral imposition by external powers. The boundaries that have been determined between Israel, Egypt, and Jordan have now taken on international status. This is the first time in Israel's history that any of its boundaries have achieved this form of legal status, as contrasted with the temporary status of armistice lines.

In the case of both Egypt and the ongoing negotiations with the Palestinian Authority, the result of the conflict-resolution process has been to undergo territorial contraction, namely to withdraw from all, or part, of the land previously controlled. The peace treaty with Jordan has not resulted in any significant territorial change. Israel's eastern boundary along the Jordan and Aravah Valleys has been ratified, with some minor transfers of parcels of land from Israel to Jordan. In most cases these land parcels have been leased back to Israeli farmers, who continue to cultivate them. Jordan made an important territorial statement when it decided not to ratify the section of the boundary that runs through the Jordan Valley and separates the West Bank, as contrasted with sovereign Israel, from Jordan. This, the Jordanians argued, was to be left for future negotiations between Jordan and an independent Palestinian entity.

The two peace treaties between Israel and its neighbors have, in effect, pushed the security boundary farther from the population centers. Those treaties forbid introduction of troops into adjacent territories. Egypt may not send any major forces into the Sinai Peninsula, while Jordan may not allow any foreign troops to enter its state territory. Thus, the security boundary has been pushed farther south and east than ever before, giving Israel an extended cordon sanitaire.

The Oslo I Agreement resulted in Israeli withdrawal from the Gaza Strip and the town of Jericho. This was extended to include further towns and some Palestinian villages under the terms of the Oslo II Agreements (Alpher 1994; Newman 1995b, 1996a). From a Palestinian perspective, the transition from initial autonomy to full statehood must be accompanied by further territorial changes, including the transfer of the whole of the West Bank to Palestinian control (Newman and Falah 1995; Falah and Newman 1996). The mutual perceptions of the West Bank as a single compact territory differs for each of the participants in the conflict. For Palestinians, accepting a Palestinian state in the West Bank and Gaza Strip is a major concession, in that it signals the abandonment of claims to the whole of pre-1948 Palestine by accepting less than 30 percent of the total land area (Newman and Falah 1997). From the Israeli perspective, Palestinian claims to the whole of the West Bank reflect a maximal claim that cannot be met, owing to a variety of strategic, water, and settlement issues (Newman 1994, 1995a). The semantic difference between "just" the West Bank or the "whole" of the West Bank reflects the major territorial differences that have yet to be resolved.

Within Israel, the transfer of autonomy has been of major symbolic significance. Despite the heated, and sometimes violent, opposition by religious nationalists to the transfer of "Land of Israel" territory to "foreign" rule, the territorial discourse has returned to the pragmatic, rather than symbolic, sphere. Numerous proposals have been submitted concerning the final territorial delineation of a West Bank–Palestinian state/entity (Heller 1997; Newman 1998a). They all accept the inevitability of some form of territorial withdrawal on the part of Israel and focus on the need to retain control of settlements and/or strategic sites. Yet again the territorial discourse has changed, with the concrete facts on the ground having modified the extent to which the symbolic dimension is taken into account as part of the pragmatic process of conflict resolution and territorial reconfiguration. The extent to which these diverse emphases can be changed in the short term has been attested by the return to power of a hard-line, right-wing government in May 1996, and the renewed focus on symbolism and religious attachment to land as a justification for adopting intransigent territorial policies.

CONCLUSION

In this chapter I have described the fluid nature of the political map of Israel and its neighbors. During the course of eighty years, five major phases of territorial change have occurred, ranging from the Mandate division of the region, the partition in Palestine west of the River Jordan, the establishment of the State of Israel in its armistice boundaries, the territorial expansion following the Six Day War and, finally, the territorial contraction taking place as part of the peace processes being negotiated between Israel and its neighbors. The significance of the last phase is that, as part of negotiated agreements between equal participants, the ultimate territorial configurations take on a more permanent legal status, the integrity of which is recognized by all sides in the conflict.

Interaction and feedback between the concrete and symbolic dimensions of the territorial discourse have surfaced at each stage of territorial change. Symbolic attachments to land have been influential in determining territorial policies, especially in the post-1967 era. But when faced with possibility of achieving immediate political gains, it is the pragmatic, rather than the symbolic, factors that have proved to be uppermost in the considerations of decision makers. This is as true of the decision to accept partition in the 1930s and 1940s as it was of the Oslo Agreements in the 1990s. The rhetoric of territorial symbolism is an effective tool for stating one's case under conditions of heightened conflict, but it is relegated to secondary significance under conditions of conflict resolution. The concrete arguments, especially those relating to security and strategic issues, lead to far greater public consensus than do the historic/religious arguments. That does not mean to say that the latter are insignificant in influencing territorial decision making, but it is the strategic and potential demographic implications of territorial change that speak to a wider section of the population. Thus it is common for religious-nationalist supporters of a Greater Israel to couch their arguments in terms of the strategic threat, while it is equally convenient for right-wing politicians to draw on support from the religious nationalists by occasionally referring to the historic nature of the claim. But the strategic argument carries the day, explaining to a great extent why public opinion is far more divided over the West Bank issue, much of which is couched in the language of symbolic territory, as contrasted with the Golan Heights and/or South Lebanon, both of which are perceived as being straightforward concrete-strategic issues. It also explains the constant use of the security rhetoric by the Netanyahu administration, whose main ideological support comes from the religious-nationalist community and its emphasis on the symbolic, rather than pragmatic, attachment to land and territory.

At the same time, where the symbolic attachment to territory comes to the forefront in political decision making, the issues are much more difficult to resolve. This is clearly evident with respect to the ideological opposition to any withdrawal from the West Bank–Judea/Samaria, and even more so with respect to the sensitive issue of Jerusalem (Romann and Weingrod 1990; Dumper 1997; Friedland and Hecht 1997). Emotional attachment to this city extends beyond any other piece of microterritory within Israel/Palestine. Its choice as the capital city of the state in 1948 was based on the symbolic attachment, while the rhetoric of a post-1967 unified city, forever to be the eternal capital of the Jewish people, never again to be divided, is a political rhetoric with which the large majority of the Jewish population of Israel identifies. The very suggestion, later to be proved false, during the 1996 election campaign that the administration of Yitzhak Rabin and Shimon Peres had prepared plans for the redivision of the city, even a functional rather than physical division, was enough to carry some important floating votes from the Peres camp to that of Netanyahu.

Clearly, an understanding of both territorial dimensions, the concrete and the symbolic, and of the interrelationships between them is necessary if a fuller understanding of territorial conflict and competing claims is to be achieved. Symbolic attachment to land in such diverse places of conflict as Bosnia, Northern Ireland, or Israel/Palestine, to name but a few, makes these conflicts all the more difficult to resolve, even when pragmatic solutions may be applicable. Decision makers and political leaders are happy to latch on to the symbolic arguments as a means of delaying pragmatic conflict resolution, at the same time raising the flag of national pride and patriotism. The internal discourse of societies undergoing ethnoterritorial conflict is as much, if not more, about symbolism than it is about concrete manifestations of territory. Moreover, once caught up in the heightened emotions of symbolic and metaphysical attachment to land, a society finds it increasingly difficult to set this attachment aside, even when, the pragmatic-tangible conditions allow mediation and negotiations with the "other" side to take place.

By contrast, the external discourse focuses solely on the concrete manifestations of territory. Symbolic elements are diametrically opposed to each other, with both sides claiming exclusive duration and priority in a particular area. Conflict resolution only begins to take place when there is a conscious decision to compromise over the tangible elements and an understanding that the symbolic attachment to land will remain unresolved. In other words, conflict resolution assumes a separation between the respective concrete and symbolic discourses.

This is true of the Israel-Palestine conflict, where the Oslo process dealt with the tangible issues of territorial separation and partition, while each side continued to argue its exclusive notions of territorial attachment. Conflict resolution came about because the political leaders accepted the need to achieve tangible benefits in the short term, accepting that no dialogue could ever take place over the diametrically opposed symbolic values held by each side. While the road to war is strewn with the minefields of symbolism and religious attachment to territory, the more difficult path to peace is largely dependent on the relegation of the symbolic manifestation of territory to the metaphysical, rather than practical, realms of decision making.

REFERENCES

Albin, Cecilia. 1991. "Negotiating Indivisible Goods: The Case of Jerusalem." *Jerusalem Journal of International Relations* 13: 45–76.

Allon, Yigal. 1976. "Israel: The Case for Defensible Boundaries." *Foreign Affairs* 55: 38–53.

Alpher, Joseph. 1994. *Settlement and Borders*. Jaffee Center for Strategic Studies, Tel Aviv University. Final Status Issues: Israel-Palestinians. Study no. 3.

Bar Gal, Yoram. 1993. "Boundaries as a Topic in Geographic Education." *Political Geography* 12: 421–435.

Beydoun, A. 1992. "The South Lebanon Border Zone: A Local Perspective." *Journal of Palestine Studies* 21: 35–53.

Billig, Michael. 1995. *Banal Nationalism*. London: Sage Publications.

Burghardt, Andrew. 1973. "The Bases of Territorial Claims." *Geographical Review* 63: 225–245.

Coakley, John, ed. 1993. *The Territorial Management of Ethnic Conflict*. London: Frank Cass.

Cohen, Saul B., and Nurit Kliot. 1981. "Israel's Place Names as Reflection of Continuity and Change in Nation Building." *Names* 29: 227–246.

———. 1992. "Place Names in Israel's Ideological Struggle over the Administered Territories." *Annals of the Association of American Geographers* 82: 653–680.

Cohen, Shaul E. 1993. *The Politics of Planting: Israeli- Palestinian Competition for Control of Land in the Jerusalem Periphery*. University of Chicago Geography Research Paper No. 236. Chicago: University of Chicago Press.

Davies, W. D. 1974. *The Gospel and the Land: Early Christianity and Jewish Territorial Doctrine*. Berkeley: University of California Press.

Diehl, Paul F., and Gary Goertz. 1988. "Territorial Changes and Militarized Conflict." *Journal of Conflict Resolution* 32: 103–122.

Dragadze, T. 1996. "Self-Determination and the Politics of Exclusion." *Ethnic and Racial Studies* 19: 341–350.

Duchacek, Ivo D. 1970. *Comparative Federalism: The Territorial Dimension of Politics*. New York: Reinhart and Winston.

Dumper, Michael. 1997. *The Politics of Jerusalem since 1967*. New York: Columbia University Press.

Eisenberg, Laura Z. 1997. "Israel's Lebanon Policy." *MERIA Journal* 3: http://www.biu.ac.il/SOC/besa/meria.html.

Falah, Ghazi. 1983. "The Development of the Planned Bedouin Settlement in Israel, 1964–1982: Evaluation and Characteristics." *Geoforum* 14: 311–323.

———. 1996a. "Living Together Apart: Residential Segregation in Mixed Arab-Jewish Cities in Israel." *Urban Studies* 33: 823–857.

———. 1996b. "The 1948 Israeli-Palestinian War and Its Aftermath: The Transformation and Designification of Palestine's Cultural Landscape." *Annals of the Association of American Geographers*. 86: 256–285.

Falah, Ghazi, and David Newman. 1995. "The Spatial Manifestation of Threat: Israelis and Palestinians Seek a 'Good Boundary.'" *Political Geography* 14: 689–706.

———. 1996. "The Dynamics of State Formation and the Geography of Palestinian Self-Determination." *Tijdschrift voor Economische en Sociale Geografie* 87: 60–72.

Fearon, J. D. 1995. "Rationalist Explanations for War." *International Organization* 49: 379–414.

Friedland, Roger, and Richard Hecht. 1997. *To Rule Jerusalem*. Cambridge, U.K.: Cambridge University Press.

Galnoor, Itzhak. 1991. "Territorial Partition of Palestine: The 1937 Decision." *Political Geography Quarterly* 10: 382–404.

Goertz, Gary, and Paul F. Diehl. 1992. *Territorial Changes and International Conflict*. London: Routledge.

Golan, Arnon. 1995. "The Transfer to Jewish Control of Abandoned Arab Land during the War of Independence." In *Israel: The Decade after Independence*, edited by Ilan Troen and Noah Lucas. Albany: State University of New York Press.

Gonen, Amiram. 1995. *Between City and Suburb: Urban Residential Patterns and Processes in Israel*. Aldershot, U.K.: Avebury Press.

Gottmann, Jean. 1973. *The Significance of Territory*. Charlottesville: University Press of Virginia.

Haim, Y. 1978. "Zionist Attitudes towards Partition, 1937–1938." *Jewish Social Studies* 40: 303–320.

Harris, William W. 1978. "War and Settlement Change: The Golan Heights and the Jordan Rift Valley, 1967–1977." *Transactions of the Institute of British Geographers* 3: 309–330.

Hasson, Shlomo, and Norman Gosenfeld. 1980. "Israeli Frontier Settlements: A Cross-Temporal Analysis." *Geoforum* 11: 315–334.

Heller, Mark. 1997. "Towards a Palestinian State." *Survival* 39: 5–22.

Hoffman, L. A., ed. 1986. *The Land of Israel: Jewish Perspectives*. Notre Dame, Ind.: University of Notre Dame Press.

Hooson, David, ed. 1994. *Geography and National Identity*. Oxford: Blackwell.

Holsti, K. J. 1991. *Peace and War: Armed Conflicts and International Order, 1648–1989*. Cambridge, U.K.: Cambridge University Press.

Horowitz, D. 1975. "Israel's Concept of Defensible Boundaries." Leonard Davis Institute of International Relations, Working Papers. Hebrew University of Jerusalem, Israel.

Huth, Paul. 1996. *Standing Your Ground: Territorial Disputes and International Conflict*. Ann Arbor: University of Michigan Press.

Inbar, Efraim, and Shmuel Sandler. 1997. "The Risks of Palestinian Statehood." *Survival* 39: 23–41.

Johnston, Ronald J. 1995. "Territoriality and the State." In *Geography, History and Social Sciences*, edited by Georges B. Benko and Ulf Strohmayer. Dordrecht, Netherlands: Kluwer Academic Publishers.

Katz, Yossi. 1994. "The Partition Plan of Palestine and Zionist Proposals for the Beisan Valley." *Jewish Journal of Sociology* 36: 1–20.

Kellerman, Aaron. 1994. *Society and Settlement: Jewish Land of Israel in the Twentieth Century.* Albany: State University of New York Press.

Kimmerling, Baruch. 1983. *Zionism and Territory: The Socio- Territorial Dimension of Zionist Politics.* Berkeley: University of California Press.

Knight, David B. 1994. "People Together, Yet Apart: Rethinking Territory, Sovereignty and Identities." In *Reordering the World: Geopolitical Perspectives on the 21st Century,* edited by George J. Demko and William B. Wood. Boulder, Colo.: Westview Press.

Kocs, S. 1995. "Territorial Disputes and International War, 1943–1987." *Journal of Politics* 57: 159–175.

Lustick, Ian S. 1993. *Unsettled States—Disputed Lands: Britain and Ireland, France and Algeria, Israel and the West Bank-Gaza.* Ithaca, N.Y.: Cornell University Press.

———. 1997. "Has Israel Annexed East Jerusalem?" *Middle East Policy* 5: 34–45.

Meir, Avinoam. 1997. *As Nomadism Ends: The Israeli Bedouin of the Negev.* Boulder, Colo.: Westview Press.

Morris, Benny. 1993. *Israel's Border Wars, 1949–1956.* Oxford: Clarendon Press.

Murphy, Alexander B. 1990. "Historical Justifications for Territorial Claims." *Annals of the Association of American Geographers* 80: 531–548.

———. 1996. "The Sovereign State System as Political-Territorial Ideal: Historical and Contemporary Considerations." In *State Sovereignty as Social Construct,* edited by T. J. Biersteker and C. Weber. Cambridge, U.K.: Cambridge University Press.

Newman, David. 1989. "The Role of Civilian and Military Presence as Strategies of Territorial Control: The Arab-Israel Conflict." *Political Geography Quarterly* 8: 215–227.

———. 1994. "Demarcating a Boundary of Peace between Israel and the West Bank." In *Political Boundaries and Coexistence,* edited by Werner A. Gallusser. Berne, Switzerland: Peter Lange.

———. 1995a. *Boundaries in Flux: The Green Line Boundary between Israel and the West Bank.* Boundary and Territory Briefing No. 7. Durham, U.K.: International Boundaries Research Unit.

———. 1995b. "Territorial Discontinuity and Palestinian Autonomy: Implementing the Oslo II Agreement." *Boundary and Security Bulletin* 3: 75–85.

————. 1996a. "Shared Spaces, Separate Spaces: The Israel- Palestine Peace Process." *Geojournal* 39: 363–376.

————. 1996b. "The Territorial Politics of Exurbanization: Reflections on Thirty Years of Jewish Settlement in the West Bank." *Israel Affairs* 3: 61–85.

————. 1997a. "Metaphysical and Concrete Landscapes: The Geopiety of Homeland Socialization in the 'Land of Israel.'" In *Land and Community: Geography in Jewish Studies*, edited by Robert O. Mitchell and Harold Brodsky. College Park: University of Maryland Press.

————. 1997b. "Israeli Security: Reality and Myth." *Palestine-Israel Journal* 4, no. 2: 17–24.

————. 1998a. "Creating the Fences of Separation: The Discourses of Israeli-Palestinian Conflict Resolution." *Geopolitics and International Boundaries* 2, no. 2: 1–35.

————. 1999, in press. *The Dynamics of Territorial Change: A Political Geography of the Arab-Israel Conflict*. Boulder, Colo.: Westview Press.

Newman, David, and Ghazi Falah. 1995. "Small State Behaviour: On the Formation of a Palestinian State in the West Bank and Gaza Strip." *Canadian Geographer* 39: 219–234.

————. 1997. "Bridging the Gap: Palestinian and Israeli Discourse on Autonomy and Statehood." *Transactions of the Institute of British Geographers* 22: 111–129.

Newman, David, and Anssi Paasi. 1997. "Fences and Neighbours in a Postmodern World: Rethinking Boundaries in Political Geography." *Progress in Human Geography* 22, no. 2: 186–207.

Norton, A. R., and J. Schwedler. 1993. "(In)security Zones in South Lebanon." *Journal of Palestine Studies* 23: 61–79.

Paasi, Anssi. 1995. "Constructing Territories, Boundaries and Regional Identities." In *Contested Territory: Border Disputes at the Edge of the Former Soviet Empire*, edited by Thomas Forsberg Edward. Aldershot, U.K.: Elgar.

————. 1996. *Territories, Boundaries and Consciousness: The Changing Geographies of the Finnish-Russian Border*. New York: John Wiley.

Peres, Shimon. 1994. *The New Middle East*. New York: Henry Holt.

Reichman, Shalom. 1990. "Partition and Transfer: Crystallization of the Settlement Map of Israel following the War of Independence, 1948–1950." In *The Land That Became Israel: Studies in Historical Geography*, edited by Ruth Kark. New Haven, Conn.: Yale University Press.

Romann, Michael. 1989. "Territory and Demography: The Case of the Jewish-Arab National Struggle." *Middle Eastern Studies* 26: 371–382.

Romann, Michael, and Alex Weingrod. 1991. *Living Together Separately: Arabs and Jews in Contemporary Jerusalem*. Princeton, N.J.: Princeton University Press.

Sack, Robert. 1986. *Territoriality: Its Theory and History*. Cambridge, U.K.: Cambridge University Press.

Schnell, Itzchak. 1993. "Israeli Palestinian Territorial Perceptions." *Environment and Behaviour* 25: 419–456.

———. 1994. *Perceptions of Israeli Arabs: Territoriality and Identity*. Aldershot, U.K.: Avebury Press.

Senese, Paul D. 1996. "Geographical Proximity and Issue Salience: Their Effects on the Escalation of Militarized Interstate Conflict." *Conflict Management and Peace Science* 15: 133–161.

Smith, Anthony D. Smith. 1981. *The Ethnic Revival*. New York: Cambridge University Press.

Sibley, David. 1995. *Geographies of Exclusion: Society and Difference in the West*. London: Routledge.

Sicker, Martin. 1992. *Judaism, Nationalism and the Land of Israel*. Boulder, Colo.: Westview Press.

Stolcke, V. 1995. "New Boundaries, New Rhetorics of Exclusion in Europe." *Current Anthropology* 36: 1–24.

Taylor, Peter J. 1994. "The State as a Container: Territoriality in the Modern World System." *Progress in Human Geography* 18: 151–162.

———. 1995. "Beyond Containers: Internationality, Interstateness, Interterritoriality." *Progress in Human Geography* 19: 1–15.

———. 1996. "Territorial Absolutism and Its Evasions." *Geography Research Forum* 16: 1–12.

Tuan, Yi-Fu. 1976. "Geopiety: A Theme in Man's Attachment to Land and Place." In *Geographies of the Mind*, edited by David Lowenthal and Martyn J. Bowden. New York: Oxford University Press.

———. 1991. "Language and the Making of Place: A Narrative-Descriptive Approach." *Annals of the Association of American Geographers* 81: 684–696.

Vasquez, John A. 1983. "The Tangibility of Issues and Global Conflict: A Test of Rosenau's Issue Area Typology." *Journal of Peace Research* 20: 179–192.

———. 1993. *The War Puzzle*. Cambridge, U.K., and New York: Cambridge University Press.

Wright, J. 1947. "Terrae incognitae: The Place of Imagination in Geography." *Annals of the Association of American Geographers* 37: 1-5.

Yiftachel, Oren. 1991. "State Policies, Land Control and an Ethnic Minority: Arabs and Jews in the Galilee Region, Israel." *Society and Space* 9: 329–352.

————. 1992. *Planning a Mixed Region in Israel: The Political Geography of Arab-Jewish Relations in the Galilee.* Aldershot, U.K.: Avebury Press.

Yishai, Yael. 1985. "Israeli Annexation of East Jerusalem and the Golan Heights: Factors and Processes." *Middle Eastern Studies* 21: 45–60.

PART II

The Origins of Territorial Conflict

2

Enduring Rivalries and Territorial Disputes, 1950–1990

Paul K. Huth

I n this article I analyze the conflict behavior of states that were involved in territorial disputes between 1950 and 1990. I test a set of
hypotheses regarding the domestic and international conditions
that lead a challenger state to become involved in an enduring rivalry
over disputed territory. A growing body of scholarship points toward
the conclusion that enduring rivalries and territorial disputes are
closely related to one another. Scholars have established that international relationships characterized by enduring rivalries are much
more likely to escalate to militarized confrontations, including the
outbreak of war, than are nonrivalry relationships (Goertz and Diehl
1992, 1993). Researchers have also argued that territorial disputes are
a central cause of wars between states (Holsti 1991; Vasquez 1993,
chap. 4; Kocs 1995). The link between enduring rivalries and territorial disputes is that the interstate conflicts which spark and drive enduring rivalries often seem to be associated with territorial disputes.
With further research it will most likely be established that territorial
disputes are a central underlying cause of enduring rivalries between
states.

A logical question to ask, therefore, is, How often do territorial
disputes develop into enduring rivalries? Put differently, when do
challenger states maintain claims to disputed territory over a protracted period of time and engage in the frequent use of diplomatic

and military pressure in an attempt to alter the territorial status quo? Empirically, in the post–World War II period of the 129 territorial disputes that existed between 1950 and 1990, 36 (about 28 percent) developed into enduring rivalries. The short answer, then, is that most territorial disputes do not become enduring rivalries—but why?

The theoretical puzzle is to differentiate between those conditions that cause foreign-policy leaders to adopt nonviolent and more flexible diplomatic policies concerning disputed territory and those that prompt leaders to pursue territorial claims in a more aggressive and confrontational manner. This is the central question I address. I begin by presenting a general theoretical framework for studying international conflict behavior, and then I derive a number of hypotheses about the causes of enduring rivalries over disputed territory. In the next section I describe the dataset to be analyzed and the operational measures for each of the variables to be tested. I then present the results of the statistical analysis and discuss the findings for each of the hypotheses tested. In the concluding section I consider the implications of the empirical results for a traditional realist approach to the study of international politics.

THEORETICAL APPROACH

The theoretical framework that I employ incorporates a number of assumptions from a conventional realist approach, but at the same time I also posit that domestic political concerns figure prominently in the foreign policy choices of state leaders. The underlying premise is that domestic politics can be incorporated into a realist framework in a logically sound and generalizable way (see Huth 1996, chap. 3, for a more complete discussion of the modified realist model presented below).

I begin by utilizing a rational-choice framework for analyzing the decisions of foreign policy leaders. In this rational-choice approach I assume that decisions are made by a single unitary actor who makes the final choice of whether to challenge the territorial status quo by some combination of military and diplomatic pressure. This assumption does not imply that this decision maker is isolated from the influence of other groups and political actors, either within or outside the government. This key decision maker, however, must choose the policy option with the greatest expected utility.

Beyond presuming rationality, the basic assumptions of the modified realist model are:

Assumption 1: In international politics, state leaders cannot depend on a recognized supranational authority to settle disputes with other countries. As a result, state leaders are ultimately responsible for protecting their country from possible military attack and other international security threats.

Assumption 2: A central concern of state leaders is to retain their position of domestic political power, and the ability of state leaders to remain in office is strongly related to maintaining the support of various domestic political groups.

Assumption 3: Domestic political groups seek to shape the policy choices of state leaders in order to advance their political and economic interests, and political opponents of a regime will attempt to mobilize political opposition when policies pursued by the regime have failed to achieve stated policy goals.

Assumption 4: State leaders believe that a foreign policy setback for their country stemming from a diplomatic retreat or military defeat will impose high domestic political costs on them.

This first set of assumptions establishes that state leaders must balance two critical political roles: they are held accountable for preserving the national security of their country; and they are politicians who seek to remain in power and thus are concerned with political opposition from counterelites. If political leaders attempt to meet the demands of both of these roles, some important implications follow. First, state leaders do not give military security issues the highest priority. The material and financial resource demands of national security policy do not have a privileged position in comparison with domestic policy needs. Second, decisions about foreign policy, including security policy, are examined in terms of what the consequences are for the domestic political position of state leaders, and security policy may be used to advance the domestic political interests of the leaders. Taken together, these two corollaries imply that political leaders will define the foreign policy agenda of their country in terms broader than just military security issues. Third, state leaders will be very sensitive to the potential costs that domestic groups and constituencies may suffer as a result of military conflict or a deterioration in political relations with other countries. Generally the public is not attentive to foreign policy issues, but if their country does become engaged in a crisis or military conflict, foreign policy issues become much more salient and the public is likely to hold their political leaders accountable for the outcome of the international confrontation (Bueno de Mesquita, Siverson, and Woller 1992, for example). As a result, decisions about security policy are influenced by leaders' estimates of anticipated domestic opposition, and elites can generally count on high levels of public support for confrontational policies with other states only if the direct material and human costs are not high (for example, Russett 1990, chaps. 2, 4; Page and Shapiro 1991, chaps. 5–6).

Assumption 5: Domestic political institutions structure and induce political elites to resolve conflict in particular ways. In some political systems, institutions permit the use or threat of violence and the imposition of decisions to settle conflict, whereas other systems delegitimize violence and promote compromise solutions to disputes.

Assumption 6: The norms and practices on which state leaders rely for resolving domestic political conflict are utilized in the resolution of international disputes.

The corollary to these two assumptions is that if regimes vary in fundamental ways with respect to norms concerning the legitimacy of coercion and compromise in dealing with political opposition, then regime type should be an important factor explaining patterns of international conflict behavior among states (for example, Doyle 1986; Bueno de Mesquita and Lalman 1992; Dixon 1993, 1994; Russett 1993).

Assumption 7: The threat or use of military power is the ultimate recourse for state leaders to resolve disputes with other countries and ensure their security.

One important corollary to this assumption is that foreign policy leaders should be selective in resorting to military threats or the use of force because state resources and military capabilities can be overextended due to an overly expansive definition of what constitutes vital national security interests. Overextension risks undermining a country's underlying base of military power, its capacity to defend vital interests, and military involvement in peripheral conflicts. The threat or use of force should therefore be reserved for those situations in which state leaders believe that compelling issues are at stake.

Assumption 8: State leaders seek to maintain diplomatic and military flexibility in their foreign relations with other states. When necessary, however, political leaders will align themselves with other states in order to advance their country's foreign and domestic policy goals.

One corollary to this final assumption is that when we observe states entering into formal alliances with other states we should expect salient foreign policy gains to be made by the agreement, since such agreements almost invariably entail some constraints on the foreign and defense policy choices of states. State leaders will seek military and diplomatic support from other countries when they believe that their country's foreign and domestic policy goals cannot be ensured by relying on their own material and financial resources (Walt 1987; David 1991; Barnett 1992; Morrow 1995). Because states often lack the resource capacity and/or political resolve to meet all of their foreign policy goals, security ties with other countries are necessary. Alliances, then, should not be entered into lightly by states and should indicate that there is a convergence of foreign policy interests between states.

Hypotheses regarding the Issues at Stake

Assumption 1 posits that decision makers should assess the utility of challenging the territorial status quo by the extent to which the military security of the country would be enhanced by gaining control of disputed territory. From this comes:

Hypothesis 1: There is a positive relationship between the strategic location of bordering territory and the probability that a challenger will be involved in an enduring rivalry over disputed territory.

The logic of this hypothesis is that control over strategically located territory should be of central concern to state leaders who are responsible for ensuring the military security of their country. Control of strategically located territory would strengthen the military position of the challenger in a number of potential ways: for example, by enhancing power projection capabilities for either defensive or offensive military operations, establishing a military presence in close proximity to narrow choke points or major trade routes on the sea, or extending a defense perimeter around important military bases. Given these potential benefits, leaders should be more resolved to escalate such disputes to higher levels of conflict over a protracted period of time in an attempt to coerce the target.

The second set of hypotheses is derived from assumptions 2–4 and their corollaries. These hypotheses focus on the fact that foreign policy makers are also domestic political leaders who seek to remain in power, which will influence their assessment of what salient issues are at stake in a territorial dispute.

Hypothesis 2: There is a positive relationship between the location of ethnic minorities within the target along its border who share ties with the predominant ethnic group within the challenger and the probability that a challenger will be involved in an enduring rivalry over disputed territory.

Hypothesis 3: There is a positive relationship between the challenger and target populations sharing ethnic ties and the probability that a challenger will be involved in an enduring rivalry over disputed territory.

The logic supporting these hypotheses consists of two main arguments. First, we should expect political leaders to consider not only the military security benefits of changing the territorial status quo but also the potential domestic political payoffs. For state leaders a fundamental concern is whether a foreign policy decision and course of action will generate domestic political support. The utility of challenging the territorial status quo is, therefore, viewed through the lens of whether the leader's domestic political position will be strengthened by confronting its neighbor. In this context, foreign policy issues that appeal to ethnic solidarity are particularly attractive because citizens often feel strong ties of affiliation based on common ethnic backgrounds.

If we extend this logic to the question of territorial disputes, we can argue that appeals to ethnic solidarity and unity will be very effective when minority populations located along the border in a target state share ethnic identities with the largest ethnic group within the challenger state. In such a situation, state leaders can legitimize their claim to bordering territory by emphasizing common linguistic and cultural ties. Furthermore, the leaders can imply or explicitly charge that the target government is mistreating the minority population. In either case, political leaders within the challenger can portray themselves as championing the rights of self-determination for the minority population within the target.

Appeals to ethnic solidarity and unity can also be invoked when both the challenger and target populations have the same ethnic backgrounds. The logic supporting hypothesis 3 is that cultural and ethnic similarity between challenger and target is also a source of political rivalry and conflict between states. The argument is that ethnic similarity can be expected to promote rivalry and competition between the political leadership of the challenger and target for the allegiance and right to rule over the populations of each country. Thus, the attempt by the challenger to achieve political unity coterminous with ethnic boundaries should be strongly resisted by the target. As a result, conflict becomes more likely as the leadership of the challenger seeks to increase its base of political power and support by expanding its territory, whereas the leadership of the target seeks to protect its domestic political power. Furthermore, appeals to national unity can be used by the challenger to sanction and legitimize coercion and violence against the target. Finally, since unification is the goal of the challenger, compromise or accommodation with the target becomes a less politically attractive policy for leaders within the challenger to pursue.

Hypotheses regarding the International Context

Assumptions 4 and 7 and their corollaries provide the theoretical foundation for a series of hypotheses:

Hypothesis 4: There is a positive relationship between the balance of conventional military forces and the probability that a challenger will be involved in an enduring rivalry over disputed territory.

The logic of this hypotheses is that the stronger the challenger, the higher the probability that it can overturn the territorial status quo by the use of military force or compel the target to accept its territorial demands backed by the credible threat of force. Conversely, the weaker the challenger, the greater the risk of a diplomatic or military defeat if the challenger confronts a strong target. Military weakness increases the risks of a foreign policy defeat that threatens the domestic political position of leaders within the challenger. It follows that challenger states with greater relative capabilities will be more likely to engage in higher levels of coercive pressure in an attempt to force concessions from the target or to take control of disputed territory.

Hypothesis 5: There is an inverse relationship between a challenger's involvement in political-military disputes with other states and the probability that the challenger will be involved in an enduring rivalry over disputed territory.

If the challenger is engaged in conflicts with other states, it is less likely to be in a strong position to apply diplomatic and military pressure against a target, because it has already committed or intends to commit some of its available resources to a dispute with another adversary. As a result, the bargaining position of the challenger will be weakened, and thus the probability of the challenger achieving its territorial goals will decrease. The challenger will then avoid escalation of an ongoing dispute with the target. Such a policy will focus available resources on the conflict with the other state(s) and avoid the risks of a foreign policy setback in the conflict with the target.

Assumption 8 provides the logical foundation for the next hypothesis:

Hypothesis 6: There is an inverse relationship between a target and a challenger that share alliance ties and the probability that a challenger will be involved in an enduring rivalry over disputed territory.

Although the political and military value of disputed territory establishes the potential benefits to be gained by the challenger, there are also potential costs involved in pursuing a confrontation with a target. If the challenger is engaged in a dispute with a target, it is possible that bilateral relations between the challenger and the target will suffer as a result. The logic of assumption 8 implies that leaders will think of potential costs in terms of the security implications of worsening relations with a target.

More specifically, the challenger will consider the contribution that the target can make to its security and foreign policy goals in confrontations that it may have with other states. If the target is viewed as an ally in security and other foreign policy issues, then there is a greater opportunity cost in engaging in a dispute with that country because the target may become a less reliable ally once the challenger presses territorial claims against it. According to assumption 8, states will generally be cautious in forming alliances, and thus they will ally with other states only if important foreign policy interests are at stake. Thus, we can conclude that a challenger is likely to believe that an ally has considerable value in strengthening its diplomatic and military position in disputes with other states. Convergent security and foreign policy interests of a challenger and a target will provide incentives to the challenger to reduce the levels of diplomatic and military conflict in a dispute in order to secure the continued support of its ally.

Hypotheses regarding the Domestic Context

The final hypothesis is derived from assumptions 5 and 6 and their corollaries and centers on the impact of democratic institutions and practices on conflict-resolution behavior.

Hypothesis 7: There is an inverse relationship between how democratic the challenger is and the probability that the challenger will be involved in an enduring rivalry over disputed territory.

The argument is that as a country's political institutions become more democratic, its political leaders are less likely to resort to the threat or use of coercion and violence to resolve domestic political conflicts. Instead, we should expect those leaders to favor hard-nosed bargaining and compromise. Bargaining and compromise are a feature of political competition in all political systems, but the mix of coercive and compromising behavior varies significantly across political systems. The acceptance of nonviolent means of conflict resolution and the need to compromise with political opponents reflect the structure of incentives produced by democratic institutions. If these democratic institutions are durable and stable in a country, we should expect political elites to accept the legitimacy of compromise and bargaining as the prevalent means by which to resolve political conflict. The implication for foreign policy is that political elites who have competed for an extended period of time in a democratic system should be less prone to the aggressive use of force to resolve international disputes and more willing to consider some form of compromise as an acceptable solution to a dispute. (For a review and critical analysis of empirical studies on the war-proneness of democracies, see Ray 1995; Rousseau, Gelpi, and others 1996.) Norms of nonviolent conflict resolution and compromise will not prevent a democratic challenger from disputing territory with a target, but they will influence the pattern of bargaining and negotiation over disputed territory. The willingness of democratic leaders to resort to threats or the use of military force will be reduced, while their propensity to propose a compromise settlement will increase compared with less democratic political systems. In other words, the moderating effects of democratic norms on conflict behavior within a territorial dispute will be present regardless of whether the adversary is democratic. I dispute both the logical basis and the empirical basis for arguing that democracies are only more pacific in their relations with other democracies. (See Rousseau, Gelpi, and others 1996 for a more detailed analysis of the theoretical and empirical basis for a nondyadic approach.)

The equation to be tested is as follows:

$$y = c + b_1x_1 + b_2x_2 + b_3x_3 + b_4x_4 + b_5x_5 + b_6x_6 + b_7x_7 + ut$$

For each variable I include the expected sign of the coefficient when it was estimated in the statistical analysis.

The endogenous variable y = the probability that a challenger state will be involved in an enduring rivalry over disputed territory in a given year

c = constant term

The exogenous variables x_1 to x_7 are specified as follows:

Issues at Stake

x_1 = strategic location of bordering territory (positive)

x_2 = support for minorities along border of target with ethnic ties to the challenger (positive)

x_3 = political unification based on common ethnic background between challenger and target populations (positive)

International Context

x_4 = the balance of conventional military capabilities between challenger and target (positive)

x_5 = challenger dispute involvement with other states (negative)

x_6 = common security ties between challenger and target (negative)

Domestic Political Context

x_7 = democratic norms of challenger (negative)

u_t = error term

RESEARCH DESIGN AND MEASUREMENT OF VARIABLES

The dataset I analyzed consists of 129 territorial disputes between states in the international system from 1950 to 1990. For each dispute information was collected annually on the level of diplomatic and military conflict initiated by the challenger state over disputed territory. (See Huth 1996, chaps. 2, 5 and app. A for a detailed description of this dataset.) The dataset is structured as a pooled time series on the conflict behavior of challengers in each of the 129 territorial dispute cases. In total, the dataset contains 3,039 years of observations in which the challenger was disputing territory.

The endogenous variable was coded 1 if the challenger was involved in an enduring rivalry for a given year; 0 if it was not. To be coded as an enduring rivalry all three of the following conditions had to be met: the territorial dispute had to have existed for at least ten years; at least one-half of the years in which a dispute existed had to have been characterized by high levels of diplomatic and/or military conflict initiated by the challenger; and the challenger had to have initiated at least two militarized confrontations over disputed territory or to have resorted to the large-scale use of military force within a militarized confrontation for at least two consecutive years. (See Goertz and Diehl 1992, 1993 for a general discussion of the concept of an enduring rivalry.)

High levels of diplomatic and political conflict over disputed territory were coded when a challenger actively confronted a target over disputed territory and when the actions of a challenger included one or more of the following: hostile rhetoric and public recriminations; solicitation of third-party support in order to pressure a target into making concessions; use of sanctions or restrictions on bilateral diplomatic, economic, or military ties as a result of the territorial dispute; or efforts to overthrow or destabilize the government of a target in an attempt to induce a change in target policy over disputed territory. Militarized confrontations over disputed territory occurred when a challenger threatened or resorted to the use of military force against a target (large-scale use of force being defined as involving 1,000 or more troops). Applying these coding rules, challenger states became involved in enduring rivalries in 36 out of the 129 territorial dispute cases between 1950 and 1990 (see Table 1). Overall, approximately 76.2 percent of the observations (2,316) equaled 0; the remaining 23.8 percent of the observations (723) equaled 1.

Table 2.1

Enduring Rivalries over Disputed Territory, 1950–1990*

Countries in a Territorial Dispute	Duration	Years of Enduring Rivalry
The Caribbean, Central, and South America		
Argentina vs. Chile	1950–90	35
Argentina vs. UK	1950–90	14
Argentina vs. Uruguay	1950–73	0
Bolivia vs. Chile	1950–90	0
Cuba vs. US	1959–90	0
Ecuador vs. Peru	1950–90	41
Guatemala vs. UK	1950–90	15
Honduras vs. El Salvador	1950–90	14
Honduras vs. US	1950–72	0
Mexico vs. US	1950–63	0
Netherlands/Suriname vs. France	1950–90	0
Netherlands/Suriname vs. UK/Guyana	1950–90	0
Nicaragua vs. Colombia	1980–90	0
Nicaragua vs. Honduras	1957–60	0
Nicaragua vs. US	1950–71	0
Panama vs. US	1950–77	0
Uruguay vs. Brazil	1950–90	0
Venezuela vs. UK/Guyana	1951–90	9
Europe		
USSR/East Germany vs. US/West Germany/France/UK	1950–71	15
France vs. UK	1950–53	0
Greece vs. Albania	1950–71	0
Greece vs. UK/Turkey	1951–90	52[a]
Ireland vs. UK	1950–90	0
Netherlands vs. Belgium	1950–59	0
Netherlands vs. West Germany	1955–60	0
Spain vs. UK	1950–90	0
West Germany vs. Czechoslovakia	1955–73	0
West Germany vs. East Germany	1955–72	0
West Germany vs. France	1955–57	0
West Germany vs. Poland	1955–70	0
Yugoslavia vs. Italy	1950–75	0
Middle East		
Egypt vs. Israel	1950–89	40
Egypt vs. UK	1950–54	0
Egypt vs. UK/Sudan	1950–90	0

Iran vs. Iraq	1950–90	8
Iran vs. Saudi Arabia	1950–68	0
Iran vs. UK/Bahrain	1950–70	0
	1979–90	
Iran vs. UK/United Arab Emirates	1950–90	13
Iraq vs. Kuwait	1950–90	20
Jordan vs. Israel	1950–90	36
Jordan vs. Saudi Arabia	1950–65	0
North Yemen vs. UK/South Yemen	1950–90	34
Oman vs. United Arab Emirates	1977–81	0
Qatar vs. Bahrain	1967–90	0
Saudi Arabia vs. Iraq	1950–81	0
Saudi Arabia vs. Kuwait	1961–90	0
Saudi Arabia vs. UK/Qatar	1950–65	0
Saudi Arabia vs. UK/United Arab Emirates	1950–74	22
Syria vs. Israel	1950–90	36

Africa

Benin vs. Niger	1960–65	0
Comoros vs. France	1975–90	0
Ethiopia vs. France/Djibouti	1950–77	0
Ethiopia vs. Sudan	1950–72	0
Ethiopia vs. UK/Kenya	1950–70	0
Ghana vs. France/Ivory Coast	1959–66	0
Lesotho vs. South Africa	1966–90	0
Liberia vs. France/Guinea	1950–58	0
Liberia vs. France/Ivory Coast	1950–60	0
Libya vs. Chad	1954–90	14
Madagascar vs. France	1960–90	0
Mali vs. Burkino Faso	1960–87	0
Mali vs. Mauritania	1960–63	0
Mauritania vs. Spain	1960–75	0
Mauritius vs. France	1976–90	0
Mauritius vs. UK	1980–90	0
Morocco vs. France/Algeria	1956–72	6
Morocco vs. Mauritania	1957–70	0
Morocco vs. Spain	1956–90	0
Seychelles vs. France	1976–90	0
Somalia vs. Ethiopia	1950–90	21
Somalia vs. France/Djibouti	1960–77	0
Somalia vs. UK/Kenya	1960–81	8
Togo vs. Ghana	1960–90	0
Tunisia vs. France	1956–62	0
Tunisia vs. France/Algeria	1956–70	0
Uganda vs. Tanzania	1972–79	0
Zaire vs. Congo	1970–90	0
Zaire vs. Zambia	1980–90	0
Zambia vs. Malawi	1981–86	0

Central Asia

Afghanistan vs. Pakistan	1950–90	10
China vs. Afghanistan	1950–63	0
China vs. Bhutan	1979–90	0
China vs. Burma	1950–60	0
China vs. India	1950–90	32
China vs. Nepal	1950–61	0
China vs. Pakistan	1950–63	0
China vs. Soviet Union	1950–90	28
India vs. Bangladesh	1973–90	0
India vs. France	1950–54	0
India vs. Portugal	1950–74	14
Pakistan vs. India	1950–90	35
USSR vs. Iran	1950–54	0
USSR vs. Turkey	1950–53	0

East and South East Asia

China vs. Japan	1951–90	0
China vs. South Vietnam/Vietnam	1951–90	22[b]
China vs. Taiwan	1950–90	26
Indonesia vs. Netherlands	1950–62	5
Indonesia vs. UK/Malaysia	1961–66	0
Japan vs. USSR	1951–90	0
Malaysia vs. China	1979–90	0
North Korea vs. South Korea	1950–90	34
North Vietnam vs. South Vietnam	1954–75	10
Philippines vs. China	1956–90	0
Philippines vs. Malaysia	1961–90	0
Portugal vs. Indonesia	1975–90	0
South Korea vs. Japan	1951–90	0
South Vietnam/Vietnam vs. Cambodia	1956–83	18[c]
Taiwan vs. Japan	1951–90	0
Thailand. vs. France/Cambodia	1950–82	37[d]
Thailand vs. Laos	1984–90	0
Vanuata vs. France	1982–90	0

* For a more complete description of each territorial dispute case including, information on the issues in dispute, the outcome of the dispute, and the dates when states initiated militarized confrontations, see Huth, 1996, App. A.

[a] The total of fifty-two years was divided between Greece and Turkey as challengers. The period 1965–1990 was coded as an enduring rivalry for Greece as a challenger against UK/Turkey, and the same years were also coded as an enduring rivalry for Turkey as the challenger against UK/Greece.

[b] The total of twenty-two years was divided between China and Vietnam as challengers. The period 1980–1990 was coded as an enduring rivalry for China as a challenger

against Vietnam, and the same years were also coded as an enduring rivalry for Vietnam as the challenger against China.

[c] The total of eighteen years was divided between Cambodia and Vietnam as challengers. The periods 1965–1970 and 1976–1983 were coded as an enduring rivalry for South Vietnam/Vietnam as a challenger against Cambodia, and the years 1980–1983 were coded as an enduring rivalry for Cambodia as the challenger against Vietnam.

[d] The total of thirty-seven years is divided between Thailand and Cambodia as challengers. Thailand as a challenger was coded as being in an enduring rivalry for the years 1955–1982, while Cambodia as the challenger was coded for an enduring rivalry from 1962 to 1970.

The exogenous variables were coded as follows (see Huth 1996, app. C for a more detailed discussion of operational measures and sources utilized):

Strategic Location of Bordering Territory: This variable was coded 1 if bordering territory was strategically located; 0 if it was not. Strategic located territory was defined by any one of the following conditions: it was in close proximity to major shipping lanes or choke points of narrow straits; it was in close proximity to the challenger's military bases; it provided an outlet to the sea for an otherwise landlocked country; it was being used as a military base by the target; it could be used to establish a second military front against the target; or control of disputed territory blocked the principal route through which a challenger could attack a target.

Minority Groups along Border with Ties to Challenger: This variable attempts to measure the presence of bordering populations that are a minority within the target state but share ties of a common language and ethnicity with the largest comparable ethnic group within the challenger state. The variable was coded 1 if groups along the border or within disputed territory, which were a minority within the target, spoke the same language and shared the same ethnic background as the largest ethnic group within the challenger; 0 if they did not.

Political Unification Based on Similarity of Challenger and Target Populations: This variable was coded 1 if the predominant language and ethnic group of the populations of the challenger and target were the same; 0 if they were not.

Balance of Conventional Military Capabilities: To measure the relative military capabilities of challenger and target, annual data were collected on national military expenditures and the number of men under arms from 1950 to 1990. The challenger's capabilities were then calculated as the percentage of the combined capabilities of challenger and target for each of three indicators of military capabilities: the number of men under arms; total military expenditures; and total expenditures per soldier. When necessary, the capabilities of challenger and target were discounted to reflect the impact of distance on the power-projection capabilities of each state (Bueno de Mesquita 1981, 105). The overall balance of forces was then calculated by averaging the percentages. The balance-of-forces variable could range from 0 to 1. A value approaching 0 indicated that the challenger had very limited capabilities, whereas a value close to 1 indicated that the challenger was much stronger militarily than the target.

Involvement of Challenger in Disputes with Other States: This variable measured, in each year, the number of territorial disputes in which the challenger was engaged with states other than the target.

Common Security Ties between Challenger and Target: A value of 1 was coded for each year in which the target and the challenger were members of the same defense pact, entente, or nonaggression/neutrality pact; 0 if they were not. A neutrality or nonaggression pact was coded as present if states had agreed that they would not attack each other or would not join adversarial alliances.

Democratic Norms of Challenger: This variable was constructed from the POLITY II dataset (Gurr, Jaggers, and Moore 1989). For each year the challenger's autocracy score was subtracted from its democracy score, generating a net democracy score. This net score (which could range in value from –10 to 10) was then converted into a dummy variable with values of 5 or greater equaling 1, indicating that the challenger was relatively democratic; 0 if it was not. The next step was to determine how often the challenger had been democratic during the past twenty-five years. The measure thus attempted to weigh the current democratic status of the challenger by the relatively recent past history of democratic rule in the country. A twenty-five-year lag was chosen because it roughly measures the generational experiences of leaders that were in power.

DATA ANALYSIS AND RESULTS

Probit analysis was used to test the equation and the coefficients, robust standard errors, and significance levels are presented in Table 2.

Overall, the results provide substantial insight regarding the conditions that played an important role in the development of enduring rivalries over disputed territory. The estimated coefficients for both domestic and international variables are uniformly in the predicted direction; several variables have moderate to large substantive effects; and the significance levels are quite high for many variables as well.

Table 2.2
Probit Estimates of Enduring Rivalry over Disputed Territory, 1950–1990*

Explanatory Variables	Coefficient	Standard Errors	Significance Level
Constant	-1.595	0.071	<.001
Issues at Stake			
Strategic location of territory	0.524	0.059	<.001
Ties to bordering minority	0.754	0.068	<.001
Political unification	0.720	0.069	<.001
International Context			
Balance of military forces	1.349	0.113	<.001
Challenger disputes	-0.129	0.017	<.001
Common security ties	-0.289	0.059	<.001
Domestic Context			
Democratic challenger	-0.018	0.004	<.001

* Number of observations = 3,039; initial Log-likelihood = -2,106.5; log-likelihood at convergence = -1,419.1; percentage of cases correctly predicted = 77.4. All significance levels based on one-tailed tests.

The Issues at Stake in Enduring Rivalries

Test results supported all of the hypotheses focusing on the military security and domestic political issues at stake. Territorial disputes involving issues of ethnic irredentism or national unification were the most likely to develop into enduring rivalries. Disputes over strategically located territory were also likely to become enduring rivalries, but the substantive effects were slightly less than they were for disputes in which ethnic irredentism and national unification were the issues at stake. Overall, the results provide solid support for the modified realist model and point out the limits of a traditional realist approach. A traditional realist approach was only partially supported, even though a consistent relationship was found between military security issues at stake and enduring rivalries. The reason is that a traditional realist model would predict that disputes involving security issues should be the most conflictual and likely to become enduring rivalries, but the probit results indicate that territorial disputes defined in terms of domestic political issues were even more prone to becoming enduring rivalries.

The first result in Table 2 to examine in greater detail is that strategically valuable bordering territory was associated with an increased likelihood of the challenger's being involved in an enduring rivalry. The positive coefficient and strong t-ratio (9.23) for this variable indicates clear support for hypothesis 1. In Table 3 we see that this variable produces a 12 percent increase in the probability of an enduring rivalry.

Table 2.3.
The Marginal Impact of Variables Measuring the Issues at Stake on the Probability of an Enduring Rivalry over Disputed Territory, 1950–1990

Change in Value of Explanatory Variable	Probability of an Enduring Rivalry (%)
STRATEGIC LOCATION OF TERRITORY Is bordering territory strategically located?	
No vs. Yes	+12.0
TIES TO BORDERING MINORITIES Do bordering minority groups within the target share ties of language and ethnicity with the population of the challenger?	
No vs. Yes	+19.2
POLITICAL UNIFICATION Do the general populations of challenger and target share ties of a common language and ethnicity?	
No vs. Yes	+18.0

* The changes in the probability of an enduring rivalry were calculated utilizing the coefficients from the equation presented in Table 2. The value of a single explanatory variable was changed, while all continuous variables in the equation were held at their mean or the modal value for dummy variables. The change in location on the cumulative normal distribution was then converted into the percentage change in the probability of an enduring rivalry (see King 1989, 106–108).

In previous research (Huth 1996, chap. 4) I found that the strategic location of bordering territory was a strong predictor of whether a challenger would become involved in a territorial dispute. The findings here build on those results by indicating that when strategic issues are at stake in territorial disputes, challenger states are more likely to adopt coercive diplomatic and military policies in an attempt to gain control of the disputed territory. Examples include the use of force by Iran to take control of the islands of Abu Musa and the Greater and Lesser Tunb in the Straits of Hormuz in 1971 and its refusal since then to withdraw (Ramazani 1975, 415–435); Iraqi diplomatic and military pressure on Kuwait to gain control of Warbah and Bubiyan Islands (Finnie 1992, chap. 10; Freedman and Karsh 1993, chaps. 1–3; Schofield 1993); Argentina's military pressure against Chile over disputed islands in the Beagle Channel during the 1960s and 1970s (Day 1982, 335–337); and Egyptian and Syrian unyielding opposition to Israeli occupation of the Sinai and the Golan Heights and their determination to regain the lost territories (Heikal 1975; Herzog 1975; Drysdale and Hinnebusch 1991, 103–108).

If we turn to the two hypotheses that focus on domestic politics, we find strong results for each. First, the presence of minority groups along the border of the target with common ethnic ties to the general population of the challenger increased the likelihood of an enduring rivalry. The positive and very significant coefficient (t-ratio = 11.12) in Table 2 strongly supports hypothesis 2. In Table 3 we see that the presence of minority groups produces a 19 percent increase in the probability of an enduring rivalry. These statistical findings converge with the conventional wisdom that when ethnic irredentism is an issue at stake in a territorial dispute, higher levels of diplomatic conflict and even armed violence are more likely. A number of examples illustrate these findings: the dispute between Pakistan and India over Kashmir; the Arab-Israeli conflict and the struggle of the Palestinians for a homeland; and Somalia's conflict with Ethiopia over the ethnic Somali population in the Ogaden.

If we compare these results for bordering minorities with those from my previous research, an interesting contrast is apparent. In another study (Huth 1996, chap. 4) I found that irredentist claims and support for the self-determination rights of minority groups were not a strong predictor of why challengers became involved in territorial disputes. One contributing factor was that prevailing international norms in the post–World War II period have not supported the rights of national groups or states to self-determination when it threatened the territorial integrity of sovereign states. The results here suggest that because this international norm is generally respected, only states that have strong domestic political forces favoring conflict with the target will become involved in territorial disputes over irredentist or self-determination claims. Therefore, higher levels of conflict over an extended period of time can be expected.

In a number of cases, then, the domestic political incentives for leaders within challenger states to dispute territory overcame the lack of international support for such claims. Examples include Somalia's claims against Ethiopia; Pakistan's dispute with India over Kashmir; Afghanistan's conflict with Pakistan over the Durand Line; and Turkey's confrontation with Greece over the fate of Turkish Cypriots since the 1974 invasion. In each of these cases the challenger was not able to generate diplomatic support for its position within either regional organizations or the United Nations, and, in some cases, these international organizations openly opposed the challenger's claims (the Organization of African Unity [OAU] and Somalia, for example, or the United Nations and Turkey). Nevertheless, political leaders in the challenger states persisted in their claims, maintained very firm diplomatic positions, resorted to the threat or use of military force, or continued to occupy disputed territory (Touval 1972, 83–89, 111–118, 133–153; Bahcheli 1990, chap. 4; Allcock, Arnold, and others 1992, 48–63, 411–426, 474–488).

The second strong finding was that disputes in which the challenger sought political unification with the target were likely to escalate into an enduring rivalry. In Table 2 the ethnic similarity variable is positive and very significant (t-ratio = 10.36), which strongly supports hypothesis 3. In Table 3 the marginal impact analysis reveals that when the populations of the challenger and target share ethnic and linguistic backgrounds the probability of an enduring rivalry increases by 18 percent.

Cases such as North Vietnam versus South Vietnam, North Korea versus South Korea, China versus Taiwan, Iraq versus Kuwait, North Yemen versus South Yemen, and India versus Portugal over Goa all illustrate how challengers that sought political unification with the target often turned to the threat or use of military force. Nevertheless, in some cases the challenger did not escalate disputes to high levels of diplomatic and military conflict despite common ethnic backgrounds across state borders. Interestingly, in only one of these cases—West Germany versus East Germany—did the challenger question the very sovereignty of the target. In the cases that did not support hypothesis 3 the disputes often centered on relatively small sections of territory along a border that otherwise had been recognized by both parties. In Central and South America examples include the disputes between Nicaragua and Honduras and between Argentina and Uruguay; in Africa, the disputes between Benin and Niger and between Tunisia and Algeria are good examples; in the Middle East relevant cases include the dispute between Jordan and Saudi Arabia or that among the smaller Persian Gulf states.

The International Context of Enduring Rivalries

The results in Table 2 for the international-level variables are all supportive of the hypotheses tested. First, the conventional balance-of-forces variable had a positive and very significant coefficient (t-ratio = 11.98), as predicted by hypothesis 4. This result indicates that challenger states became more likely to engage in higher levels of diplomatic and military pressure against a target as their relative military position improved. As Table 4 shows, a change in the balance of forces from a one-to-nine disadvantage to a nine-to-one advantage for the challenger is associated with an approximate 22 percent increase in the likelihood of an enduring rivalry.

Closer examination of the results reveals that the effects of the military balance are actually somewhat curvilinear. That is, very weak as well as very strong challengers were often less likely to engage in high levels of escalation compared with challengers that were closer to parity or held a clear but not overwhelming edge in military capabilities. Very weak challengers lacked the military means to pose a credible threat to the target and therefore seldom initiated militarized confrontations. For example, successive Bolivian governments failed to threaten Chile despite a strong desire to gain direct access to the Pacific Ocean; Spanish governments did not attempt to use military force to dislodge the British from Gibraltar; and Japan did not contest with military force Soviet control of the disputed Kurile Islands.

Table 2.4

The Marginal Impact of Variables Measuring the International Context on the Probability of an Enduring Rivalry over Disputed Territory, 1950–1990*

Change in Value of Explanatory Variable	Probability of an Enduring Rivalry (%)
BALANCE OF MILITARY FORCES	
The ratio of challenger to target capabilities varies from:	
$\frac{1}{9}$ to $\frac{1}{3}$	+2.2
$\frac{1}{3}$ to $\frac{1}{1}$	+5.4
$\frac{1}{1}$ to $\frac{3}{1}$	+8.0
$\frac{3}{1}$ to $\frac{9}{1}$	+6.1
	Total +21.7
CHALLENGER DISPUTE INVOLVEMENT	
How many other territorial disputes is the challenger involved in?	
0 vs. 1	-2.5
1 vs. 2	-2.2
2 vs. 5	-4.5
5 vs. 10	-3.0
	Total -12.2
COMMON SECURITY TIES	
Are challenger and target military alliance partners?	
No vs. Yes	-4.0

* See the note to Table 2.3 for a description of how the changes in the probability of an enduring rivalry were calculated.

In each of these cases, challenger governments maintained a very firm policy of diplomatic opposition, but their military weakness required that they be cautious about becoming involved in any armed confrontation (DeSota 1962; Jain 1981; Shumavon 1981; Levie 1983; Morales 1984; Nimmo 1988, chaps. 1–2). Some relatively weak states have adopted quite tough and inflexible negotiating positions regarding their territorial demands, but they have rarely escalated the conflict to the military level despite the refusal of the much stronger target to make territorial concessions. Cuba, for example, has maintained a policy of unyielding opposition to the U.S. military base at Guantánamo Bay for decades but has not attempted to compel the United States to withdraw by militarily challenging the U.S. forces positioned there (Allcock, Arnold, and others 1992, 582–585). When weaker states have become involved in militarized confrontations they have typically engaged in limited military probes to test the resolve of the target (for example, Guatemala versus the United Kingdom or Ecuador versus Peru), and there were no examples of very weak challengers initiating the large-scale use of force against a much stronger target that was expected to respond in kind.

Even though very strong challengers had the military capabilities to seize disputed territory, they often did not resort to the use of force since no vital security interests were at stake. The reason was that because the challenger had such a decisive military advantage, control of disputed territory was of only minimal strategic importance. For example, China did not rely on coercive pressure against neighbors such as Afghanistan, Burma, or Nepal, and the Soviet Union did not resort to military pressure to force Iran to make territorial concessions. In each of these cases the challenger had an overwhelming military advantage, but only relatively small sections of territory were in dispute. Therefore, it would seem that the strategic issues at stake were quite limited for the challenger. However, when much stronger challengers did believe that strategically valuable territory was at stake then diplomatic and military pressure was used (Iraq versus Kuwait, Iran versus the United Arab Emirates, or China versus India).

In many of the cases with the highest frequency of years involving the threat or use of force, either the challenger and the target possessed roughly equal military capabilities or the challenger enjoyed a clear but not overwhelming advantage. Furthermore, when the challenger did resort to the large-scale use of military force, it had a clear military advantage in a minority of cases (Turkey versus Greece/Cyprus in 1974; China versus India in 1962; India versus Portugal in 1961; China versus Vietnam in 1979; North Korea versus South Korea in 1950; Vietnam versus Cambodia in 1977; Iraq versus Kuwait in 1990). In the majority of cases the challenger was evenly matched or inferior to the target (Argentina versus Great Britain in 1982; Egypt versus Israel in 1967, 1970, and 1973; Iraq versus Iran in 1980; Jordan versus Israel in 1967; Syria versus Israel in 1967 and 1973; Somalia versus Ethiopia in 1977; Uganda versus Tanzania in 1978; Pakistan versus India in 1965; Indonesia versus Malaysia 1964; North Vietnam versus South Vietnam in 1965).

In sum, assessments of relative military strength seem to be one important component of a challenger's decision to become involved in an enduring rivalry. Weak challengers did not resort to the large-scale use of military force against powerful targets, and when weaker challengers did threaten the use of force against stronger targets they did so through limited military actions designed to probe the resolve of the target. As a result, the challenger could pull back from further escalation if the target responded in a forceful manner. In disputes in which the challenger maintained rough parity or enjoyed a military advantage, enduring rivalries were more likely to emerge over time. In these disputes the use of military force was a viable option that state leaders frequently exercised when the incentives to act were strong.

Moreover, the propensity of the challenger to become involved in an enduring rivalry was clearly related to its involvement in conflicts with other states. In particular, the challenger was less likely to escalate against a target if it was involved in territorial disputes with other states. The negative coefficient for this variable is quite significant (t-ratio = -7.55), which strongly supports hypothesis 5. In Table 4 the results indicate that as the number of other territorial disputes for the challenger increases from zero to ten, the likelihood of an enduring rivalry decreases by about 12 percent.

A number of examples illustrate these general findings. China was involved in multiple disputes throughout the 1950s and 1960s. In the late 1950s it was a party in ten disputes involving India, Pakistan, Burma, Nepal, Afghanistan, Taiwan, the Soviet Union, South Vietnam, Japan, and the Philippines. During the late 1950s and early 1960s, however, China pursued an active and confrontational policy only toward India and Taiwan (Whiting 1975, chap. 1; Jetly 1979; Stolper 1985; Sandhu 1988; Long 1991). Saudi Arabia had simultaneous disputes with Iran, Jordan, Iraq, Kuwait, and the British but pursued a tough diplomatic policy combined with limited military pressure only toward the British in the dispute over Abu Dhabi (Albaharna 1975, 196–238, 261–263). In the 1960s Morocco had disputes with Spain, Algeria, and Mauritania but was careful to avoid escalation of all three disputes at the same time. For example, a sharp deterioration in relations with Algeria in the early to mid-1960s was accompanied by relatively stable relations with both Spain and Mauritania (Touval 1972, 255–269). Somalia had territorial claims against Ethiopia,

Kenya, and Djibouti, but after a period of high levels of conflict with Ethiopia and Kenya in the early 1960s, it deescalated its dispute with Kenya while maintaining a more confrontational policy toward Ethiopia (Touval 1972, chap. 9; Day 1982, 114–118, 131–136).

Two related reasons explain why challengers were less likely to become involved in enduring rivalries when they were involved in multiple territorial disputes. First, challengers often lacked the military capabilities to project their military forces across several borders simultaneously. If a state was a challenger in multiple disputes it could not generally pose a credible threat of military pressure on multiple fronts. Conversely, if a state was both a challenger and target in different cases, it had to worry that if it escalated a dispute with one state it would risk weakening its defensive position along its other borders and therefore undercut its ability to deter potential attacks. For example, Ethiopia's primary concern was the threat of Somalia, and therefore it did not aggressively press its claims against Sudan or Kenya.

Second, challengers involved in multiple disputes had incentives to avoid confrontation with some states and thereby convince those states to support their claims in a dispute with another adversary. For example, China in part sought cooperative relations with Pakistan in the hope that Pakistan would support China in its dispute with India, and an accommodative policy toward Japan in the 1970s over the disputed Senkaku Islands was linked to the goal of trying to induce Japan to form an anti-Soviet coalition in the Far East (Syed 1974; Barnett 1977, chap. 2; Rais 1977; Jain 1980, chaps. 6–7; Vertzberger 1983). In December 1970 Iran retreated from its claim to Bahrain in an attempt to secure support from Saudi Arabia and other Persian Gulf states for its claim to the islands of Abu Musa and the Greater and Lesser Tunb which it occupied in November 1971 (Ramazani 1975, 411–415). As an extension of this second point, challengers also pursued accommodative policies in disputes with some states in order to foster an image of reasonableness and peaceful intentions and thus to build greater international support for their territorial claims in other disputes. An excellent example was China's policy of accommodation toward Afghanistan, Burma, and Nepal in the early 1960s. Chinese leaders believed that peaceful and friendly relations with many of its neighbors would help to convince other states that the failure of

China to reach a settlement with India was due to India's intransigence and thereby would isolate India diplomatically (Pettman 1973;
Husan and Anwar 1979; Ghoble 1986).

The final result for the international context variables concerns
the effects of common security interests between challenger and target. In Table 2 we see that if the challenger had military alliance ties
with the target, it was less likely to become involved in an enduring
rivalry. As predicted by hypothesis 6, the negative coefficient is significant (t-ratio = –4.88) but in Table 4 we see that an enduring rivalry
is only 4 percent less likely between allies. The probit results are supportive, but only moderately so.

A number of examples illustrate the effects of common security interests between challenger and target. In Western Europe, North Atlantic Treaty Organization (NATO) allies were involved in several territorial disputes (France versus the United Kingdom, Netherlands
versus Belgium and West Germany, and West Germany versus
France), but all of these disputes were short-lived, and in none of the
cases did the challenger resort to high levels of diplomatic or military
pressure. The common perception of a threat posed by the Soviet
Union and the Warsaw Pact probably contributed to the belief among
the allies that their disputes should not drive a serious wedge between
them and thus weaken NATO's ability to oppose the Warsaw Pact. In
the Middle East, Iran and Saudi Arabia were involved in a dispute
from 1950 to 1968, but neither side engaged in high levels of diplomatic or military pressure. The avoidance of conflict can be attributed
in part to a shared interest in confronting their common adversaries of
Iraq and Great Britain, with which they both had territorial disputes.
Similarly, Saudi Arabia and Kuwait had a common interest in avoiding serious conflict in their territorial disputes so that their powerful
neighbor Iraq could not play one off against the other in pursuit of its
own territorial claims (Ramazani 1975, 398–399, 406, 409–414; Abdulghani 1984, 80, 86–87; Razi 1984, 406–410). In Africa, the common
threat of Somali irredentism provided the impetus for Ethiopia and
Kenya to form a military alliance and to develop and maintain close
cooperative relations (Touval 1972, 141–142, 248–249). Finally, in
Central Asia China and Pakistan avoided conflict in their territorial
dispute as part of a general policy of diplomatic and military cooperation against their common adversary, India. China, for example, pro-

vided substantial amounts of conventional arms to Pakistan beginning in the mid-1960s and is believed to have provided assistance to
Pakistan's nuclear weapons program (Syed 1974, 139–144; Rais 1977,
99–106; Vertzberger 1983, 88–90; Spector 1987, 105).

While common security ties generally served to mitigate conflict
between challenger and target, in several examples such ties did not
deter the challenger from high levels of diplomatic and military escalation: common alliance ties within NATO did not prevent Greece
and Turkey from actively competing for influence and control over
Cyprus; despite their common membership in the Rio Pact, Argentina
frequently resorted to military threats against Chile; and Iraq pursued
a confrontational policy toward Kuwait even though they were both
members of the Arab League. In each of these cases the target was a
relatively weak ally that could provide little in the way of military aid
to support the challenger in conflicts with other states. As a result,
there were minimal security risks associated with the loss of the target as a potential military ally. For example, Iraq's primary security
threat was Iran, but Kuwait was not capable of posing a military threat
to Iran. Similarly, the Soviet Union was a security concern for Turkey,
but Greece could do little to assist Turkey in the event of a military
confrontation with the Soviet Union.

Common security interests can be a powerful force pushing the
challenger to avoid conflict with a target. The statistical findings un-
derstate this effect because the degree of common security interests
represented by alliance ties varies considerably across disputes and is
not adequately captured by a measure that codes only the presence of
alliance ties. The estimated coefficient reflects the general effect of
this variable and therefore includes cases in which the challenger's
likely estimate of the value of the target as a military and diplomatic
ally was moderate, if not low. However, when a challenger viewed a
target as a valuable ally, common security interests provided strong
incentives for the challenger to avoid becoming involved in an enduring rivalry with the target.

The Domestic Context of Enduring Rivalries

In hypothesis 7 it was posited that democratic challengers are less
likely to engage in escalatory actions against the target and become

involved in an enduring rivalry. In Table 2 the coefficient for the democratic norms variable is negative, as expected, and significant (the t-ratio = 4.59). The substantive effect of this variable, however, is not that large, as indicated by the results in Table 5: as one moves from a case in which the challenger has no history of democratic rule to one in which it has been democratic for the past twenty-five years, the likelihood of an enduring rivalry decreases by about 6 percent.

Table 2.5
The Marginal Impact of Variables Measuring the Domestic Context on the Probability of an Enduring Rivalry over Disputed Territory, 1950–1990*

Change in Value of Explanatory Variable	Probability of an Enduring Rivalry (%)
DEMOCRATIC CHALLENGER	
For how many years has the challenger been democratic in the past twenty-five years?	
0 vs. 5	-1.6
5 vs. 10	-1.4
10 vs. 15	-1.2
15 vs. 20	-1.1
20 vs. 25	-1.0
	Total -6.3

* See the note to Table 2.3 for a description of how the changes in the probability of an enduring rivalry were calculated.

More detailed examination of the cases reveals an interesting pattern. Among the thirty-six enduring rivalries, only one (India versus Portugal) involved a challenger state with a well-established pattern of democratic rule. Thus, in all but one of the enduring rivalries the challenger was nondemocratic, clearly supporting hypothesis 7. Furthermore, in disputes in which the challenger had a high democracy score, the percentage of cases with relatively high levels of escalation is very low (one out of twenty, or only 5 percent). Once again, hypothesis 7 receives strong support. However, in dispute cases in which the challenger had a low democratic coding, fewer than one-half of the disputes were characterized by relatively high levels of escalation. Thus, in a substantial number of cases nondemocratic states did not resort to high levels of diplomatic or military pressure, contrary to the expectations of hypothesis 7. The modest results in Table 5 are, therefore, a reflection not of the fact that democratic states often engaged in high levels of escalation over a protracted period of time but that a good number of nondemocratic states failed to do so.

The one common feature of cases in which nondemocratic challengers did not engage in high levels of escalation is that many of them faced more pressing security threats from states other than the target. As a result, either the challenger gave a low priority to the dispute with the target and therefore was not very active in pursuing its claim, or the challenger and target shared an adversary and the challenger decided to build friendly relations with the target in an attempt to solidify the target's support as an ally. For example, in the dispute between Iran and Saudi Arabia both countries were entangled in more confrontational territorial disputes with other states, and they therefore had a mutual interest in avoiding high levels of escalation in their own conflict. Similarly, Ethiopia's conflict with Somalia provided a strong impetus for Ethiopia to pursue accommodative policies toward its other neighbors, Kenya and Sudan. Both of these examples illustrate the more general point that external security considerations often seemed to be pivotal in determining how flexible and accommodative the challenger was, despite the presence of opposing domestic political forces.

Up to this point I have examined only the separate effects of each variable, which is useful in clarifying and highlighting the specific impact of each variable. State leaders, however, make decisions in response to the combined set of incentives and disincentives they face. Thus, certain combinations of variables have a very powerful effect on the probability of an enduring rivalry. For example, if we begin with the "baseline" territorial dispute in which the variables in Table 2 assume their mean/modal values, then the equation in Table 2 would predict the overall probability of an enduring rivalry to be about 9 percent. However, if we change the values for each of the variables in the equation so that they are set to increase the chances of an enduring rivalry by the maximum amount, we find that the probability of an enduring rivalry surges to more than 80 percent (see Case Two or Three in Table 6). Compared with the baseline case, the marginal difference in probability levels is about 72 percent (81 percent minus 9 percent). Put differently, there is a ninefold increase in the predicted probability of an enduring rivalry (from 9 percent to 81 percent). Conversely, if we set the equation at values designed to minimize the likelihood of an enduring rivalry (see Case One in Table 6), the chances of an enduring rivalry plummet to almost 0 percent—a marginal decrease of about 9 percent and about a ninefold decrease in the absolute value of the predicted probability level.

Table 2.6.
The Probability of an Enduring Rivalry over Disputed Territory Under Different Sets of Conditions, 1950–1990*

CASE ONE: Equation Set at Values to Minimize Chance of Enduring Rivalry

---

Values of the Explanatory Variables:
Strategic location of territory = 0
Ties to bordering minority = 0
Political unification = 0
Balance of military forces = $\frac{1}{9}$
Challenger disputes = 10
Common security ties = 1
Democratic challenger = 25
Probability of an enduring rivalry given the values of the explanatory variables = 0.0%

CASE TWO: Equation Set at Values to Maximize Chance of Enduring Rivalry

---

Values of the Explanatory Variables:
Strategic location of territory = 1
Ties to bordering minority = 1
Political unification = 0
Ratio of balance of military forces = $\frac{9}{1}$
Challenger disputes = 0
Common security ties = 0
Democratic challenger = 0
Probability of an enduring rivalry given the values of the explanatory variables = 81.5%

CASE THREE: Equation Set at Values to Maximize Chance of Enduring Rivalry

---

Values on the Explanatory Variables:
Strategic location of territory = 1
Ties to bordering minority = 0
Political unification = 1
Ratio of balance of military forces = $\frac{9}{1}$
Challenger disputes = 0
Common security ties = 0
Democratic Challenger = 0
Probability of an enduring rivalry given the values of the explanatory variables = 80.6%

---

* For each case the probability of an enduring rivalry was calculated utilizing the coefficients from the equation presented in Table 2. For each case the values of each explanatory variable were set at the levels specified, and then the equation was estimated. From the estimated equation the value of the cumulative normal distribution was then converted into the probability of an enduring rivalry (see King 1989, 106–108).

CONCLUSION

In this research I empirically tested the power of a modified realist model to find the circumstances under which challenger states became involved in enduring rivalries over disputed territory. The statistical results indicated that decisions by challenger states to escalate disputes were shaped by the interplay of domestic and international factors. Hypotheses cast at each level of analysis received varying degrees of empirical support, and, as a result, the principal claim of the modified realist model—the necessity to consider carefully both domestic and international factors in the study of international conflict behavior—was clearly supported by the evidence.

When the findings of this article are coupled with the results of my prior research (Huth 1996, chap. 4) on the causes of territorial disputes between states in the post–World War II period, the limits of a traditional realist approach become quite clear. In my prior study I found that strategically situated bordering territory was a powerful predictor of whether challengers would be involved in disputes. Nevertheless, fewer than 20 percent of all disputes involved claims to strategic territory. Challengers were also not likely to become embroiled in disputes with their military allies and were reluctant to dispute territory if that meant risking damage to their political reputation for honoring international commitments by having to discard previously signed border agreements. An important negative finding was that the relative military strength of the challenger was a poor predictor of whether the challenger became involved in a territorial dispute. The weak results reflected the fact that in many disputes the challenger was in a very unfavorable military position.

I also found that the domestic political incentives to dispute territory were multifaceted for foreign policy leaders. In many cases the decision to dispute territory could be linked to the expected political benefits of increased popular support and legitimacy when claims were directed at achieving national unification, at recovering lost national territory, or at gaining access to valuable economic resources. Just as important, however, was the desire of leaders in many cases to avoid the political costs of failing to support a long-standing policy of disputing territory.

The strong findings for domestic political variables in explaining both why territorial disputes are initiated and why some develop into enduring rivalries point to an important general conclusion: foreign policy leaders adopt or maintain policies that risk conflict with other states largely because of domestic political concerns. The traditional realist expectation that international conflict is fundamentally a result of the clash between states over issues of national security is incorrect. Military security issues may come close to being sufficient conditions for conflict and rivalry between states, but they are by no means a necessary condition. As a result, many of the issues that become the underlying source of political and even military conflict between states have few clear and compelling military security implications.

These findings, coupled with my previous research on territorial disputes, indicate that the explanatory power of domestic and international-level variables depends on the theoretical questions being addressed. The particular strength of a domestic-politics perspective lies in explaining why territorial disputes emerge and why they persist over time. The international strategic environment, on the other hand, best explains why territorial disputes escalate to varying levels and why political leaders sometimes make the difficult choice of offering concessions to settle a dispute.

What do these findings say more broadly about the modified realist model? First, the traditional realist assumption that the threat or use of military force is indeed the most important means by which states can advance and protect their foreign policy interests is appropriate. Other sources of state power and influence doubtless exist, but military strength and the credible threat of its use remains essential for understanding the conflict behavior of states. Second, the traditional realist assumption that conflict and competition in international politics centers around issues of military security is inaccurate. When security issues are at stake, leaders will place a high priority on protecting them, but political and military conflict is by no means limited to such issues, as these findings indicate. Military security issues are only one of several high-priority issues for foreign policy leaders. Indeed, one of the strengths of the modified realist model is its ability to explain the range of issues over which states become embroiled in conflict.

This comparative advantage of the modified realist model reflects the fact that in the model, domestic politics can provide a far richer explanation and understanding of why certain issues are on the policy agenda of foreign policy leaders. Thus, the basic argument of the modified realist model that foreign policy is closely linked to the domestic political needs and concerns of leaders was well supported. In sum, the modified realist model represents a clear advance over traditional realist approaches. With further work and refinement, this type of model promises to capture more fully the reciprocal influences of both domestic politics and the international strategic environment of states on international conflict behavior.

I would like to thank the National Science Foundation for its financial support of this research project and John Vasquez for his comments on an earlier draft of this chapter.

REFERENCES

Abdulghani, J. M. 1984. *Iraq & Iran: The Years of Crisis.* London: Croom Helm.

Albaharna, Husain. 1975. *The Arabian Gulf States: Their Legal and Political Status and Their International Problems.* Rev. 2d ed. Beirut: Libraire du Liban.

Allcock, John, Guy Arnold, Alan Day, D. S. Lewis, Lorimer Poultney, Roland Rance, and D. J. Sagar. 1992. *Border and Territorial Disputes.* 3d ed. London: Longman.

Bahcheli, Tozun. 1990. *Greek-Turkish Relations since 1955.* Boulder, Colo.: Westview Press.

Barnett, A. Doak. 1977. *China and the Major Powers in East Asia.* Washington D.C.: Brookings Institution.

Barnett, Michael. 1992. *Confronting the Costs of War: Military Power, State, and Society.* Princeton, N.J.: Princeton University Press.

Bueno de Mesquita, Bruce. 1981. *The War Trap.* New Haven, Conn.: Yale University Press.

Bueno de Mesquita, Bruce, and David Lalman. 1992. *War and Reason.* New Haven, Conn.: Yale University Press.

Bueno de Mesquita, Bruce, Randolph Siverson, and Gary Woller. 1992. "War and the Fate of Regimes." *American Political Science Review* 86: 638–646.

David, Steven. 1991. *Choosing Sides: Alignment and Realignment in the Third World.* Baltimore, Md.: Johns Hopkins University Press.

Day, Alan, ed. 1982. *Border and Territorial Disputes.* 2d ed. London: Longman.

DeSota, Anthony. 1962. *Bolivia's Right to an Access to the Sea.* Pasadena, Calif.: Jensen Publishing.

Dixon, William. 1993. "Democracy and the Management of International Conflict." *Journal of Conflict Resolution* 37: 42–68.

———. 1994. "Democracy and the Peaceful Settlement of International Conflict." *American Political Science Review* 88: 14–32.

Doyle, Michael. 1986. "Liberalism and World Politics." *American Political Science Review* 804: 1151–1161.

Drysdale, Alasdair, and Raymond Hinnebusch. 1991. *Syria and the Middle East Peace Process.* New York: Council on Foreign Relations Press.

Finnie, David. 1992. *Shifting Lines in the Sand: Kuwait's Elusive Frontier with Iraq.* Cambridge, Mass.: Harvard University Press.

Freedman, Lawrence, and Efraim Karsh. 1993. *The Gulf Conflict, 1990–1991: Diplomacy and War in the New World Order.* Princeton, N.J.: Princeton University Press.

Ghoble, T. R. 1986. *China-Nepal Relations and India.* New Delhi: Deep and Deep Publications.

Goertz, Gary, and Paul Diehl. 1992. "The Empirical Importance of Enduring Rivalries." *International Interactions* 18: 151–163.

———. 1993. "Enduring Rivalries: Theoretical Constructs and Empirical Patterns." *International Studies Quarterly* 37: 147–172.

Gurr, Ted Robert, Keith Jaggers, and Will Moore. 1989. *Polity II Codebook.* Center for Comparative Politics, Department of Political Science, University of Colorado.

Heikal, Mohammed. 1975. *The Road to Ramadan.* New York: Ballantine Books.

Herzog, Chaim. 1975. *The War of Atonement.* Boston: Little, Brown.

Hodges, Tony. 1983. *Western Sahara: The Roots of Desert War.* Westport, Conn.: Lawrence Hill.

Holsti, Kalevi. 1991. *Peace and War: Armed Conflict and International Order, 1648–1989.* Cambridge, U.K.: Cambridge University Press.

Husan, Asad, and Asifa Anwar. 1979. *Conflict in Asia: A Case Study of Nepal.* New Delhi: Classical Publications.

Huth, Paul. 1996. *Standing Your Ground: Territorial Disputes and International Conflict.* Ann Arbor: University of Michigan Press.

Jain, Rajendra. 1980. *China and Japan, 1949–1980.* Rev. 2d ed. London: Martin Robertson.

———. 1981. *The USSR and Japan, 1945–1980.* Atlantic Highlands, N.J.: Humanities Press.

Jetly, Nancy. 1979. *India China Relations, 1947–1977: A Study of Parliament's Role in the Making of Foreign Policy.* New Delhi: Radiant Publishers.

King, Gary, 1989. *Unifying Political Methodology: The Likelihood Theory of Statistical Inference.* Cambridge, U.K.: Cambridge University Press.

Kocs, Stephen. 1995. "Territorial Disputes and International War, 1945–1987." *Journal of Politics* 57: 159–175.

Levie, Howard. 1983. *The Status of Gibraltar.* Boulder, Colo.: Westview Press.

Long, Simon. 1991. *Taiwan: China's Last Frontier.* New York: St. Martin's Press.

Morales, Waltraud. 1984. "Bolivian Foreign Policy." In *The Dynamics of Latin American Foreign Policies,* edited by Jennie Lincoln and Elizabeth Ferris. Boulder, Colo.: Westview Press.

Morrow, James. 1995. "Arms versus Allies." *International Organization* 47: 207–234.

Nimmo, William. 1994. *Japan and Russia: A Reevaluation in the Post-Soviet Era.* Westport, Conn.: Greenwood Press.

Page, Benjamin, and Robert Shapiro. 1991. *The Rational Public: Fifty Years of Trends in American's Policy Preferences.* Chicago: University of Chicago Press.

Pettman, Ralph. 1973. *China in Burma's Foreign Policy.* Canberra: Australian National University Press.

Rais, Rasul. 1977. *China and Pakistan: A Political Analysis of Mutual Relations.* Lahore, Pakistan: Progressive Publishers.

Ramazani, Rouhollah. 1975. *Iran's Foreign Policy, 1941–1973.* Charlottesville: University Press of Virginia.

Ray, James. 1995. *Democracy and International Conflict: An Evaluation of the Democratic Peace Proposition.* Columbia: University of South Carolina Press.

Razi, Gholam. 1984. "Relations in the Persian Gulf." In *International Relations of the Middle East and North Africa,* edited by Abid Al-Marayati. Cambridge, U.K.: Schenkman Publishing.

Rousseau, David, Chris Gelpi, Dan Reiter, and Paul Huth. 1996. "Assessing the Dyadic Nature of the Democratic Peace, 1918–88." *American Political Science Review* 90, no. 3: 512–533..

Russett, Bruce. 1990. *Controlling the Sword: The Democratic Governamce of National Security.* Cambridge, Mass.: Harvard University Press.

———. 1993. *Grasping the Democratic Peace: Principles for a Post–Cold War World.* Princeton, N.J.: Princeton University Press.

Sandhu, Bhim. 1988. *Unresolved Conflict: China and India.* New Delhi: Radiant Publishers.

Schofield, Richard. 1993. *Kuwait and Iraq: Historical Claims and Territorial Disputes.* 2d ed. London: Royal Institute of International Affairs.

Shumavon, Douglas. 1981. "Bolivia: Salida al Mar." In *Latin American Foreign Policies: Global and Regional Dimensions,* edited by Elizabeth Ferris and Jennie Lincoln. Boulder, Colo.: Westview Press.

Spector, Leonard. 1987. *Going Nuclear.* Cambridge, Mass.: Ballinger.

Stolper, Thomas. 1985. *China, Taiwan, and the Offshore Islands.* Armonk, N.Y.: M. E. Sharpe.

Syed, Anwar Hussain. 1974. *China & Pakistan: Diplomacy of an Entente Cordiale.* Amherst: University of Massachusetts Press.

Touval, Saadia. 1972. *The Boundary Politics of Independent Africa.* Cambridge, Mass.: Harvard University Press.

Vasquez, John A. 1993. *The War Puzzle.* Cambridge, U.K., and New York: Cambridge University Press.

Vertzberger, Yaacov. 1983. *The Enduring Entente: Sino-Pakistani Relations, 1960–1980.* New York: Praeger.

Walt, Stephen. 1987. *The Origins of Alliances.* Ithaca, N.Y.: Cornell University Press.

Whiting, Allen. 1975. *The Chinese Calculus of Deterrence: India and Indochina.* Ann Arbor: University of Michigan.

3

Border Configuration and Conflict: Geographical Compactness as a Territorial Ambition of States

John P. Vanzo

COMPACTNESS AND INTERNATIONAL RELATIONS

Academic attention to territorial factors as a key variable in the incidence and intensity of wars has increased greatly in recent years. A primary factor that has emerged from the research is the importance of proximity (Boulding 1962; Cobb and Elder 1970; Diehl 1985; Bremer 1993; Vasquez 1993; Lemke 1995); more concretely, the history and character of the borders between contiguous states. Because borders are the most obvious physical manifestation of the political, economic, and military interface between contiguous states, their nature may serve to either constrain or encourage the opportunities for interactions in general, and war in particular (Richardson 1960; Wesley 1962; Weede 1970; Midlarsky 1974; Starr and Most 1976; Most and Starr 1980; Siverson and Starr 1991; Starr 1996).

This chapter aspires to contribute to the literature concerning borders in international relations. However, whereas most of the previous research has centered on the number or type of borders, this study joins only a very small group that examines the configuration of borders as a key variable of interest. More specifically, it explores the question of whether states in the international system pursue a goal of geographical compactness when adjusting their borders; that is, all things being equal, whether countries prefer to expand in directions that form borders of more nearly round or rectangular shape, spread evenly around a central core.

For instance, when the European powers negotiated the boundaries of their colonial possessions in Africa, the maximization of the colonies' size and the compactness of the borders were their top two priorities (Whittlesey 1944; Muir 1975). The relevance of compactness noted in this historical anecdote has been supported by research in various academic fields. In terms of political administration, a compact shape provides the most efficient configuration for internal communication and control (Glassner 1993). A compact shape also affects a nation's macroeconomic performance, especially in regard to the organization of labor, the size of markets, and the extraction of rents (Pounds and Ball 1964; Nystuen 1967; Friedman 1977). The configuration of a nation's borders can also influence its political viability and acceptance by the international community (Christopher 1994). Finally, and most importantly, the compactness of borders directly affects a nation's ability to defend itself, and therefore may be a contributing factor in the incidence of war (Fifield and Pearcy 1944; Richardson 1961; Ratzel 1965). Given these advantages, compactness emerges as a potentially important, though understudied, territorial ambition of states.

Aside from abstract academic interest, the concept of compactness may also have important practical applications for the conduct of foreign policy, especially during the delicate early phases of nation building. Besides the bizarre U.N. configuration analyzed in this study, there have been several other instances of extravagantly uncompact borders suggested for emergent states: for instance, the patchwork borders recommended by the Vance-Owen plan for Bosnia-Herzegovina, the bisected form of old East-West Pakistan, and the scattered islands of quasi-sovereignty for the Palestinian state. Third-party brokers, such as the United Nations or the United States, apparently wished to minimize the dislocation of populations by blindly creating new political borders that corresponded to preexisting ethnic borders. Also, they may have hoped that such scrambled configurations would lead to mutually beneficial cooperation between rival political or ethnic groups.

Unfortunately, the history of bitter conflict that has spatially concentrated on these uncompact areas should dispel any such utopian notions in the future: new states have tended to straighten out their borders through the time-honored methods of war and ethnic cleansings. The compactness approach strongly recommends that when forming new borders for emergent states, exclaves, enclaves, protrusions, intrusions, choke points, and areas of confused sovereignty should be avoided to the maximum extent feasible. By including compactness concerns in the early stages of negotiations, much bloodshed and human misery may be avoided. Aside from the humanitarian interests involved, financial inducements for the resettlement of peoples into compact, defensible borders may actually be more cost-effective than are expensive and potentially dangerous peacekeeping missions designed to stabilize uncompact borders.

COMPACTNESS AS A CONCEPT

In the abstract sense, the most compact shape of any two-dimensional geometric figure is that of a circle. First, a circle minimizes the length of border perimeter for a given surface area. For a country, this means that a circular shape minimizes the length of frontier that must be defended, thus maximizing the density of its armed forces. A circular shape also maximizes the distance any invader must travel to the geographical center of a state, as well as simultaneously minimizing the length of friendly supply lines from the core to its defensive borders. Because of these factors, Nicholas Spykman (1938) flatly stated that, "Obviously, the ideal territorial shape for a state is that of a circle" (34).

This is not to say that countries will literally strive to achieve circular borders; they will "satisfice" with a roughly circular or rectangular configuration as a compromise with other local, political and/or geographical situational factors. Indeed, a hexagonal shape is the most compact shape for a gridded field without voids or overlaps of territory. Nevertheless, as the ideally compact shape, the circle remains the best mathematical measure of compactness. In general, then, we should expect states to endeavor to selectively expand in directions that increase their compactness, especially in terms of eradicating narrow pinches of borders, broadening long protrusions of its shape, and incorporating exposed exclaves of territory surrounded by potentially hostile neighbors (all of which serve to increase their mathematical approximation of a circle).

This is also not to dismiss traditional explanations for the territorial expansion of states, such as the acquisition of raw materials, markets, and militarily strategic areas or the integration of culturally allied populations (Diehl and Goertz 1991). The objective here is to add compactness to this list of classical motivations, not to replace them. At this point we may merely assume that the quest for compactness is coequal with these other traditional geopolitical objectives; that is, with all other factors held constant, we should expect a nation to prefer to expand in directions that increase its configurational compactness. A victorious country may occasionally expand in directions that decrease the compactness of its borders, but only when the loss of compactness is more than offset by gains in other political, economic, or strategic areas (Van Valkenburg 1939).

Based on these general assumptions, one may deduce some preliminary testable propositions regarding the behavior of states in instances of territorial change:

1. Nations will tend to expand in directions that increase their configurational compactness, ceteris parabis. Therefore, on average, in instances of territorial gain we should expect compactness to increase.
2. Militarily victorious nations, especially those with an already satisfactory level of compactness, may translate their victory into territorial changes that decrease the compactness of their defeated enemies, thus increasing their relative configurational advantage. Therefore, in instances of territorial loss we should expect compactness to decrease.
3. Although it is beyond the scope of this limited study, we may also hypothesize about the role that compactness motives play in the territorial ambitions of specific states. We may suppose that compactness concerns will affected by the preexisting level of compactness, the presence of threatening neighbors, or the degree of competing territorial interests, such as ideological considerations or the need for raw materials. Therefore, compactness will assume a higher priority when it is already low, when the likelihood of conflict is high, and when competing territorial motivations are relatively absent.

Naturally, competing hypotheses could be inferred from these assumptions. For instance, the second proposition is based primarily on an analysis of Germany's borders, but one could also postulate that military defeat may act to eventually increase the compactness of a state, rather than decrease it. If a country is strong, it may be able to bear the costs of maintaining convoluted, uncompact borders. But if the country is weak, territorial protrusions and exclaves may make particularly tempting targets for foreign aggression. The loss of these exposed territories should act to (unwillingly) increase the compactness of defeated states. Over time, a weak country may be whittled down to a size and level of compactness that it can militarily maintain against external pressures. Complicating the situation is the fact that victorious nations may adjust their compactness strategies toward defeated nations in accordance with their expectation of future relations: the Allies' attitude toward Germany in the postwar era may be an example of this shift in geopolitical strategy. Definitive answers to these questions must obviously await a large-scale quantitative analysis.

Another obvious question that arises is whether a country would voluntarily abandon territory in its quest to achieve greater compactness. In general we may assume the answer to be negative, for a number of reasons. First, to cede sovereignty over an area would not be rational, because any surrender of land necessarily results in the loss of some of the previously discussed territorial resources. Perhaps more importantly, the maintenance of sovereignty over territory is intimately tied to a country's international prestige and the political survival of its leadership. As perfectly illustrated by the Falklands War, the sociopolitical importance of defending one's territory often overrides more objective evaluations of its actual economic or military value. Given these reasons, we may assume that a country will prefer to maintain its territorial integrity except in the most extraordinary of circumstances, even if its borders are not compact, and that a country will always prefer to expand in order to increase compactness, rather than to contract.

When a country does cede territory in a nonmilitary context, land can be conceptualized merely as another commodity that the nation can exchange for other monetary or security-related values. The Israeli surrender of the Sinai Peninsula in exchange for an Egyptian peace treaty and guarantees of further U.S. support may be an example of this. Even here, however, one would surmise that a country would prefer to cede territory that would not result in an unacceptable loss of compactness. Indeed, one could imagine circumstances in which two neighbors peacefully negotiate a mutual exchange of territory in order to increase the compactness of both states. The resolution of the 1963 Chamizal dispute between Mexico and the United States, caused by a meandering of the Rio Grande, is an example of this optimal outcome.

One may even extrapolate compactness propositions from the national to the regional or systemic level of analysis. Compactness alone will seldom be a sufficient cause for war, but it may affect the likelihood of war, especially when analyzed at the aggregate level. For instance, if a low level of compactness does indeed provide strong countries with a motive for aggression or invite attack against the weak, we should expect a negative correlation between the regional level of compactness and the incidence of war. Furthermore, if each nation acts to maximize its compactness, the contesting states in a region may eventually reach a state of homeostasis, in terms of size and compactness, in which geographical configuration no longer provides a significant motive for territorial aggression—a spatial corollary to balance of power. As long as there are no dramatic changes in the distribution of power, with all countries maintaining borders of defensible size and compact configuration, we should expect the region to be relatively peaceful. This "Compactness Peace Proposition" also implies that bipolar configurations of global politics will generally be more peaceful, at least in terms of international war, than will multipolar configurations, because of the lower number of relevant actors, borders, and aggregate border length.

Although definitive evidence regarding the veracity of these propositions must await further study, the present work may provide a heuristic glimpse of the potential value of the compactness approach in analyzing international relations.

COMPACTNESS MEASURES

Scholars have long attempted to describe and measure compactness. The oldest and most elementary means of conveying shape is comparison to familiar shapes and objects. Although evocative and clear, descriptions like the "boot shape" of Italy are clearly inadequate for a rigorous study of the configuration of states. During the 1950s, White and Renner (1957) took a step forward by popularizing a nominal-level typology of five basic shapes, including one described as "compact," but it was still inadequate because it did not allow for quantification (Boyce and Clark 1964).

With the behavioral revolution in the social sciences came mathematical quantification of shape and compactness, but virtually all of it was applied to analysis of U.S. congressional districts in an attempt to determine the degree of gerrymandering (Reock 1960; Taylor 1973). Exhaustive typologies of compactness equations have been compiled recently, with heated debates regarding the most effective (Niemi, Grofman, and others 1990; Horn, Hampton, and Vandenberg 1993). The consensus is that no single measure of compactness is totally satisfactory in all situations.

Despite the interest in compactness in U.S. politics, the present generation of international relations researchers has largely ignored the concept. Earlier political geographers like Samuel Van Valkenburg (1939) and S. Whittemore Boggs (1940) devoted some attention to compactness in their analyses of the shape of nations. Their simple formulas focused on the ratio between the circumference of a circle containing the area of a country and the true border length, but their coarseness of measurement made the formulas inadequate for serious scholarship.

The best and most developed measure of compactness, at least from the standpoint of international relations, was offered by the famous pioneer of quantitative social science analysis, Lewis Fry Richardson (1993). In an appendix to his seminal *Statistics of Deadly Quarrels*, Richardson maintained that nations pursue geographical compactness and that the length and number of borders is directly related to the incidence of war. Like Van Valkenburg and Boggs, Richardson's elegant yet succinct compactness formula measures the deviation of a country's borders from the ideal, circular shape:

$$(2\sqrt{\pi A})P \text{ (where A = area and P = perimeter)}$$

Richardson's formula has the advantage of mathematically controlling for size: a large geometric shape will intrinsically have a higher area-to-perimeter ratio than will a smaller version of the same shape, distorting simpler ratio formulas. His formula also produces a convenient index value bounded between 1 and 0, with 1 representing perfect circular compactness and 0 representing perfect uncompactness, or a country with infinitely long borders or zero area. Although a sample distribution of nations' compactness indexes is needed to put a particular compactness value in true relative perspective, an informal comparison of Richardsonian values for some common polygons may give the reader an intuitive sense of scale: circle = 1.00; hexagon = .95; square = .89; equilateral triangle = .78; and 1 x 10 rectangle = .51.

Unfortunately, Richardson was frustrated in his attempt to obtain sufficiently accurate and reliable measures of nations' perimeters and areas because of the relatively crude analog cartographic equipment then available. In the end, he abandoned his quest to directly measure compactness and instead concentrated his efforts on the "cellulation" of maps into hexagonal cells. Through this method he obtained his estimate of a .77 correlation between the number of borders and the incidence of war (Richardson 1960; Starr and Most 1978).

Richardson died before the second edition of *Statistics of Deadly Quarrels* was published, and the appendix with his examination of compactness was not even included in the 1960 edition. Eventually, in 1961, it was published under the title "The Problem of Contiguity." Although generally disappointing, his method of portraying the international environment as a field of hexagonal blocks did become a common practice in conflict simulations (Bremer and Mihalka 1977; Starr 1996).

With modern technology the geographical values necessary for calculating compactness can now be measured accurately. Richardson's compactness formula will therefore form the basis for one of the versions of compactness tested in this paper: perimeter compactness. In this view, the operative variable affecting a nation's interest in compactness is the length of the borders; nations desire to shorten their border length in order to maximize the density of their defensive forces. In terms of the propositions mentioned earlier, we should expect a nation to increase its perimeter–compactness index in instances of territorial gain and to lose compactness in instances of territorial loss.

Even though academics, and perhaps practitioners, of international relations have concentrated on border length as the most important component of compactness, a review of political propaganda indicates that the threat posed by a border's proximity to the core of a nation is much more likely to be emphasized. Obviously designed to motivate a population for war, such examples of provocative propaganda have included portraying Czechoslovakia as a mailed fist thrusting into Germany, Korea as a sword aimed at Japan's heart, and Communist Cuba as a bayonet thrusting into the United States' sphere of influence.

Attention to the size of a nation's core has not been entirely ignored by geopolitical theorists. The concept was originally developed by Friedrich Ratzel in his organic interpretation of a state's growth, and it was later embellished by Derwent Whittlesey (Glassner 1993). Sir Halford Mackinder extrapolated the concept to the global level in his writings on the heartland, which Alexander P. deSeversky (1950) updated for his airpower-oriented interpretation of superpower conflict. In each of these cases, it is the proximity of borders to a nation's core or center that presents a threat, rather the length of its borders.

This view is not entirely without merit. For instance, one can imagine a state with an undulating river border, but otherwise very compact. The bends in the river would cause a dramatic decrease in its compactness as measured by the Richardsonian perimeter index. Yet a second country, with relatively straight borders that intrude dangerously toward the core, would be calculated as relatively compact. The first country also has the advantage of short lines of communication to the farthest reaches of its borders, whereas the second country has long, narrow, exposed lines of communication.

In light of the inability of the Richardsonian perimeter-compactness formulation to take into account the threat posed to a nation's core by intrusive and/or protruding borders, a second version, radial compactness, will be utilized in this paper as a comparison. Radial compactness is a combination of two measures. The first, the intrusion ratio, is the radial distance from the nation's core to the closest border, divided by the radius of a circle with the same area as the country. Based on a compactness formula proposed by J. P. Cole (1977), it in essence operationalizes the core as the largest circle that will fit within a nation's borders. The second measure, the protrusion ratio, is the radial distance from the nation's core to the farthest extent of its borders, which is then divided into the radial distance of a circle with the same area as the country. Loosely based on a compactness formula proposed by J. P. Gibbs (1977), it essentially operationalizes protrusion as the smallest circle that will contain all borders of a nation. Values for the intrusion ratio and the protrusion ratio are arithmetically averaged to indicate the overall radial compactness index. In equation form, the radial compactness index is as follows:

$$\frac{\left(\dfrac{\text{Intrusion Distance}}{\text{Circle Distance}}\right) + \left(\dfrac{\text{Circle Distance}}{\text{Protrusion Distance}}\right)}{2}$$

Naturally, there are alternative interpretations of what constitutes the core of a country. The national capital, the country's largest city, its industrial regions, and the geographical centroid have all been proposed as cores of states. Unfortunately, both Israel and Germany had multiple/disputed capitals, and changes in the populations of cities could cause spurious changes in a country's compactness measure. Furthermore, multiple industrial regions could be problematic. Lastly, in the case of early Israeli stages, the geographical centroid of the country was actually located outside its borders. In the end, the Gibbs-Cole formula was chosen because it reliably produces clear, reproducible, nonnegative values, and, like Richardson's formula, provides an index based on comparison with a circle, bounded between 0 and 1.

The Richardsonian perimeter-compactness index and the Gibbs-Cole radial compactness index will therefore form the two basic mathematical measures of compactness compared in this paper. As a check on the two quantitative measures, each of the historical stages analyzed in this study will also be qualitatively assessed for the degree of compactness relevance. More specifically, each stage will be examined for the degree to which compactness concerns figured in the territorial motivations of states relative to other competing objectives, not merely the expected magnitude of compactness gain. It is hoped that these three methodologies will complement each other and add to understanding of the compactness-influenced behavior of states.

RESEARCH DESIGN

Fortunately for this study, the problem of inaccurate maps and unreliable cartographic measurement tools that confounded Richardson's initial attempt to measure compactness has been solved. Satellite photometry now allows extremely accurate maps to be drawn. Because of the potential for partisan distortions of national dimensions, especially where borders are contested by the international community or are a matter of domestic politicization (Bar-Gal 1993), this study obtained independent data from third-party maps rather than relying on previously published data. Actual distance and area measurements were obtained through GIS technology.

The methods used to operationalize the compactness indexes are relatively straightforward. First, a comprehensive set of maps detailing the historical evolution of Israeli and German borders between 1900 and 1992 was compiled for each of the geopolitical phases (Freytag and Bernt 1938; National Geographic 1940a, 1940b, 1944; Berliner Lithographisches Institut 1944; U.S. Department of State 1946; Israeli Office of Information 1954, 1957, 1966, 1971, 1975, 1984; Central Intelligence Agency 1978; Wolfsohn 1987; Pitt and Pitt 1989; Nahkleh 1991; *New York Times* 1996). The information regarding the evolution of the borders was then combined into master maps for Israel and Germany. Which and how many phases to utilize was decided on the basis of chronological durability and representativeness. Intermediate, temporary steps between obvious break points were ignored: for example, Israel's phased withdrawal from the Suez Canal was distilled down to the starting and end lines.

Several coding decisions were then implemented to translate the literal boundaries into theoretically and operationally satisfactory form to portray the central elements of the compactness approach. First, a twelve-mile territorial-waters buffer zone was added to control for the fractal quality of coastlines (Nystuen 1967; Gleick 1987) and to take into account the need for offshore sea control. Although this results in inflated areas, the ensuing higher compactness values better reflect the added security afforded by sea boundaries versus land borders.

Second, demilitarized zones, no-man's-lands, and U.N. buffer zones were excluded from the territorial boundaries of the states. The standard coding rule demands that the area must be claimed as part of the national territory and be under its military control. This avoids the problem of grandiose claims over uncontrolled lands, as well as territory only temporarily occupied by the military within the context of battle. This dual requirement gives meaning, for instance, to the German reoccupation of the Rhineland.

Lastly, one-and-a-quarter-mile-wide lines of communication were drawn from the main corpus of the state to any isolated exclaves. These lines of communication represent, in compactness terms, the military and logistical costs associated with maintaining exclaves surrounded by potentially hostile neighbors. Lines of communication were drawn to follow primary road or rail lines; in the absence of land routes, sea lanes were drawn.

Each master map was then digitized into electronic vector-type maps representing each of the historical phases (see Mapsets 1 and 2), using a Calcomp 9500 digitizer operating with "Microstation" computer-assisted design software (Intergraph Corporation). This translated each map into a roughly 1,800- sided polygon in electronic data form. The data were then exported in the DXF file format and saved to diskettes, which were then imported into a computer and analyzed, using the "MapInfo" GIS computer program (MapInfo Corporation). Control trials indicated that human error was negligible to nonexistent, with border-length error never exceeding .007 and area error calculated as zero out to four decimal places.

The area and perimeter values for each historical phase were then inserted into the Richardsonian perimeter-compactness and Gibbs-Cole radial compactness formulas and computed (see SPSS data spreadsheet in Appndix 2). Because the geopolitical stages are neither randomly chosen nor numerous enough to make statistical assumptions, simple two-by-three tables were constructed in order to provide a rough approximation of how well the data confirmed the propositions. As an added check, prior to the calculation of the compactness values, a content analysis was performed on the historical stages in order to qualitatively assess the degree of compactness concerns in the decision makers' territorial priorities vis-à-vis other traditional explanations.

REVIEW OF CASE STUDIES

Although this study lacks the scope and rigor necessary for definitive conclusions, the results do provide a significant basis for belief that states do, at times, include compactness concerns among their territorial priorities.

Israel

The Israeli subset of case studies comprises four historical phases. (For an expanded description of each historical stage, see Appendix 1.)

Phase 1 (MANDATE): This initial Israeli configuration represents the U.N. Mandate borders of the prospective state. They are extremely uncompact, having the lowest compactness values for any historical stage in this study.

Phase 2 (INDEP): The Israeli War of Independence resulted in a profound increase in compactness, especially in terms of ending its geographical fragmentation. Both indexes demonstrated dramatic increases as a result of these territorial gains.

Phase 3 (6DAYWAR): Israel's territorial gains in the 1967 Six Day War resulted in a tremendous increase in size and compactness. For instance, compared with its MANDATE configuration, Israel's perimeter index values increased from an analogous $\frac{1}{26}$ rectangle to a very compact $\frac{1}{5}$ rectangle.

Phase 4 (TREATY): Israel's peace treaty with Egypt basically involved trading land for peace, resulting in net territorial loss. The research propositions correctly predicted the resultant compactness loss, though Israel was careful to limit the loss to a very modest level.

Analysis of the (admittedly limited in number) Israeli historical phases seems to strongly indicate that Israel's leadership consciously translated military victories into clear geopolitical payoffs in terms of size and configurational compactness. Of the three instances of territorial change, one case was qualitatively rated as demonstrating a high concern for compactness; the other two demonstrated a moderate concern for compactness (see Table 1). In terms of the quantitative analysis, both the radial and perimeter indexes correctly predicted the direction of changes in compactness for every case (see Tables 2 and 3). The indexes also strongly correlate regarding the magnitude of change in compactness: over the historical span of the Israeli cases, both compactness indexes increased by approximately 50 percent. Even within the radial index, both Cole's intrusion measure and Gibbs's protrusion measure perfectly predicted the direction of change in compactness. The small sample size notwithstanding, the Israeli case studies provide an impressive indication of the relevance of compactness to the territorial concerns of states.

Mapset 1. **Israeli Case Studies**

ISR47 (UN Mandate Status Quo)   ISR49 (War of Independence)

ISR67 (Six Day War)   ISR82 (Egyptian Peace Treaty)

Table 3.1
Qualitative Analysis Summary

High concern	INDEP
	VERSAILL
	CZECH
Moderate concern	6DAYWAR
	TREATY
	RHINELND
	POLAND
	COLDWAR
Low concern	AUSTRIA
	SUDETEN
	MEMEL
	ALSACE
	UNIFIED

Table 3.2
Richardson Perimeter Compactness Summary

	Compactness Increase	Compactness Neutral	Compactness Decrease
Territorial Gain	INDEP	RHINELND	AUSTRIA
	6DAYWAR	MEMEL	
	SUDENTEN		
	CZECH		
	POLAND		
	ALSACE		
	UNIFIED		
Territorial Loss			TREATY
			VERSAILL
			COLDWAR

Table 3.3
Gibbs-Cole Radial Compactness Summary

	Compactness Increase	Compactness Neutral	Compactness Decrease
Territorial Gain	INDEP 6DAYWAR SUDENTEN CZECH POLAND ALSACE UNIFIED	AUSTRIA MEMEL ALSACE	RHINELND
Territorial Loss	VERSAILL		TREATY COLDWAR

The positive assessment of compactness in these cases is bolstered by the relative lack of competing explanations found in the qualitative analysis. For instance, in their list of traditional explanations for territorial expansion, Paul Diehl and Gary Goertz (1991) specifically mention the seizure of the Golan Heights as being motivated by what may be interpreted as radial compactness concerns. But other motivations listed by them are relatively lacking. Overcrowding, for example, does not seem to be a plausible explanation: the spatial placement of Israeli settlements seems to indicate religious/ideological or military-consolidation goals. The economic rationale also seems implausible, for raw materials are scarce in the annexed areas. Acquisition of markets is clearly not convincing, because Israeli expansionism resulted in vast boycotts rather than increased access. Indeed, Israel's superpower patron, the United States, often provided strong incentives for Israel to restrain its expansionist policies. Finally, Israel clearly had no interest in uniting neighboring peoples of common heritage: its expansion had the opposite effect of incorporating relatively huge, hostile populations into the confines of the state.

The lack of compelling alternative explanations enhances the confidence one may place in the compactness approach as a competing rationale. In the language of Harvey Starr, Israeli military superiority may have provided the opportunity to expand, but aside from the compactness issue, few other plausible reasons exist for their willingness to conquer (Starr and Most 1978). On the other hand, Israel's surrender of the Sinai Peninsula was obviously an example of a state's treating nonessential territory as a commodity to be traded for other concrete political and economic goals. Although both indexes correctly predicted the loss of compactness for this territorial transfer, it is equally obvious that Israel's configurational compactness was not compromised to any significant degree by the deal. Overall, the Israeli case studies provide a textbook example of compactness concerns.

Germany

The German subset of cases comprises eleven historical phases. (For an expanded description of each historical stage, see Appendix 1.)

Phase 5 (PREWWI): The starting point of the German historical case study is the pre–World War I borders of Germany. Large and relatively compact, the borders reflect the acquisition of the Alsace-Lorraine region from France as a consequence of the Franco-Prussian War.

Phase 6 (VERSAILL): The Treaty of Versailles, which followed World War I, imposed catastrophic territorial penalties on Germany. Not only did the defeated nation lose a colossal amount of land, but it was fragmented by the Polish Corridor. Richardson's perimeter index dropped significantly in the predicted direction, but the radial compactness index moved marginally in the counterpredicted direction because of an anomaly in Germany's configuration.

Phase 7 (RHINELND): Germany's reestablishment of sovereignty over the Rhineland clearly added to the nation's compactness at the strategic level. However, the added length caused by convolutions in the new Rhine River border caused the perimeter index to show no change. The radial index once again moved marginally in the counterpredicted direction because of the anomaly.

Phase 8 (AUSTRIA): Austria's incorporation into the Third Reich provided Richardson's perimeter index with its only mispredicted change, a small drop in compactness. The Gibbs-Cole radial measure showed no net change.

Phase 9 (SUDETEN): The German 1938 annexation of the Sudetenland, the mountainous border region of Czechoslovakia, resulted in correctly predicted increases in both types of compactness measures.

Phase 10 (CZECH): Germany's bloodless conquest of the region we now know as the Czech Republic provides a perfect example of compactness-driven territorial gain. Both compactness indexes showed very significant increases in the predicted direction. The compactness explanation is bolstered by a lack of other convincing objectives.

Phase 11 (MEMEL): The peaceful reincorporation of this tiny sliver of Lithuanian-occupied territory into Germany resulted in no change in either compactness measure.

Phase 12 (POLAND): The German invasion and partial incorporation of Poland, generally regarded as the start of World War II in Europe, resulted in dramatic increases in both compactness measures. The German willingness to risk war over the elimination of the Polish Corridor may have been a vindication of an Allied intention to direct German territorial ambitions eastward through the Treaty of Versailles.

Phase 13 (ALSACE): After the successful western campaign of 1940, Germany annexed portions of France, Luxembourg, and Belgium. The effect on compactness was minimal, with a small increase in perimeter compactness and no change in radial compactness.

Phase 14 (COLDWAR): In the aftermath of World War II, the Allies once again imposed catastrophic territorial penalties on defeated Germany. The balkanization and eventual division of Germany into opposing political entities had severe consequences in terms of compactness. Both compactness measures dropped in the predicted direction for a territorial loss, with the Richardsonian perimeter measure showing a particularly large change.

Phase 15 (UNIFIED): With the elimination of internal borders after the reunification of Germany, both compactness indexes demonstrated very large increases in the predicted direction for a territorial gain. The radial compactness rating for this phase was the highest of any in this study, and the perimeter index showed its greatest increase for any case. Whether by design or accident, modern Germany has been eroded to a very compact configuration, virtually removing compactness as a factor in the territorial ambitions of that state.

Unlike the Israeli example, which was relatively uncomplicated by competing territorial motivations, the German experience, especially during the interwar period, demonstrated a wide variety of objectives. The qualitative assessment of compactness salience reflects this dilution of purpose: only two phases seemed to demonstrate a

Mapset 2. **German Case Studies**

GER14
(pre-WWI status quo)

GER18
(Treaty of Versailles)

GER14
(Rhineland remilitarization)

GER38a
(Austrian anschluß)

GER38b
(Sudentenland annexation)

GER38c
(Czech annexation)

GER39a
(Memel reincorporation)

GER39b
(Polish reincorporation / annexation)

GER40
(Fr-Be-Lux
reincorporation/
annexation)

GER60x
(Combined E&W Germany)

GER96
(Reunified Germany)

high compactness concern; three phases demonstrated moderate compactness concern; and five phases demonstrated little or no compactness concern (see Table 1). Nevertheless, compactness often seems to have been a factor in decision makers' calculations of territorial objectives, occasionally an important one.

The quantitative measures were also less definitive and consistent in their results compared with the Israeli cases (see Tables 2 and 3). The Richardsonian perimeter index performed rather well, with only one compactness change (the Austrian *Anschluss*) moving against the predicted direction, though two others showed no change. Seven changes were correctly predicted. The radial index performed less well in regard to predicted direction of change: two compactness changes were in the wrong direction; three others showed no change; and only five predicted correctly. If we break down the index into its two components, however, we see that the peculiar configuration of Germany caused problems with Cole's intrusion measure, which in turn degraded the performance of the overall index. The Gibbsian protrusion measure was clearly superior in producing expected results, though a definitive test of the two measures must await more cases.

The German experience is also complicated by the fact that, unlike Israel, Germany faced catastrophic defeat in two major wars. Especially in the aftermath of World War I, Germany's geopolitical strategy is a virtually unbroken sequence of territorial revisions of the Versailles Treaty. Because of the tremendous compactness penalty, one should expect a bias toward increased compactness as Germany regresses toward the mean with each successive territorial gain. Nevertheless, although clouded by a much more complex environment, the German case studies concur with the Israeli cases in providing anecdotal evidence that compactness concerns occasionally hold a prominent place in the territorial ambitions of states.

ANALYSIS OF RESULTS

Although this study lacks the scope and depth needed to draw conclusions with any degree of statistical certainty, the results do provide strong evidence that compactness does play a role, at least in certain circumstances, in the territorial ambitions of states.

On the methodological level, this study has, at the very least, demonstrated the feasibility of utilizing GIS technology to achieve precise and reliable measures of compactness at the national level. The quality and accuracy of maps, and the instrumentation for their reliable measurement, have finally caught up with Richardson's demands. The data also provide the raw material for the calculation of a second, complementary interpretation of compactness. Perhaps as important, good progress has been made in creating a coherent set of coding rules for converting raw boundary data into a form that avoids the problem of fractal boundaries while capturing the essence of the compactness interpretation of spatial relationships in international relations.

In terms of the substantive interpretation of results, there are solid grounds, I believe, for believing that configurational compactness does indeed matter to some states in some circumstances. For instance, the qualitative analysis of the case studies, which examined the relative degree to which compactness concerns were present in the territorial priorities of states compared with other traditional motivations, found a high level of concern in three (23 percent) of the thirteen cases. Moderate concern was found in five (38 percent) of the cases, and little or no concern was found in the final five (38 percent) cases. In order to minimize allegations of bias, I utilized a very conservative grading criteria for evaluating the cases. In the end, the distribution of cases within the three categories provides one with the plausible conclusion that, like other, more traditional factors comprising the territorial ambitions of states, configurational compactness only occasionally becomes the dominant variable motivating behavior; much more often it is diluted by the presence of other factors, or is not a significant factor at all. Nevertheless, one is left with the feeling that compactness as a variable is (or should be) in the same general magnitude category of territorial ambitions as the quest for natural resources, the conquest of militarily significant terrain, the incorporation of culturally allied populations, and so forth. Confidence that compactness concerns have behavioral consequences in the international system is enhanced by the simulations performed by Thomas Schelling (1978), which indicated that even very mild spatial micromotive preferences by actors on a grid can translate to surprisingly strong patterns of compactness-related macrobehavior.

The quantitative data also provide compelling evidence for the face validity of the compactness approach. For instance, in the analysis of the average change in compactness, there was a mean increase in perimeter compactness of +.08 for the Richardsonian perimeter index in cases of territorial gain. In cases of territorial loss, the average was a decrease in compactness of –.15. For the Gibbs-Cole radial index, compactness increased an average of +.08 in cases of territorial gain, whereas the index dropped an average of –.10 in cases of territorial loss. It is significant that both indexes showed changes in compactness overwhelmingly in accordance with the predicted direction of change, and in impressive magnitude.

If we categorize the cases into two-by-three tables according to whether the case was a territorial gain or loss and according to whether the result was a compactness increase or loss or neutral, the results are similarly encouraging. For the Richardsonian perimeter index, ten of the thirteen cases (77 percent) fall into the predicted cells, with only one case (8 percent) falling into a clearly mispredicted cell. If we ignore the two cases of neutral compactness change, the correctly predicted percentage jumps to 91 percent. The Gibbs-Cole radial index preformed less impressively, due to previously discussed idiosyncratic convolutions in Germany's interwar configuration. However, even here eight of the cases are correctly predicted (62 percent), and only two clearly are mispredicted (15 percent). Ignoring the three cases of compactness-change neutrality, the correctly predicted number jumps to 80 percent. The results here give credence to the notion that both of the indexes have some explanatory power and that the two original propositions regarding the direction of compactness change have some credibility.

The scope of this study was too limited to determine whether both compactness indexes are needed to adequately measure the concept. The perimeter index performed marginally better than did the radial one, but the arithmetic correlations between the two are in a comfortable range, which suggests to me that they are associated but not redundant (Pearson correlation = .533). Because of the vastly different methods for their computation, at this stage I feel we may reasonably consider them complementary measures of compactness, though this will surely be a topic of study at a later stage of research. The same points may be said to be true for the two components of the radial measure, intrusion and protrusion compactness. The protrusion measure seems to be the marginally better predictor, but this may be a mere situational artifact caused by the peculiar shape of Germany's interwar border with Czechoslovakia.

Indeed, the limited evidence of this paper provides as least as many new questions as it does answers. For instance, there still remains the question of whether, and in which circumstances, victors impose compactness penalties on losers, versus gerrymandering acceptably compact borders in order to promote chances of future peace. Another important question is, At what point do nations consider themselves sufficiently compact? Surely this is at least partly contingent on the level of local threat felt by the nation's leadership, but exactly when is a border considered settled? Another paradox, mentioned by Richardson (1993) in his six-sentence exploration of the compactness concept, is that whereas nations pursue compactness, overseas empires tend to become less compact. Is this a sign that imperial nations have solved their regional security problem and hence reverse their configurational ambitions in order to take advantage of the commercial advantages conferred by a less compact shape (Nystuen 1967)? Lastly, how does the compactness concept compare, in terms of explanatory weight, with other, more traditional territorial objectives?

Obviously, many other facets remain to be examined by further research on the compactness concept. Beyond mere academic interest, however, the compactness approach could have some important consequences for the citizens and neighbors of newly emergent states. The notorious Nazi-era political geographer Karl Haushofer once asserted that it was the geopolitical scholar's task to "prepare the way of the statesman by investigating the prerequisites of a just division of areas on our planet" (Parker 1985, 84). The prestige of the geopolitical approach to international relations could be restored by turning its tools from swords to plowshares, erasing the nightmare of lebensraum and replacing it with Richardson's dream of using political science to decrease the chances of war. By understanding the role compactness plays in the territorial ambitions of states, we may have that opportunity.

APPENDIX 1
Historical Case–Study Descriptions

Mandate

This first geopolitical phase represents the initial 1947 British Mandate partition borders drawn for the prospective state of Israel prior to its War of Independence. Even the most naive observer cannot escape noticing the extremely uncompact configuration. Especially problematic from the compactness perspective is the fragmentation of the state, bizarre X-shaped intersections of Arab and Israeli quadrants, narrow lines of communication to isolated exclaves, and enclaves of Arabs perforating the state. My qualitative analysis of this phase is that the first priority of the U.N. Special Committee on Palestine was the minimization of population transfers, with the optimistic hope that the exotic borders would lead, in some functionalist fashion, toward cooperation between the Arabs and Israelis. From the compactness perspective, these borders are clearly untenable: they provided the Israeli leadership with a powerful incentive—a virtually irresistible imperative—for territorial expansion.

The quantitative analysis utilizing the two compactness formulas is equally pessimistic regarding this configuration. Both the Richardsonian perimeter formula and the Gibbs-Cole radial formula rate this phase as having the lowest compactness index of any of the fifteen cases in this study (.33 and .39, respectively). The Richardsonian index value is analogous to a rectangle with the dimensions of $\frac{1}{26}$.

Indep

In the aftermath of its War of Independence, Israel widened several narrow pinches of territory, eliminated some threatening intrusions of Arab territory, and incorporated all exclaves into a single geopolitical corpus. Although Israel's land area increased by 30 percent, the total length of its borders was actually shortened. My qualitative judgment is that Israel consciously expanded in directions intended to reduce the threat to its survival presented by its uncompact configuration. Traditional explanations for territorial expansion, such as the quest for natural resources or the incorporation of culturally allied populations, do not seem relevant. I rate this historical phase as containing a high degree of compactness concern.

In terms of the quantitative measures, both compactness indexes show very significant increases. The radial measure increases to a level of .49, a rise of more than 25 percent. The perimeter measure posts an even more impressive gain, increasing by a full one-third to .44. In this case there is a very strong correlation between the conclusions of all three methods of analysis—a classic example of compactness-driven territorial expansion.

6 Day War

This third stage represents Israeli borders after the 1967 Six Day War. Here Israel reached the pinnacle of its size, reflecting the capture of the Sinai Peninsula, the West Bank, and the Golan Heights. Israel added significantly to its compactness with wider buffer zones between its core and its potential enemies, as well as straightening the large Jordanian indentation formed by the West bank. On the other hand, the new borders were now anchored either on water courses or mountain ranges—archetypal geomilitary barriers predicted by traditional theories of territorial objectives. The consolidation of Jerusalem also had religious/ideological considerations attached to it. Because of the mixture of traditional and compactness motives, I qualitatively rate this phase as having only moderate compactness concerns.

The quantitative indexes show very dramatic increases in compactness. The radial index rises to .64, a full one-third increase in compactness, the largest in any of the fifteen cases for this measure. The perimeter index shows an impressive .22 increase, achieving a compactness level analogous to a $\frac{1}{5}$ rectangle. This results in an exactly 50 percent increase in the measure, making it the second largest increase for that index. Although the large compactness increases are in the predicted direction of change for cases of territorial expansion, the quantitative measures do not demonstrate any sensitivity to the mixed motives of the Israeli decision makers described in the qualitative analysis. This highlights the notion that mere quantitative measures cannot achieve the subtlety of interpretation that a qualitative analysis can achieve, at least on a case-by-case basis.

Treaty

The final Israeli case illustrates the political arrangements arrived at in the aftermath of the Yom Kippur War and the Lebanese civil war, most notably the return of the Sinai to Egypt and the establishment of a narrow security zone in southern Lebanon. Although Israel was victorious in the Yom Kippur War, the Egyptian peace treaty resulted in a large net loss of territory. The Israeli willingness to trade territory for peace was probably the result of several factors: U.S. political pressure coupled with guarantees of future economic and military aid, international demands to reopen the Suez Canal, development of a regional nuclear weapon monopoly, and the fear that its previous size was too extensive to adequately defend. Israel's previous configuration was very large and compact, but the nation was responsible for the defense of more than 1,000 miles of hostile borders; and the successful Egyptian assault across the Suez Canal may have convinced Israeli decision makers that its size was not sustainable in that military-political environment. Although diluted by several other attractive competing objectives, I rate this case as an instance of moderate compactness concern because of the dramatic shortening of border length and because no significant compactness goals were sacrificed in the bargain.

The quantitative measures move in the direction predicted for territorial loss. The radial index loses .11, and a .07 loss is registered for the perimeter index. Notwithstanding the losses in compactness, both measures remain at a satisfactory level, with the Richardsonian index comparable to a $\frac{1}{6}$ rectangle. Despite the successful prediction of direction, however, there are some troubling doubts regarding the measures' validity. For instance, the perimeter measure shows a drop in compactness, despite the fact that this phase registers the shortest absolute border of any of the Israeli phases—a clear indication of perimeter-compactness concern. The reduction in the radial index reflects the loss of the enormous Sinai Peninsula, but the true political, economic, and demographic core of Israel suffered no actual reduction in its buffer distance. As in the previous case, I believe that the quantitative measures must be supplemented by qualitative analysis in order to properly assess the role of compactness concerns.

Pre WWI

The starting point for the German case studies is its pre–World War I configuration (see Mapset 2). At this stage, Germany enjoyed relatively high compactness: its radial compactness index is an impressive .59, and its perimeter compactness is .52, analogous to a rectangle of approximately $\frac{1}{9}$ shape. Size was relatively large, with a good coincidence between political and ethnic borders (with the partial exceptions of the ethnically mixed provinces of Alsace, northwestern Lorraine, and Schleswig-Holstein). Although its borders were compact, Germany's position in the center of the European landmass, with no clearly defined natural borders in the east and only partial ones in the west, made its strategic geopolitical situation a precarious one.

Versailles

The second historical phase shows the severe territorial ramifications of the Treaty of Versailles. Essentially, all German national territories that had ever been disputed since 1772 (and more) were returned to the rival party. Alsace-Lorraine was returned to France, Schleswig-Holstein was returned to Denmark, Belgium received the Malmedy region despite its lack of claims to the area, and Lithuania unilaterally seized the Memel region of northeastern Prussia. All overseas colonies were forfeited, and the Ruhr was demilitarized and occupied by France to guarantee payment of war reparations. The most politically intolerable (and the most problematic from the compactness standpoint) territorial loss was the transfer of Posen–West Prussia to Poland in order to create a corridor to the sea for the new state. Not counting colonies and the French-occupied Ruhr, the Treaty of Versailles deprived Germany of more than 10 percent of its population and 13 percent of its territory. My qualitative analysis of these transfers is that the Allies were consciously aiming to disrupt and delay the rebuilding of German economic and military power and, much more interesting from the geopolitical standpoint, to redirect future German territorial ambitions eastward toward Russia and away from France. By creating the extremely problematic Polish corridor across Prussia and politically encouraging Polish intransigence in the interwar period, the Allies could achieve the classical Mackinderan goal of splitting the Eastern European heartland. I therefore rate this phase as illustrating a high level of compactness concern (on the part of the Allies, who dictated the changes). In the next several historical stages, the desire to reincorporate former lands and Germanic peoples into the Reich would dominate the interwar geopolitical agenda of the Hitler regime, but compactness concerns were clearly present in a few of the cases.

The quantitative measures of compactness for this historical phase show mixed results. The Richardsonian perimeter index moves significantly in the predicted direction, dropping from .52 to a .42 level. The Gibbs-Cole radial measure, however, shows a small change in the opposite direction, counterpredictedly moving up from .59 to .60. In some ways, this can be interpreted as a spurious measure due to the limitations of the radial method of calculation in this specific situation: the radial core of Germany does not actually change from the 1914 phase to the 1918 phase, but the smaller area of the state outside the core in the second phase causes the unchanged core to have a relatively higher compactness ratio. If the radial index is broken down into its constituent parts, Gibbs's protrusion component changes significantly in the predicted direction (–.08) but is overshadowed by Cole's previously mentioned 'spurious' intrusion radial change of .09. Generally, the Gibbs protrusion index performs better in terms of the predicted direction of change in the German cases, but this could be an artifact of the idiosyncratic configuration of Germany's borders rather than a systematic superiority (the Cole and Gibbs methodologies agreed in direction for every Israeli case).

Rhineland

The third German historical phase represents the reestablishment of sovereignty and military control over the Rhineland, a step generally regarded as Hitler's first significant move in his sequential revision of the Treaty of Versailles. Irredentism (the desire to reclaim lost national territory and peoples), economic interests, and the attainment of a clearly defined geographical barrier, the Rhine River, were obviously the predominant objectives for this territorial gain. At the strategic level, the remilitarization of the Rhineland erased a large indentation from its configuration and hence did contribute to the overall compactness of the state. The addition also contributed to the buffer between the boundaries and Germany. However, because of the presence of other compelling objectives, I rate this phase as having only moderate compactness concerns.

The quantitative measures concur neither with the predicted direction of compactness change nor with my qualitative evaluation. Because of the peculiar configuration of Germany's borders, especially the Czech indentation, the intrusion component of the radial index decreases for the reasons explained in the previous phase. The protrusion component does increase in the predicted direction, but not enough to offset the intrusion loss in value. The net change for the radial index is −.02. The Richardsonian perimeter index shows a zero change in compactness because of the convolutions of the Rhine River, as opposed to the straight lines of the demilitarized zone, which exactly canceled out the more compact, strategic-level curve of the river line. Once again, peculiarities of the specific German configuration in this phase work to undermine the apparent validity of the quantitative measures.

Austria

The fourth territorial phase is the incorporation, or *Anschluss*, of Hitler's native Austria into Germany. Although the annexation of Austria conferred definite geographical advantages vis-à-vis the later move into Czechoslovakia, the *Anschluss* was clearly dominated by ideological and economic motives. I therefore rate this phase as having little or no compactness salience.

The quantitative indexes agree with my qualitative assessment of the phase's motivations, although they are mildly against the predicted direction for a territorial gain. Once again, the unchanging intrusion distance creates another negative shift for Cole's measure (−.05), which is exactly offset by a .05 increase in the Gibbsian protrusion measure. The net change in radial compactness, then, is a neutral zero. This phase provides the Richardsonian perimeter index with its only mispredicted direction of change in the entire study, a minor loss of −.01 in this case of territorial gain. Both the quantitative and qualitative assessments agree that compactness concerns were overridden by other, more traditional territorial motivations in this particular case.

Sudeten

The fifth German historical stage is the annexation of the Sudetenland, a mountainous, ethnically German region surrounding the western borders of Czechoslovakia. Interestingly, the Allies resisted German demands for a plebiscite for the Sudeten districts because their loss would reduce the Czech state to very slender proportions, another hint that Allied planners considered compactness concerns in the formulation of the post–World War I borders of Europe (Fifield and Pearcy

1944). For Germany, however, the addition of the Sudetenland was overwhelmingly for ethnic, economic, and military reasons. Accordingly, I rate this phase as containing little or no compactness concern for the decision makers.

The quantitative measures both move slightly in the predicted direction for a case of territorial gain. For the radial index, the annexation finally provides an increase in the intrusion core size, echoed by an increase in the protrusion measure. Overall, the radial compactness increases a modest .03. The perimeter compactness also slightly increases by a mere .01. In general, the prediction of direction is successful, with the small change in compactness agreeing with my minimal qualitative evaluation of its importance.

Czech

The German annexation of the western half of the rump state of Czechoslovakia is one of the clearest examples of compactness concerns by states. The western regions of Moravia and Bohemia were incorporated into the Reich, while the remainder, Slovakia, gained nominal independence (other portions of eastern Czechoslovakia were ceded to Poland and Hungary). For the first time, Germany exceeded the bounds of what could be considered its legitimate territory; hence, the pan-Germanistic ideological motivations noted in previous stages are absent here. Absent also are convincing economic or military motivations, for the Sudetenland contained the most valuable lands in these categories. What this annexation did provide was an enormous shortening of Germany's borders, as well as the final elimination of the Czech border indentation that had so constrained earlier measurements of the intrusion index. My evaluation is that this stage illustrates a high degree of compactness concern, especially because the spectacular compactness gains are relatively undiluted by competing motivations.

The two mathematical indexes correspond closely to the strong qualitative assessment of compactness concern in this case. The radial measure jumps .07 to .69, the entire increase due to the added buffer between border and core. This increased measure of security addresses the frequent propaganda point that Czechoslovakia's border intrusion presented a threat to Germany's heartland. The perimeter index also shows a significant rise, up .09 to .51, which is virtually identical to Germany's pre–World War I level of compactness. In terms of standardized rectangles, this represents a jump from a $\frac{1}{16}$ to a $\frac{1}{9}$ shape. Here, then, is a clear case of high compactness concern undiluted by other significant competing explanations, with both qualitative and quantitative assessments in strong agreement.

Memel

What is surely the least known of the interwar territorial gains by Germany is the reincorporation of the tiny, wedge-shaped Memel region. This reversed the unauthorized seizure of the East Prussian port by Lithuania in the immediate aftermath of World War I. The actual land area is minuscule, and I judge the gain to have had little or no compactness concern for Germany's leadership.

Both quantitative indexes concur with the insignificance of the Memel reincorporation; neither measure shows any compactness change for this phase.

Poland

The invasion of Poland was, at its root, designed to eliminate the most intolerable aspect of the Treaty of Versailles—the physical dismemberment of East Prussia from the rest of Germany. Usually considered the starting point of World War II in Europe, the invasion has been characterized as having several motivations: ideological, economic, military, demographic, political, and even psychological. From the compactness perspective, the creation of the Polish Corridor increased German borders by 350 miles, disrupted transportation nets, created a dangerous intrusion toward the capital, and created problematic areas of disputed political sovereignty. Because of the wide variety of powerful, compelling motivations, I rate this phase as having a moderate level of compactness concern.

The quantitative measures of compactness show mixed results in terms of magnitude, though both indexes change in the predicted direction. Because of the peculiar configuration of Germany at this time, the radial measure shows little change, with a mere .01 increase in compactness. Once again, the protrusion component of the radial index is a better predictor than the intrusion component. On the other hand, the Richardsonian perimeter index shows a significant increase in compactness, a full .10 rise, reflecting a dramatic relative shortening of the Reich's borders. This increase is equivalent to an increase in compactness from a $\frac{1}{9}$ rectangle to a very compact $\frac{1}{6}$ rectangle.

Alsace

The final wartime increase in the official territorial limits of Germany occurred in the aftermath of its successful campaign against France and the Low Countries. Luxembourg, Alsace-Lorraine, and a small ethnically German area of southeastern Belgium were annexed by the Reich. The economic value of the region was marginal, but it has been viewed as militarily valuable because of the broken terrain. A more important quality for the Nazi leadership was the partially Germanic demographics of the population, but the region's main value seems to have been as a symbol of victory over Germany's traditional rival, France. In compactness terms, the region had some value as an added buffer against invasion, but I rate this factor as having little or no salience as an issue.

The quantitative measures show very little change in compactness terms: the radial index shows no change at all, and the perimeter index shows only a very slight increase of .01 in the predicted direction for a territorial gain. Overall, this phase demonstrates agreement among all three methodologies: compactness was not a significant concern in this case.

Cold War

The tenth territorial stage represents the post–World War II cold war configuration of a divided Germany. Once again, Germany paid a catastrophic territorial penalty for losing a major war, conceding all of the territories affected by the Treaty of Versailles, as well as the entire eastern third of its land. By reducing Germany to a small, rump state, the compactness value for all German territory remained rather high, but the political division of the country into capitalist West Germany and communist East Germany had the enormously heavy impact of reducing it to a balkanized weakling. The isolated enclave of West

Berlin buried deep in East German territory is especially problematic from the compactness perspective, for the tenuous line of communication to the city became a flash point during the cold war. It is a matter of historical controversy whether the victorious Allies intended the division to be permanent or merely transitional. From the compactness perspective, a permanently divided Germany implies a conscious compactness penalty imposed in order to once again hobble German recovery. If a united Germany was envisioned by the Allies, its overall rather compact shape seems to imply a desire to remove compactness concerns as a territorial motivation for future German aggression. Either way, I rate this phase as demonstrating moderate compactness concern. Interestingly, there is also evidence that President Harry S. Truman personally attempted to configure the German-Polish border to form "a short and more easily defensible frontier" between the states (DeZayas 1977, 159).

The unique circumstances of an internally divided country was also problematic from the quantitative coding perspective. In the end, it was decided to portray the political balkanization of Germany by combining the areas and perimeters of both East and West Germany in the compactness formulas, essentially accepting the permanent-division interpretation of Germany's status. The isolated West Berlin enclave was given a line of communication along the single rail line allowed by the Soviets. Though it may seem awkward to double count East and West Germany's common border, it was felt that this coding decision most accurately reflects the mirror-image burden paid by the German people during their period of political division. The radial index shows a relatively small drop of –.05, and the perimeter index shows a stupendous –.28 drop in compactness. Although the quantitative measures differ widely in terms of magnitude, both compactness indexes move in the predicted direction for a territorial loss.

Unified

The final historical phase analyzed in this study represents the recent reunification of East and West Germany. Although Germany's external international borders did not change, the elimination of the double counted borders separating the two Germanies had a significant effect on its compactness. This final, relatively small, and very compact configuration may be an example of a relatively weak state's being whittled down to a size and a level of compactness that it can militarily sustain over time. (Although it may seem strange to some to call Germany a weak nation, it was clearly outclassed in all categories of national power by the coalitions of nations allied against it.) This erosion hypothesis, which predicts that territorial loss will result in higher compactness, seems to contradict the penalty hypothesis, which predicts compactness loss in instances of territorial loss, but perhaps the choice of strategies pursued by victor nations is conditioned by their expectations of future relations with their defeated rival. Specifically, if victor nations expect future hostilities they may impose compactness penalties in order to weaken their potential enemy, but if they expect peaceful relations they may configure the defeated enemy's borders to remove compactness as a territorial ambition. Certainly the draconian relocation of ethnically German peoples from Eastern Europe by communist authorities in the aftermath of World War II is an example of applying geopolitical strategies to ensure a more peaceful future; Germany's political and ethnic borders were finally made to match—the hard way. Compactness motivations of the Allies aside (which were reflected in the rating for the previous phase), the Germans were obviously preoccupied with the political and economic aspects of reunification. I therefore rate this phase as demonstrating little or no compactness concerns.

The quantitative measures reflect the removal of internal borders with large, positive increases in compactness. The radial index increases by .06, the entire change due to the greatly expanded intrusion measure. This gives Germany the highest radial compactness rating of any case in the study. The Richardsonian perimeter index shows an enormous increase, rising a full .24 to .58, the largest increase in any case in the study. Although much of this increase is an artifact of the debatable double-counted East-West border, it does seem to reflect the tangible economilitary benefits Germany has accrued from the end of its cold war political division.

APPENDIX 2
SPSS Data Spreadsheet

	phase	result	area	perim	circdist	intdist	prodist
1	MANDATE	start	10587	1387	58	30	213
2	INDEP	gain	14837	1229	69	45	213
3	6DAYWAR	gain	64720	1731	143	120	325
4	TREATY	loss	20656	1086	81	58	234
5	PREWW1	start	597700	8509	436	230	665
6	VERSAILL	loss	433600	8837	372	230	640
7	RHINELND	gain	485300	9373	393	230	665
8	AUSTRIA	gain	569200	10523	426	230	665
9	SUDETEN	gain	603800	10550	438	255	665
10	CZECH	gain	650300	8930	455	315	665
11	MEMEL	gain	654500	8920	456	315	665
12	POLAND	gain	753700	8102	490	325	665
13	ALSACE	gain	771400	8045	496	325	675
14	COLDWAR	loss	365500	10224	341	1956	470
15	UNIFIED	gain	365500	5949	341	240	470

	intratio	proratio	radindex	perindex	radchng	perchng	qualitat
1	.52	.27	.39	.33			start
2	.65	.32	.49	.44	.10	.11	high
3	.84	.44	.64	.66	.15	.22	moderate
4	.72	.35	.53	.59	−.11	−.07	moderate
5	.53	.66	.59	.52			start
6	.62	.52	.60	.42	.01	−.10	high
7	.59	.59	.59	.42	−.01	.00	moderate
8	.54	.64	.59	.41	.00	−.10	moderate
9	.58	.66	.62	.42	.03	.01	low
10	.69	.68	.69	.51	.07	.09	high
11	.69	.69	.69	.51	.00	.00	low
12	.66	.74	.70	.61	.01	.10	moderate
13	.66	.73	.70	.62	.00	.01	low
14	.57	.73	.65	.34	−.05	−.28	moderate
15	.70	.73	.71	.58	.06	.24	low

VARIABLES LIST

PHASE = Historical border phase
RESULT = Effect on territory (start, gain, loss)
AREA = National area in square kilometers
PERIM = National border perimeter in kilometers
CIRCDIST = Radius of ideal circle with an equal area

INTDIST = Intrusion radius (largest circle within borders)
PRODIST = Protrusion radius (smallest circle enclosing borders)
INTRATIO = INTDIST divided by CIRCDIST
PRORATIO = CIRCDIST divided by PRODIST
RADINDEX = Radial compactness index $(\frac{\text{INTRATIO + PRORATIO}}{2})$
PERINDEX = Perimeter-compactness index ($2\sqrt{\pi A}$) perim
RADCHNG = Change in RADINDEX from previous phase
PERCHNG = Change in PERINDEX from previous phase
QUALITAT = Qualitative compactness role (high, moderate, low)

REFERENCES

I could not end this chapter without expressing my most profound gratitude to Professor Douglas Lemke, without whose magnanimous contributions this work literally would not have been possible. Many sincere thanks also to Professors James L. Ray, Paul Hensel, Patrick O'Sullivan, and Marilyn Ruiz, for their very generous assistance.

Bar-Gal, Yoram. 1993. "Boundaries as a Topic in Geographic Education: The Case of Israel." *Political Geography* 2: 421–425.

Berliner Lithographisches Institut. 1944. "Postleit Gebeitkarte" (map). Berlin: Reichspostzentralamt.

Berry, Joseph K. 1993. *Beyond Mapping: Concepts, Algorithms, and Issues in GIS*. Fort Collins, Colo.: GIS World.

Beukema, Herman. 1966 [1942]. "Introduction." In *The World of General Haushofer: Geopolitics in Action*, by Andreas Dorpalen. New York: Kennekat Press.

Boggs, S. Whittemore. 1940. *International Boundaries: A Study of Boundary Functions and Problems*. New York: Columbia University Press.

Boulding, Kenneth E. 1962. *Conflict and Defense: A General Theory*. New York: Harper and Row.

Boyce, Ronald, and W. A. V. Clark. 1964. "The Concept of Shape in Geography." *Geographical Review* 54: 561–572.

Bradley, John. 1978. *The Illustrated History of the Third Reich*. New York: Grossett and Dunlap.

Bremer, Stuart. 1992. "Dangerous Dyads." *Journal of Conflict Resolution* 36: 309–341.

Bremer, Stuart, and Michael Mihalka. 1977. "Machiavelli in Machina; or Politics among Hexagons." In *Problems of World Modeling: Political and Social Implications*, edited by Karl W. Deutsch et al. Cambridge, Mass.: Ballinger.

Central Intelligence Agency. 1978. "Israel and Occupied Territories" (map #5676509). Washington D.C.: Central Intelligence Agency.

Christopher, A. J. 1994. "South Africa: The Case of a Failed State Partition." *Political Geography* 13: 123–136.

Cobb, R. and C. Elder. 1970. *International Community*. New York: Holt, Rinehart and Winston.

Cole, J. P. 1977. "The Study of Major and Minor Civil Divisions in Political Geography" (1960). Reported in *Locational Methods*, by Peter Haggett, Andrew D. Cliff, and Allan Frey. Vol. 2 of *Locational Analysis in Human Geography*. 2d ed. London: Edward Arnold; New York: John Wiley and Sons.

"Das Grossdeutsche Reich" (map). 1938. Vienna: G. Freytag and Berdt.

Dawson, William H. 1972 [1933]. *Germany under the Treaty*. Freeport, N.Y.: Books for Libraries Press.

deSeversky, Alexander P. 1950. *Airpower: Key to Survival*. New York: Simon and Schuster.

DeZayas, Alfred M. 1977. *Nemesis at Potsdam: The Anglo-Americans and the Expulsion of the Germans*. 3d ed., rev. Lincoln: University of Nebraska Press.

Diehl, Paul. 1985. "Continuity and Military Escalation in Major Power Rivalries, 1816–1980." *Journal of Politics* 47: 1203–1211.

Diehl, Paul, and Gary Goertz. 1991. "Interstate Conflict over Exchanges of Homeland Territory, 1816–1980." *Political Geography Quarterly* 10:342–355.

Dupuy, R. Ernest, and Trevor Dupuy. 1970. *The Encyclopedia of Military History*. New York: Harper and Row.

Emmerson, James Thomas. 1977. *The Rhineland Crisis, 7 March 1936: A Study in Multilateral Diplomacy*. London: Temple Smith, for the London School of Economics and Political Science.

Fifield, Russell L. and G. Etzel Pearcy. 1944. *Geopolitics in Principle and Practice*. Boston: Ginn.

Friedman, David. 1977. "A Theory of the Size and Shape of Nations." *Journal of Political Economy* 85: 59–77.

Gibbs, J. P. 1977. "Urban Research Methods" (1961). Reported in *Locational Methods*, by Peter Haggett, Andrew D. Cliff, and Allan Frey. Vol. 2 of *Locational Analysis in Human Geography*. 2d ed. London: Edward Arnold; New York: John Wiley and Sons.

Glassner, Martin Ira. 1993. *Political Geography*. New York: John Wiley and Sons.

Gleick, James. 1987. *Chaos: Making of a New Science*. New York: Penguin Books.

Gochman, Charles. 1991. "Interstate Metrics: Conceptualizing, Operationalizing, and Measuring the Geographic Proximity of States since the Congress of Vienna." *International Interactions* 17: 93–112.

Grunberger, Richard. 1964. *Germany, 1918–1945.* New York: Harper and Row.

Haggett, Peter, Andrew Cliff, and Allan Frey. 1977. *Locational Methods.* Vol. 2 of *Locational Analysis in Human Geography.* 2d ed. London: Edward Arnold; New York: John Wiley and Sons.

Hitler, Adolf. 1927. *Mein Kampf.* Sentry ed. Boston: Houghton Mifflin.

Hoggan, David L. 1989. *The Forced War: When Peacdful Revision Failed.* Costa Mesa, Calif.: Institute for Historical Review.

Horn, David, Charles Hampton, and Anthony Vandenberg. 1993. "Practical Application of District Compactness." *Political Geography* 12: 103–120

Intergraph Corporation. "Microstation version 4.0" (software). Huntsville, Ala.: Intergraph Corporation.

Irving, David. 1975. *Hitler's War.* London: Butler and Tanner.

Israeli Office of Information. 1954, 1957, 1966, 1971, 1975, 1984. "Facts about Israel" (maps). New York: Israeli Office of Information.

Johannson, Rune. 1988. *Small State in Boundary Conflict: Belgium and the Belgian-German Border, 1914–1919.* Lund, Sweden: Lund University Press.

Lange, Friedrich. 1925. *Der Kampf um die Deutschen Grenzen.* Berlin: Verlag Deutsche Volksgemeinschaft.

Lemke, Douglas. 1995. "The Tyranny of Distance: Redefining Relevant Dyads." *International Interactions* 21: 23–38.

Louis, William R. 1967. *Great Britain and Germany's Lost Colonies: Great Britain and Germany's Lost Colonies, 1914–1919.* Oxford: Clarenden Press.

Mann, Aldo. 1967. "Versailles Oppressed the Republic." In *The Creation of the Weimar Republic: Stillborn Democracy?* edited by Richard N. Hunt. Lexington, Mass.: D. C. Heath.

Map Info Corporation. "Map Info version 3.0.5" (software).

Midlarsky, Manus. 1974. "Power, Uncertainty, and the Onset of International Violence." *Journal of Conflict Resolution* 18: 395–431.

Most, Benjamin A., and Harvey Starr. 1980. "Diffusion, Reinforcement, Geopolitics, and the Spread of War." *American Political Science Review* 74: 932–946.

Most, Benjamin A., Harvey Starr, and Randolf Siverson. 1989. "The Logic and Study of the Diffusion of International Conflict." In *Handbook of War Studies,* edited by M. Midlarsky. Ann Arbor: University of Michigan Press.

Muir, Richard. 1975. *Modern Political Geography.* New York: John Wiley and Sons.

Nakhleh, Issa. 1991. *Encyclopedia of the Palestine Problem.* Vol. 2. New York: Intercontinental Books.

National Geographic Society. 1940a. "Europe and the Middle East" (map). Washington, D.C.: National Geographic Society.

———. 1940b. "Europe and the Near East" (map). Washington. D.C.: National Geographic Society.

———. 1944. "Germany and Its Approaches" (map). Washington, D.C.: National Geographic Society.

Natkiel, Richard. 1989. Maps. In *The German Homefront, 1939–45,* by Terry Charman. New York: Philosophical Library.

New York Times. 1996. "A Country Pushed, Pulled and Torn" (map). *New York Times,* regional ed., April 17.

Niemi, Richard, Bernard Grofman, Carl Carlucci, and Thomas Hofeller. 1990. "Measuring Compactness and the Role of a Compactness Standard in a Test for Partisan and Racial Gerrymandering." *Journal of Politics* 52: 1155–1181.

Nystuen, John D. 1967. Peace Reasearch Society Papers, 7th Conference, Chicago 1967.

Parker, Geoffrey. 1985. *Western Geopolitical Thought in the Twentieth Century.* London: Croom Helm.

Pitt, Barrie, and Frances Pitt. 1989. *The Chronological Atlas of World War II.* London: Macmillan.

Pounds, Norman J. G., and Sue Simons Ball. 1964. "Core Areas and the Development of the European State Systems." *Annals of the Association of American Geographers* 54: 24–40.

Prescott, J. R. V. 1965. *The Geography of Frontiers and Boundaries.* Chicago: Aldine Publishing.

Rapoport, Anatol. 1957. "Lewis F. Richardson's Mathematical Theory of War." *Journal of Conflict Resolution* 1: 249–299.

Ratzel, Friedrich. 1965. *Politische Geographie* (1895). Noted in *The Geography of Frontiers and Boundaries,* by J. R. V. Prescott. Chicago: Aldine Publishing.

Reock, Ernest. 1961. "A Note: Measuring Compactness as a Requirement of Legislative Apportionment." *Midwest Journal of Political Science* 5: 70–74.

Richardson, Lewis Fry. 1960. *Statistics of Deadly Quarrels.* Chicago: Quadrangle Publications.

———. 1993. "The Problem of Contiguity: An Appendix to Statistics of Deadly Quarrels" (1961). In *Collected Papers of Lewis Fry Richardson,* edited by Oliver M. Ashford et al. Vol. 2. New York: Cambridge University Press.

Richardson, Stephen. 1957. "Lewis Fry Richardson: A Personal Biography." *Journal of Conflict Resolution* 1: 300–304.

Schelling, Thomas C. 1978. *Micromotives and Macrobehavior*. New York: W. W. Norton.

Shirer, William L. 1959. *The Rise and Fall of the Third Reich*. New York: Simon and Schuster.

Siverson, Randolph, and Harvey Starr. 1991. *The Diffusion of War: A Study of Opportunity and Willingness*. Ann Arbor: University of Michigan Press.

Spykman, Nicholas J. 1938. "Geography and Foreign Policy, I." *American Political Science Review* 32: 28–50.

Starr, Harvey. 1996. "The Analysis of Geopolitics: Reconceptualizing International Borders through the Application of GIS." Paper presented at the Southern Political Science Association meeting, Atlanta, Ga.

Starr, Harvey, and Benjamin Most. 1976. "The Substance and Study of Borders in International Relations Research." *International Studies Quarterly* 20: 581–650.

———. 1978. "A Return Journey: Richardson, 'Frontiers,' and Wars in the 1946–1965 Era." *Journal of Conflict Resolution* 22: 441–467.

Taylor, A. J. P. 1946. "Allied Power Sustained the Republic." In *The Creation of the Weimar Republic: Stillborn Democracy?* edited by Richard N. Hunt. Lexington, Mass.: D. C. Heath.

———. 1961. *The Origins of the Second World War*. London: Atheneum.

Taylor, Peter J. 1973. "A New Shape Measure for Evaluating Electoral District Patterns." *American Political Science Review* 67: 947–950.

U.S. Department of State. 1946. "Germany: Zones of Occupation" (map). Washington, D.C.: Division of Intelligence and Cartography.

Van Valkenburg, Samuel. 1939. *Elements of Political Geography*. New York: Prentice Hall.

Vasquez, John. 1993. *The War Puzzle*. Cambridge, U.K., and New York: Cambridge University Press.

Weede, Erich. 1970. "Conflict Behavior of Nation States." *Journal of Peace Research* 7: 229–235.

Wesley, James. 1962. "Frequency of Wars and Geographical Opportunity." *Journal of Conflict Resolution* 6: 387–389.

White, C. Langdon, and George Renner. 1957. *College Geography: Natural Environment and Human Society*. New York.

Whittlesey, Derwent S. 1944 [1939]. *The Earth and the State: A Study of Political Gergraphy*. New York.: H. Holt and Company.

Wolfsohn, Michael. 1987. *Israel: Polity and Society*. Atlantic Highlands, N.J.: Humanities Press.

PART III

The Dynamics of Territorial Conflict

4

Charting a Course to Conflict: Territorial Issues and Interstate Conflict, 1816–1992

Paul R. Hensel

T he scholarly literature on interstate conflict has, for the most part, paid little attention to the impact of contentious issues, or the "disputed points or questions" that are "the subject of a conflict or controversy" (Diehl 1992, 333). Scholars generally recognize that militarized conflict happens for some reason, usually developing out of some conflict of interest or underlying tension between states (see, for example, Snyder and Diesing 1977; Lebow 1981; Vasquez 1993). Despite this recognition, few scholars have incorporated contentious issues into their studies of interstate conflict and war. Mansbach and Vasquez (1981), for example, called for the development of an issue-based paradigm to challenge realpolitik—but as Diehl (1992, 337) noted, "despite initial positive reviews and more than a decade of time, the issue paradigm approach has not germinated such that its use is seriously evident, much less widespread, in the discipline." This lack of explicit attention to the issues at stake in relations between states may constitute an important limit on our ability to explain and predict conflict behavior. That is, decision makers may be expected to behave in fundamentally different ways when dealing with an issue they consider highly salient than when dealing with a less salient concern. Leaders would seem likely to respond quite differently to the incarceration of one of their state's citizens abroad than to the seizure of a strategic piece of land.

Territory is widely seen as a type of issue that is especially salient to decision makers. Vasquez (1993, 123–124), for example, suggests that "In the modern global system, and long before then, it has been territorial issues, particularly issues involving territorial contiguity, that are the source of conflict most likely to end in war." Yet the general lack of scholarly attention to contentious issues is mirrored by the absence of serious study of territorial issues and interstate conflict. Most of the existing research on geography and conflict has treated geography as a "facilitating condition for conflict," rather than a "source of conflict" in the sense of contentious issues (Diehl 1991). Examples of work on geographical factors as a facilitating condition for conflict include Boulding's (1962) loss-of-strength gradient and studies of proximity and the initiation, escalation, or spread of war (for example, Most and Starr 1980; Diehl 1985; Bremer 1992; Lemke 1995; see also Diehl 1991).

In the present research I study territorial issues as a source of conflict. After a brief review of the literature I present and test several hypotheses regarding the effects of territory on interstate conflict. As will be seen, territorial issues produce forms of conflict behavior that are very different from those produced by less salient issues. Confrontations involving territory are more escalatory than are nonterritorial confrontations, and territorial disputes are also more likely than nonterritorial disputes to be followed by renewed conflict between the same adversaries in the future. In this sense, territorial questions between states can be seen as setting the stage for serious conflict between them, essentially charting a long course of potential conflict if the questions are not resolved quickly and peacefully.

THEORETICAL DEVELOPMENT

A number of descriptions of interstate conflict processes begin with conflicts of interest between two or more states. Snyder and Diesing's (1977) model of interstate crises, for example, begins with a conflict of interest and mild conflict behavior between the adversaries, potentially developing into a crisis if the two sides begin to employ more coercive means to pursue their interests. Lebow (1981) offers a model of crisis and war that begins with underlying hostility between the adversaries, which may lead to manifestations of tension and eventually the outbreak of a crisis between them. Holsti (1991) also describes a peace and war cycle in which contentious issues can generate conflicts between adversaries, possibly leading to war. For each of these scholars, interstate conflict begins with a disagreement over one or more contentious issues.

Contentious issues can involve a wide variety of disagreements. Holsti (1991), for example, identifies twenty-four specific types of issues that have produced conflict since 1648, ranging from national unification to supporting an ally to maintaining a balance of power. For the purposes of the present study, though, I focus on territory as an issue that is considered by many scholars and policymakers to be especially salient.[1] Hill (1945, 3), for example, argued that "International relations, in their more vital aspects, revolve about the possession of territory." Territorial issues have been described as "conspicuous among the causes of war" (Hill 1945, 3) and as "perhaps the most important single cause of war between states in the last two or three centuries" (Luard 1970, 7).

Territory can be seen as important for nation-states for several reasons (Diehl 1991, for example). In the most basic sense, territory may be important because of what it contains. Many disputed territories have contained (or have been thought to contain) valuable commodities or resources, such as strategic minerals or oil. A territory may be seen as important because of its population, particularly when the population includes members of an ethnic or religious group that inhabits a neighboring state. Territory may also be important to states as a way to increase their perceived security by providing advance warning of an impending attack and contributing to national defense, particularly to the extent that the territory in question contains defensible geographical features like rough terrain or mountains. Territory in this tangible sense contributes to a state's power and security, which are important elements in a realist worldview (for example, Morgenthau 1978).

Beyond any physical elements that it may contain, territory is also seen as important to states for less tangible reasons. Territory is argued to lie at the heart of national identity and cohesion, with the very existence and autonomy of a state being rooted in its territory (for example, Murphy 1990, 531). Similarly, Bowman (1946, 177) argued that there is a "profound psychological difference" between the transfer of territory and other types of interstate interactions or treaties:

Territory is near and plain and evokes personal feelings and group sentiments. To a people conscious of its individuality, "how sweet the silent backward tracings." Such people endow the land itself with a mystical quality, hearing revered ancestors, the authors of past grandeurs and the doers of heroic deeds, speak from their graves in its soil. . . . It is title to sentiments like these, and not merely to so-and-so many square miles of land, that is transferred when there is a change of boundaries and rule. (Bowman 1946, 177)

In short, territory is argued to have "a psychological importance for nations that is quite out of proportion to its intrinsic value, strategic or economic," and territorial disputes seem to arouse sentiments of pride and honor more rapidly and more intensely than does any other type of issue (Luard 1970, 7; see also Vasquez 1993).

Hastings and Jenkins (1983) demonstrate the symbolic or intangible importance of territory in discussing Argentina's claim to the Falkland (Malvinas) Islands:

The islands were of no economic and only limited strategic significance. . . . Nevertheless, all Argentine schools were instructed to teach "The Malvinas are Argentine," a cry which was even set to music. A generation of Argentinians thus grew up regarding the British occupation as an affront to their nationhood. Repossession was not a matter of legal or diplomatic nicety. It was a challenge to national honor. (Hastings and Jenkins 1983, 9)

Levy and Vakili (1992, 130–131) note the importance that Argentina's President Leopoldo Galtieri attached to the Malvinas as "a national symbol shared by nearly all segments of society," which made the islands seem to be an ideal tool for increasing the unity and legitimacy of the ruling regime. After Argentine forces invaded the islands in 1982, the Argentine news media and political parties—even those that had vigorously opposed Galtieri's regime in the past—rallied behind the president in celebrating the end of what *La Prensa* termed "an intolerable insult to Argentine independence and nationhood" (Lebow 1985, 114).

Similar sentiments appeared on the British side after Argentina's invasion, despite the limited economic and strategic value of the islands themselves. British public opinion blamed Prime Minister Margaret Thatcher for what was considered a serious blow to national honor and prestige. A Gallup survey shortly after the invasion found that 48 percent of the British public saw Thatcher as the worst prime minister in British history. Only 12 percent saw Neville Chamberlain—the traditional "winner" whenever the question was asked—as the worst prime minister, despite the seemingly much lower importance of the Falklands compared with Chamberlain's losses in Central Europe (Lebow 1985, 116–117).

Other territorial disputes also offer plentiful examples of the symbolic importance of territory (Hensel 1996, chap. 5). During the war between Bolivia and Paraguay over the Chaco Boreal, Bolivia's minister to the United States wrote that "Perhaps if the Chaco dispute has been merely a territorial controversy, Bolivia . . . might have resigned herself to the loss of her patrimony in order to preserve peace. . . . But the question involved is not only the possession of territories more or less valuable, but also the right to life, the necessity of breathing and of recovering the attributes of an independent and sovereign nation" (Finot 1934, 23). The Bolivian and Paraguayan media and opposition parties pressured their respective governments to take a firm stance on the Chaco question, criticizing any hint of accommodation that might be seen as surrendering national territory to the enemy (even if these opposition parties had tried to reach similar accommodations while previously in power). Paraguay's National Council of Education even adopted an official textbook with the title *The Chaco Boreal Was, Is, and Will Be Paraguayan* (Warren 1949; Rout 1970). Similarly, France and Germany both came to view the disputed territory along the Rhine River as a national symbol or "deity," leading to patriotic literature and songs with lyrics like "They shall not have it, the free German Rhine" (Mann 1968, 43, 72–73).

Beyond these tangible and intangible reasons, territory can also be important for reasons of reputation. That is, if a leader gives in to an adversary on territorial issues despite the tangible and intangible importance of the territory, other adversaries may be encouraged to press their own demands on other issues. Huth (1988) and Fearon (1994), among others, discuss similar notions regarding the impact of reputation on deterrence crises. There is evidence, for example, that reputational considerations affected the British reaction to Argentina's invasion of the Falklands. Lebow (1985, 117–118) notes concerns by the British defense ministry and the *Economist* about the risks to British interests in Gibraltar, Belize, Guyana, Diego Garcia, Hong Kong, and Antarctica if Britain were to back down over the Falklands. Even if behavior in previous crises against other adversaries may not have much overall impact on deterrence (Huth 1988), behavior in crises over such highly salient issues as territory may be expected to produce important reputational effects.

These examples, along with the observations about the tangible and intangible importance of territory that were presented above, suggest a series of implications for the study of interstate conflict. That is, if territorial issues are treated differently from other issues because of their physical or psychological importance, then conflict over territory should be different from conflict over other issues.

CONFLICT SEVERITY

For one thing, territorial issues are unusual among contentious issues in their proneness to violence, with disagreements over territorial issues being more likely than disagreements over other issues to end up in crisis or war (Vasquez 1993, 133, 151). Thus we should find that territorial disputes tend to reach higher levels of conflict severity than disputes in which policymakers are not pushed by the territorial imperative. That is, disagreements over economic relations or treaty ratifications do not seem likely to lead to all-out war, and disagreements over the disposition of one state's citizen in another state's prison rarely lead to serious conflict or war. Even when one state threatens to use force to resolve such issues, the resulting disputes would seem likely to end quickly, with little escalation and little perception that war is likely. Neither side in such a confrontation would seem likely to accept the risks and potential costs inherent in violent conflict over issues that are of such low salience for both sides.

In territorial disagreements, however, policy makers may be expected to be more active in pursuing and protecting their states' vital interests, because the risks or costs of losing the disputed stakes to the enemy may be too great. As Brecher (1993, 153) argues, the more basic the values at stake in a crisis situation, "the higher the cost crisis actors are willing to incur to protect them, and the more extreme will be their crisis management (value-protecting) technique." As a result, leaders are expected to be less likely to ignore escalatory moves by the adversary, and more likely to take escalatory actions of their own in order to protect their territorial interests.

Hypothesis 1: Militarized disputes involving territorial issues will reach higher severity levels than will disputes over other types of issues.

Several recent studies have supported similar hypotheses. In their analysis of conflict behavior in Latin American dyads, Hensel and Diehl (1994) find that militarized disputes involving territorial issues were much more likely to feature a militarized response by the target state than were disputes over less salient issues. Gochman and Leng's (1983) study of thirty interstate crises finds that those involving "vital issues"—that is, issues of territory or national independence—typically showed higher levels of escalation than did crises over less salient issues. Senese (1996) also finds that disputes over territorial issues have typically produced a greater number of fatalities than have disputes over other issues.

In this study I examine two dimensions of dispute escalation, at the low end and the high end of the escalation spectrum, in order to gain a more detailed understanding of the impact of territorial issues. The first dimension involves the target state's response to a militarized challenge by a dispute initiator. That is, once one state threatens, displays or uses force in pursuit of its interests, does the target of that action respond with military threats or actions of its own? As Hensel and Diehl (1994) note, the general category of "nonmilitarized response" by the target state in a dispute includes a wide variety of possible diplomatic or economic activities, as well as the absence of any response to the initiator's provocations. Nonetheless, the threshold between militarized and nonmilitarized responses is an important one, because the risks and costs of interstate war can be avoided by a simple refusal to employ militarized means in pursuing one's goals— even if this refusal risks losing one's interests by not standing firm militarily. If territorial issues are indeed different from other types of contentious issues, then we should expect to find that target states in disputes over territorial issues are much less likely than targets in nonterritorial disputes to refrain from a militarized response when challenged militarily, because the territorial stakes are likely to be seen as important enough to justify the risks of escalation.

The second dimension of conflict severity is the escalation of militarized disputes to war, or a protracted clash between two states' military forces that lead to substantial loss of life. If territorial issues are involved in a confrontation, we may expect that the adversaries to be more likely to take violent actions in support of their (territorial) interests than they would be in a confrontation over less salient issues— even if this leads them to full-fledged interstate war.

Conflict Outcomes

If territorial issues are as important (physically or psychologically) as I have suggested, then we may expect militarized confrontations to be more likely to end in decisive outcomes when territorial stakes are involved than otherwise and less likely to end in stalemated or compromise outcomes. Each side will be more likely to take serious action and less likely to let the matter drop without some resolution (albeit temporary, because—as will be suggested shortly—the resolution of one dispute may lead to the outbreak of another).

I also expect most of these resolutions to involve decisive outcomes (that is, a victory for one side and a defeat for its adversary) instead of negotiated compromises. To the extent that territory is seen as a vital part of a nation-state's self-identity or psychological being, as suggested above, leaders will be less likely to reach satisfactory concessionary agreements with their opponents, because of the difficulty of trading away part of the national soul. France and Germany were unwilling to pursue a negotiated settlement over Alsace and Lorraine, for example, and the territory in question changed hands several times through military conquest (a decisive outcome, if only temporary). Although compromise outcomes may be possible or even likely in disputes over less salient issues, such outcomes would seem unlikely in disputes over highly salient issues such as territory.

Hypothesis 2: Militarized disputes involving territorial issues will be more likely to end in decisive outcomes and less likely to end in stalemated or compromise outcomes than will disputes over other types of issues.

Conflict Recurrence

Dyads that contend over issues with the importance attributed to territory are arguably more likely to become involved in recurrent confrontations in the aftermath than are dyads that contend over less inflammatory issues. If an early confrontation fails to resolve an issue of relatively low salience, the adversaries may be prone to drop the matter entirely, without pursuing conflict over the issue, because the costs and risks of conflict may exceed the value attached to the issues at stake. Such issues may be one-time problems, which may be resolved quickly in a single confrontation or which may be abandoned without any type of formal resolution if the involved issues are sufficiently unimportant. Where territorial issues are involved, though, the adversaries may be expected to pursue the issue until they have achieved their goals. And when one side manages to achieve its goals over territorial issues, the other side may then have a powerful incentive to try to regain its lost territory and to overcome some of the damage to its national pride or honor, should the opportunity arise in the future.

Bowman (1946, 178), for example, noted that any territorial solution—no matter how fair it may seem—carries with it the risk of future attempts to regain lost territory. Arguments may always be raised in the future about past historical claims to the lost territory, especially in border zones of mixed ethnic or linguistic composition, and subsequent incidents may always be used to refocus attention on such historical claims. Bowman (1946, 180–181) further suggested that two or more states can often have irreconcilable claims to the same piece of territory and that in some territorial disputes there may be no logical solution acceptable to each side. It is thus reasonable to expect that recurrent conflict will be more likely when territorial issues are involved in the dispute.

Hypothesis 3: Militarized disputes involving territorial issues will be more likely to be followed by recurrent militarized conflict than will disputes over other types of issues.

In a study of conflict recurrence in Latin American dyads, Hensel (1994) finds that territorial issues have seemed to make recurrent conflict more likely than other issues; my study examines whether this relationship holds for the remainder of the world as well. Another factor that Hensel (1994; see also Maoz 1984; Brecher 1993) finds to be important in the recurrence of militarized conflict involves dispute outcomes. Specifically, Hensel (1994, 283) suggests that recurrent conflict will be more likely after a stalemate than after either a decisive outcome or a negotiated compromise, because "neither side was able to produce the desired changes in the status quo, neither was defeated and rendered unable or unwilling to mount another serious challenge, and no mutually satisfactory settlement was reached to resolve the two sides' differences." Similarly, Brecher (1993) expects that crises ending in (formal or semiformal) voluntary compromise agreements are more likely to produce mutual satisfaction in their wake than will crises with in other types of outcomes and that crises ending without such agreements are likely to be followed by greater levels of tension and instability between the adversaries.

The effects of outcomes may also be influenced by the issues at stake in a dispute. Vasquez (1993, 147) argues that unless one side is able to achieve an overwhelming victory over the other or the two sides are able to reach a diplomatic accommodation, territorial issues will tend to fester and will often produce long-term adversarial relationships. The possible interaction between the effects of dispute outcomes and contentious issues forms the basis of my final hypothesis.

Hypothesis 4: Militarized disputes involving territorial issues will be more likely to be followed by recurrent militarized conflict than will disputes over other types of issues, while controlling for the differences between decisive, stalemate, and compromise outcomes.

RESEARCH DESIGN

Spatial-Temporal Domain

My study covers the years 1816–1992, the period currently included in the Correlates of War (COW) Project's Militarized Interstate Dispute dataset. The basic unit of analysis is the militarized interstate dispute, a confrontation that involves the explicit threat, display, or use of militarized force between the regular forces of two or more nation-states (Gochman and Maoz 1984). The 2,035 militarized disputes in the

dataset are disaggregated into the individual pairs of states that confronted each other, in order to examine the conflict behavior of dyadic
adversaries.[2] Breaking down the dataset into conflictual dyads produces a total of 3,043 dyadic adversaries in the dataset's 2,035 disputes.[3]

The dyadic breakdown of the dataset did not alter the direction or
strength of the results presented in this chapter, despite possible concerns about the statistical independence of cases in which several
dyadic disputes are extracted from the same original militarized dispute
case. In fact, the dyadic breakdown allows a more detailed study of
the effects of territorial issues than might otherwise be possible. In
multilateral disputes, not all participants necessarily contend over
territorial issues, so a dyadic breakdown allows us to distinguish between those participants in the dispute that did contend over territory and those that did not. My analyses of dispute escalation and
outcomes are conducted at the level of the aggregated militarized dispute as well as the disaggregated dyadic dispute, and—as the reported
results indicate—the results do not change in strength or direction.
Furthermore, this dyadic breakdown allows us to study whether each
pair of adversaries in the dispute confronted each other in a recurrent
dispute, which is not possible if the data are not broken down dyadically to indicate which states are involved in disputes against each
other and when.

Methodology

The results of my analyses are presented in the form of contingency tables, which offer a cross-tabulation of the issues at stake in a given dispute with the severity, outcome, or aftermath of that dispute. Beyond
the tables themselves, these analyses include both a chi-square test
statistic and the odds ratio associated with the table. The chi-square
(X^2) statistic offers a conventional indicator of the statistical significance of the results, or the likelihood that the distribution of cases in
the table could have arisen by chance if the two variables in the table
are actually statistically independent. The value of the X^2 statistic is
limited, though, particularly because of its vulnerability to the size of
the sample being tested. If the number of cases is increased but the
proportion of cases in each cell does not change, the X^2 statistic will

increase in value even though the strength of the observed relationship has not been altered (Reynolds 1984).

The odds ratio offers insight into the practical or theoretical substantive significance of the results, or the strength of the relationship between two variables, as opposed to the statistical significance measured by the X^2 statistic (Reynolds 1984). The odds ratio gives us the ratio of the statistical odds of a certain value of the dependent variable, given the value of the independent variable. In my analyses, an odds ratio of 1.0 tells us that the odds of the dependent variable—for example, dispute escalation to war—are identical for disputes involving territorial issues and disputes involving other types of issues. An odds ratio of greater than 1.0 indicates how much greater are the odds of the dependent variable for one value of the independent variable than for the other. The odds ratio is not affected by the number of cases presented in a table, and it offers an easily interpretable comparison of the strength of the differences between territorial and other issues in interstate conflict.

Operationalization of Variables

Territorial Issues
The recently updated COW Militarized Interstate Dispute dataset includes a variable that indicates the primary issue at stake for each dispute participant, based on the type of alteration to the status quo ante (if any) being pursued by the participant. Four types of issues are coded. Territorial issues involve explicit contention over territory, ranging from the demarcation of a mutual border (such as questions arising from rivers that change course over time) to the ownership of an entire piece of territory (such as Alsace-Lorraine or the Chaco Boreal). Regime issues involve the disposition of a state's government or regime, which typically involves covert or overt attempts to remove a government from power. Policy issues deal with government policies, ranging from economic activities to the detention of a foreign national. The fourth type of issue is a residual category that captures issues not included in these first three.[4] For the purposes of this study, the second, third, and fourth types of issues are collapsed together, producing a dichotomous indicator of whether the dispute involved territorial issues for at least one of its participants.

Conflict Severity

My measures of dispute escalation are derived from the COW dispute data's "level of hostility" variable, which reflects the highest level of militarized action employed by each participant in a militarized dispute (Gochman and Maoz 1984). Two dichotomous escalation measures are used, based on thresholds of militarized activities by the dispute participants. The first indicator, nonmilitarized response, is based on the actions taken by the target state in the dispute. If the target state does not respond militarily to the dispute initiator's actions, that state is considered to have made a nonmilitarized response to the initiator's actions. The other measure indicates whether a dispute escalated to full-scale interstate war, which involves sustained combat between regular military forces leading to at least 1,000 battle deaths (Small and Singer 1982).

Conflict Outcomes

The COW militarized-dispute data includes a coding for the outcome of each dispute. For my purposes, I narrowed the eight-category COW outcome coding to three categories of interest. Decisive outcomes are those in which there was a clear winner in the dispute, in terms of either a battlefield victory or the clear ability to alter the status quo ante at the end of the dispute. Compromise outcomes are those in which the two sides were able to reach a mutually agreeable settlement of the dispute. Stalemate outcomes are those in which neither of the above conditions applies, with neither a victory for one side nor a mutual settlement.[5]

Conflict Recurrence

The recurrence of militarized conflict is measured dichotomously, by whether the same two adversaries engaged in at least one more militarized dispute within fifteen years of the conclusion of their previous dispute.[6] Longer periods of stability reach into times when the next dispute may not be related closely to the previous dispute. Analyses run without such a cutoff also risk a serious skewing of the results because some disputes in the early nineteenth century have had 150 years or more in which to be followed by further conflict, whereas more recent cases have had a much shorter time period in which recurrent conflict could arise.

FREQUENCY OF TERRITORIAL ISSUES

I begin by examining the relative frequency of territorial issues as a cause of conflict in the modern interstate system. Few scholars have attempted to classify the overall prevalence of territorial issues in the form of opposing territorial claims, short of classifying cases of militarized conflict by the types of issues involved in the conflict itself. A recent exception is the work of Huth (1996), who identifies 129 cases of opposing territorial claims since 1945 and studies the effects of these claims on the conflict propensity of the involved states. Similarly, Kocs (1995) identifies twenty-one contiguous-territory disputes in the 1945–1987 period that have never been resolved, as well as twenty more that had been resolved but were reopened as the result of subsequent events.

Territorial claims thus seem to have been common in the modern interstate system. Beyond their frequency, though, we might consider how territorial issues affect relations between the involved states, or how frequently such issues give rise to militarized conflict. Kocs (1995) finds that interstate war has been much more likely between adversaries with territorial claims against each other than between other adversaries, accounting for eighteen of the twenty-nine wars included in his study. Huth (1996) notes that territorial disputes were a primary cause of the armed conflict in fourteen of the twenty-one interstate wars fought during the 1950–1990 period. Holsti (1991) finds that territorial or border-related issues were the most common source of warfare in four of the five historical periods in his study of war since 1648, with 47 to 77 percent of the wars in each period involving territorial issues. Furthermore, as Vasquez (1993) notes, when territoriality-related issues are added to the list of explicitly territorial issues in Holsti's study, the proportion of wars in each historical period involving territory ranges from 79 to 93 percent. Territorial issues have thus been prominent as a source of interstate conflict and war, both over the past five centuries (in Holsti's study) and in the post–World War II period (in the Kocs and Huth studies).

Using the COW militarized-dispute data on contentious issues, we find that fewer than one-third of all militarized interstate disputes involve primarily territorial issues. The COW Militarized Interstate Dispute dataset includes 2,035 disputes between 1816 and 1992. In 28.7 percent of these disputes (585), at least one participant sought to alter the territorial status quo ante. Furthermore, although Luard

(1986) and Holsti (1991) have suggested that—especially since 1945—
territory is becoming less prominent as an issue leading to conflict or
war, the proportion of all disputes involving contention over territory
has not changed significantly over time (X^2 = 1.23, 1 d.f., p < .27). Territorial concerns were involved in 30.1 percent of all disputes between
1816 and 1945 and in 27.8 percent of all disputes since 1945.

Using the dyadic disaggregation of the militarized-dispute data,
795 (or 26.1 percent) dyadic disputes feature one or both parties' contending over primarily territorial issues in the dispute, whereas 2,248
are limited to nonterritorial issues.[7] As with the aggregated dispute-
level data mentioned above, these dyadic disputes show no appreciable difference in the frequency of territorial issues over time (X^2 =
0.01, 1 d.f., p < .92). Territorial issues were involved in 26.0 percent of
all dyadic disputes between 1816 and 1945 and in 26.2 percent of all
the disputes since 1945.

Territory is certainly not at stake in all militarized disputes, then,
which allows my analyses to produce meaningful results. If territorial
issues were coded as being involved in nearly all militarized confrontations, then a territory-conflict relationship would be tautologi-
cal; we could learn little by studying the escalatory effects of territorial issues because there would be few nonterritorial disputes or wars
to use for comparison. Using the COW dispute data, though, fewer
than one-third of the militarized disputes and—as will be seen
shortly—fewer than two-thirds of the interstate wars examined in this
study feature explicit contention over primarily territorial issues,
leaving us with a large number of both territorial and nonterritorial
confrontations. The identification of territorial issues in the militarized-dispute data thus was not done tautologically, as would have
been the case had all serious disputes or wars been coded as territorial because of some prior theoretical bias. As a result, we can interpret
this study's results with greater confidence that the findings result
from real differences between territorial and nonterritorial disputes,
rather than from poorly coded data.

EMPIRICAL ANALYSES
Conflict Severity

Table 1 examines the impact of territorial issues on the likelihood of
militarized response by the target state in a dispute. The target state

failed to respond militarily in 186 of 795 disputes involving territorial issues (23.4 percent) and in 1,146 of 2,248 disputes involving other types of issues (51.0 percent). Nonmilitarized response is thus more than twice as likely in disputes that do not involve territorial issues, and this difference is highly significant (X^2 = 181.54, 1 d.f., p < .001).[8] The odds ratio of 3.41 also indicates that the odds of a militarized response are nearly three and one-half times greater when territorial issues are at stake than when other types of issues are at stake.

Table 4.1
Nonmilitarized Response in Militarized Disputes

Territorial Issues at Stake?	Response by Target State:		Total
	Nonmilitarized	Militarized	
No	1,146 (51.0%)	1,102	2,248
Yes	186 (23.4%)	609	795
Total	1,332 (43.8%)	1,711	3,043

$X2$ = 181.54 (1 d.f., p < .001), odds ratio = 3.41

The results presented in Table 1 offer strong support for the importance of territorial issues in interstate conflict. Target states are much more likely to respond by militarized means when provoked militarily in disputes over territorial issues than in disputes over other issues. This result supports my hypothesis, indicating that decision makers are much more willing to risk dispute escalation in order to protect their interests on issues of high salience than when less salient issues are at stake. Even if threats over less salient issues can be ignored, the tangible and intangible importance of territory seems to be great enough that a challenge over territorial issues is almost always met with a militarized response.

Table 2 presents the impact of territorial issues on the escalation of militarized disputes to full-scale interstate war. Whereas Table 1 examined a low threshold of severity, Table 2 examines the highest threshold of severity. Militarized disputes that escalate to war represent the most severe, most escalatory confrontations identified by the COW Project, and this analysis allows us to tell whether territorial issues affect this last threshold of escalation as well as the lower thresholds identified earlier.

Table 4.2
Militarized Dispute Escalation to War

Territorial Issues at Stake?	Nonwar Disputes	Interstate War	Total
No	1,414	36 (2.5%)	1,450
Yes	541	44 (7.5%)	585
Total	1,955	80 (3.9%)	2,035[a]

$X2 = 28.02$ (1 d.f., $p < .001$), odds ratio = 3.19

[a] This table reports results for the aggregated dispute-level data (2,035 cases), rather than the dyadically disaggregated data (3,043 cases).

Table 2 employs the aggregated dispute-level data rather than the dyadically disaggregated data that are examined in the remainder of my analyses. This was done to minimize the effects of multilateral wars involving dozens of participants, which have been found to obscure the effects of other conflictual phenomena such as arms races (see, for example, Siverson and Diehl 1989). The aggregated dispute-level dataset presented in Table 2 includes 80 disputes that escalated to interstate war, or 3.9 percent of the 2,035 disputes. In contrast, the dyadic disaggregation results in 342 dyadic disputes in which both participants reach the level of full-scale war, or 11.2 percent of the 3,043 dyadic disputes. This inflation of the number of disputes escalating to war results in large part from the world wars and the Korean War, each of which involved numerous combatant dyads. The results presented in Table 2 do not change substantially when the dyadic disaggregation is used, but the absolute likelihood of dyadic escalation to war would be misleadingly high when compared with the overall proportion of all disputes that escalate to war, as presented here.[9]

As Table 2 reveals, militarized disputes are nearly three times as likely to escalate to war when territorial issues are involved as when only nonterritorial issues are at stake. Forty-three of 586 disputes over territorial issues (7.3 percent) escalated to war, compared with 36 of 1,456 disputes over other issues (2.5 percent). This difference is highly significant in the statistical sense ($X^2 = 26.59$, 1 d.f., $p < .001$). The odds ratio of 3.19 indicates a strong substantive difference as well, with the odds of escalation to war more than three times higher for disputes involving territorial issues than for disputes over other types of issues. In absolute numbers, there also appears to be a close connection between contention over territorial issues and escalation to interstate war. Forty-four of the eighty wars included in the dispute dataset (55 percent) involved contention over territorial issues, which is disproportionately high when we consider that only 28.7 percent of the 2,035 disputes involved territory. These results in Table 2 complement the finding in Table 1.

These first two tables together paint a consistent picture of the impact of territorial issues on dispute escalation. Militarized disputes involving territorial issues tend to reach higher severity levels than do disputes over other issues, using either militarized response or interstate war as an indicator of severity. Disputes involving territorial issues are more likely than disputes over other issues to involve militarized actions by both sides, as well as to escalate to full-scale interstate war. Territory thus seems to be seen by leaders as highly salient, justifying the risks of escalation in order to protect or advance one's interests much more than do other types of issues. Another dimension of conflict behavior that should be affected by contention over territorial issues involves the outcome of confrontations.

Conflict Outcomes

Table 3 portrays the relationship between territorial issues and dispute outcomes. Disputes in which territorial issues are at stake are much less likely to end in stalemated outcomes, with the proportion of stalemates declining from 1,268 of 1,792 (70.7 percent) to 417 of 715 (58.3 percent) when territorial issues are present. Similarly, disputes in which territorial issues are at stake are more likely to end in decisive outcomes, with the proportion of decisive outcomes increasing from 22.7 percent to 32.0 percent for territorial disputes. Both results are in the expected direction, although compromises show an unexpected increase in likelihood when territorial issues are at stake, from 6.6 percent to 9.7 percent of the dispute outcomes. These differences between outcome frequencies in territorial and nonterritorial disputes are significant at the .001 level (X^2 = 35.92, 2 d.f.).

Further analysis with individual two-by-two tables for each outcome type also showed these differences to be significant at the .001 level for all three outcome types. Decisive outcomes are much more likely in disputes over territorial issues, both statistically and sub-

Table 4.3
Militarized Dispute Outcomes

Territorial Issues at Stake?	Decisive Outcome	Stalemate Outcome	Compromise Outcome	Total
No 406 (22.7%)	1,268 (70.7)	118 (6.6)		1,792
Yes	229 (32.0%)	417 (58.3)	69 (9.7)	715
Total	635 (25.3%)	1,685 (67.2)	187 (7.5)	2,507

X2 = 35.92 (2 d.f., p < .001), [no odds ratio?]

stantively (X^2 = 23.73, 1 d.f., p < .001; odds ratio = 1.61), with the odds of a decisive outcome being more than one and one-half times greater in disputes over territorial issues. Compromise outcomes are also more likely in territorial disputes than in disputes over other issues (X^2 = 6.96, 1 d.f., p < .001; odds ratio = 1.52), with the odds again being one and one-half times greater in disputes over territorial issues. Finally, stalemates are much less likely in territorial disputes (X^2 = 35.87, 1 d.f., p < .001; odds ratio = 0.58). The odds ratio of 0.58 for stalemates indicates that the odds of a stalemate are .58 as high in disputes over territorial issues as in disputes over other issues, or (inverting the figure) the odds of a stalemate are 1.72 times higher for disputes over nonterritorial issues.

The results in Table 3 offer further support for the earlier characterization of territorial issues as highly salient and as important influences on conflict behavior. The outcome results complement the above findings on dispute escalation, that states were found to be unlikely to ignore territorial threats and conflict behavior was found to be more escalatory when territorial issues are involved. The decreased likelihood of stalemates and increased likelihood of decisive outcomes in territorial disputes seem to be related to this tendency not to ignore threats over territorial stakes, with each side attempting to achieve its goals (or protect its interests) by force and appearing unwilling to let matters fade away without some type of resolution (even if that resolution comes in a form that sets the stage for renewed conflict in the future).

The observation that negotiated compromises are more likely over territorial questions than over other issues appears surprising at first, given the characterization of territorial issues as difficult to settle to the satisfaction of both sides. Nonetheless, further reflection suggests an explanation, based on leaders' reasons for agreeing to the compromise solution. Leaders may agree to a compromise under domestic or international pressure, in order to avoid losing political support or economic backing by continuing an unpopular confrontation. They may also see a compromise as a stopgap measure, particularly if they are faring poorly in the current dispute or—as has been common in territorial disputes, given the findings in Tables 1 and 2—the current dispute is becoming too costly. A compromise outcome meant as such a temporary measure could minimize the state's losses in the current confrontation and might perhaps buy valuable time to help achieve a better outcome in the future. In either of these situations, a compromise outcome would not necessarily reflect a desire to settle the state's long-term territorial questions amicably, and it may actually be meant as a short-term ploy to end one confrontation while planning or preparing for another. Goertz and Diehl (1992) suggest that territorial changes imposed by treaty may be seen as less legitimate than changes that occur through other means, for similar reasons.

The results in Tables 1 through 3 suggest that contention over territory affects both the outcome and the escalation level of a confrontation between states. As hypothesized earlier, disputes involving territorial issues are significantly less likely to end in stalemates than disputes over other issues, and significantly more likely to end in decisive outcomes. In combination with the results presented above for dispute escalation, then, it seems clear that contention over territorial issues is significantly different from contention over other types of issues. The next question to be dealt with involves the impact of contentious issues on subsequent relations between two adversaries—that is, beyond affecting the severity and outcome of one confrontation, do the issues at stake affect the likelihood of future conflict between the same states?

Conflict Recurrence

Table 4 presents an analysis of conflict recurrence after disputes over territorial and nonterritorial issues. Regardless of the type of issues involved, more than half of all militarized disputes—1,859 of 3,043, or

61.1 percent—are followed by another dispute between the same adversaries within fifteen years. Nonetheless, the issues at stake in a confrontation also make a substantial difference in the likelihood of recurrent conflict. When territorial issues are at stake, nearly three-fourths of all disputes are followed quickly by another dispute (567 of 795, or 71.3 percent), as compared with 1,292 of 2,248 disputes over nonterritorial issues (57.5 percent). This difference is statistically significant ($X^2 = 47.38$, 1 d.f., $p < .001$), and the odds ratio of 1.84 indicates that the odds of a recurrent dispute are nearly twice as great for disputes involving territorial issues. These results offer further support for the important impact of contentious issues on conflict behavior. A one-way analysis of variance also revealed that the next militarized dispute tends to happen sooner after a dispute over territorial issues than after a nonterritorial dispute, with territorial issues producing almost two years less of stability before the outbreak of the next dispute than other types of issues (5.56 years versus 7.22; $F = 39.85$, $p < .001$).[10]

Table 4.4
Militarized Dispute Recurrence

Territorial Issues at Stake?	No Dispute within 15 Years	Followed by Recurrent Dispute	Total
No	956	1,292 (57.5%)	2,248
Yes	228	567 (71.3%)	795
Total	1,184	1,859 (61.1%)	3,043

$X2 = 47.38$ (1 d.f., $p < .001$), odds ratio = 1.84

The final set of analyses expands on the relationship between contentious issues and dispute recurrence by adding in the effects of dispute outcomes. Both territorial and nonterritorial disputes produce similar relationships between outcomes and recurrence, and both effects are statistically significant ($X^2 = 66.25$, 2 d.f., $p < .001$ for territorial issues; $X^2 = 111.45$, 2 d.f., $p < .001$ for nonterritorial issues). For both territorial and nonterritorial issues, stalemated outcomes are the most likely to produce recurrent conflict in their aftermath, followed by compromises and decisive outcomes.

Nonetheless, there are important differences between territorial and nonterritorial issues, as revealed in Table 5. In particular, for each type of outcome, disputes over territorial issues are more likely to be followed by recurrent conflict than are disputes over other issues that ended in the same type of outcome. These differences are most notable after decisive outcomes, for which the likelihood of recurrence increases from 36.2 percent to 52.8 percent when territorial issues are involved, and stalemates, for which the likelihood of recurrence jumps from 65.9 percent to 82.7 percent. These differences between territorial and nonterritorial disputes with the same outcome are statistically significant at the .001 level for both stalemates and decisive outcomes, and the odds ratios indicate that the odds of recurrence after each of these outcomes are roughly twice as great when territorial issues are at stake. Compromises produce very little change when territorial issues are involved: the likelihood of recurrence increases only from 57.6 percent to 65.2 percent, which is not statistically significant (p < .31) and which produces a relatively low contingent odds ratio of 1.38. Nonetheless, compromises see a somewhat higher likelihood of recurrence when territorial issues are involved than when adversaries are contending over nonterritorial issues, even if the differences are not great.

Tables 4 and 5 suggest that both contentious issues and dispute outcomes exert important influences on relations between adversaries in the aftermath of a confrontation. The differences between decisive outcomes, stalemates, and compromises that have been identified in earlier studies (for example, Hensel 1994) hold up for both territorial and nonterritorial issues. Similarly, for each type of outcome the likelihood of recurrence is greater for disputes over territorial issues than for disputes over other issues, particularly for decisive and stalemated outcomes. Future conflict is almost assured after a stalemate over territorial issues, and even decisive and compromise outcomes are followed by recurrent conflict more than half the time when territory was involved—although the latter two outcome types are more effective at avoiding recurrence when nonterritorial stakes are involved.

CONCLUSIONS AND IMPLICATIONS

Even though territorial issues account for the primary issues at stake in fewer than one-third of all interstate disputes in the past two centuries, they have been shown to exert an important impact on conflict behavior. Adversaries engaged in a confrontation over territorial issues have been shown to behave much differently from adversaries engaged in confrontations over other types of issues. For example, disputes over territorial issues were shown to be much more escalatory than nonterritorial disputes. Territorial disputes were less than half as likely to see nonmilitarized responses by the target state, with fewer than one-fourth of all targets responding without military means, compared with one-half of all target states in disputes over nonterritorial issues. Similarly, territorial disputes were nearly twice as likely to escalate to the level of full-scale interstate war. Disputes over territory were also much more likely to end in compromise or—particularly—decisive

Table 4.5
Militarized Dispute Outcomes and Dispute Recurrence

A. Decisive Outcomes

Territorial Issues at Stake?	No Recurrent Dispute	Followed by Recurrent Dispute	Total
No	259	147 (36.2%)	406
Yes	108	121 (52.8%)	229
Total	365	268 (42.2%)	635

$X2 = 16.60$ (1 d.f., $p < .001$), odds ratio = 1.97

B. Stalemate Outcomes

Territorial Issues at Stake?	No Recurrent Dispute	Followed by Recurrent Dispute	Total
No	433	835 (65.9%)	1,268
Yes	72	345 (82.7%)	417
Total	505	1,180 (70.0%)	1,685

$X2 = 42.61$ (1 d.f., $p < .001$), odds ratio = 2.49

C. Compromise Outcomes

Territorial Issues at Stake?	No Recurrent Dispute	Followed by Recurrent Dispute	Total
No	50	68 (57.6%)	118
Yes	24	45 (65.2%)	69
Total	74	113 (60.4%)	187

$X2 = 1.05$ (1 d.f., $p < .31$), odds ratio = 1.38

outcomes than were nonterritorial disputes and were found to be much less likely to end in stalemates.

These findings suggest some serious implications for future studies of interstate conflict. The empirical importance of territorial issues in this and other studies suggests that many research on interstate conflict could benefit by incorporating the effects of contentious issues. Including the effects of territorial issues helped Gochman and Leng (1983), Hensel and Diehl (1994), and Hensel (1994, 1996) account for the escalation of crises, the likelihood of nonmilitarized response in militarized disputes, and the recurrence of conflict. Even though these studies did not focus exclusively on territory, incorporating the effects of territorial issues helped to strengthen their findings and to increase their resulting understanding of the phenomena being studied.

My findings also offer some direction in the question of whether contiguity or contention over territorial issues is largely responsible for conflict between neighbors (Vasquez 1995). Few studies have been able to examine the impact of territorial issues directly, so most research in this area has been forced to draw inferences from the occurrence of conflict between bordering states—some of which involves territorial issues, and some of which does not. The findings of this study suggest that territorial issues do seem to make a great deal of differences in conflict behavior, beyond the effect of contiguity. Using a distinction between territorial disputes (some of which involved noncontiguous adversaries) and nonterritorial disputes (some of which involved contiguous adversaries), the present study identifies substantial differences in patterns of conflict escalation and recurrence. We would not expect to find such striking differences between territorial and nonterritorial disputes if contiguity, rather than territorial issues, were largely responsible for the escalation or recurrence of militarized dispute.

Additionally, my findings—along with those of other recent work on territory and territorial claims—suggest that further research should be devoted to contentious issues such as territory. Kocs (1995) and Huth (1996) suggest that unresolved territorial claims are fairly common and that states with competing claims are more likely than are other states to become involved in militarized disputes or wars. The present study and Senese (1996) also suggest that confrontations involving territorial issues tend to be more escalatory than do confrontations over other issues, as well as being more likely to be followed by recurrent conflict between the same adversaries. Given this greater escalation and greater likelihood of conflict recurrence, then, it would seem especially important to understand how territorial claims lead to conflict over territorial issues—and to attempt to manage or prevent such confrontations if at all possible.

One important direction for future research involves the study of how territorial issues lead to the initial outbreak of militarized conflict, beyond the effect of territory on conflict escalation or recurrence. That is, following the example of Huth (1996), it would be useful to study the differences between states that turn to militarized means to resolve their territorial differences and states that are able to manage their territorial questions peacefully. Huth has assembled a valuable dataset for studying such questions in the post–World War II era, identifying 129 cases of territorial claims. He finds that around half of these 129 cases saw the outbreak of militarized conflict at least once between 1950 and 1990, featuring aggressive diplomatic and political behavior in 32 percent of those years and militarized confrontations in about eleven percent (Huth 1996, 103, 106). It would be useful to extend the collection and analysis of territorial claims data to a longer time frame, perhaps going back to the traditional starting point for most empirical work on world politics in 1816, which would allow us to study the impact of territorial questions over a longer period.

Research on territorial issues could also be improved by developing a finer distinction between different territorial issues. Empirical research on territory has tended to treat all territorial issues as similar, focusing on the distinction between territorial and other issues but overlooking differences among types of territorial claims. It is doubtful that all territorial issues are equally salient, and it is not even certain that each side in a single territorial dispute views the dispute as equally salient. Goertz and Diehl (1992) and Huth (1996) make some progress along these lines, distinguishing between different territorial claims or territorial exchanges on the basis of the size, population, economic value, and location of the territory involved. Future research could benefit from the identification of additional components of territorial salience, as well as from the collection of data on these factors for a larger set of cases (beyond those cases where territory actually changed hands, as with Goertz and Diehl, or the past fifty years, as in Huth's work).

Another useful extension of research on contentious issues and interstate conflict would involve the collection of data on additional types of issues separating states. Most of the existing work on issues has focused on territorial matters, as I have (Goertz and Diehl 1992; Kocs 1995; Huth 1996; Senese 1996). Research on contentious issues could benefit from the identification and study of other types of issues, as well, which could greatly increase our understanding of the general role of issues in world politics. It may prove to be difficult or impossible to construct a single scale of issue salience that would be meaningful for most (or all) issue types and spatial-temporal domains (Diehl 1992, 341–342), but any movement in this direction would represent a potential improvement in the study and understanding of conflict processes.

With regard to policy implications, my findings also suggest that state leaders need to be careful in their dealings with each other over territorial issues. Confrontations over territorial issues were found to be more escalatory than confrontations over less salient issues. Disputes involving territory were also found to be more likely than other types of disputes to be followed by renewed conflict between the same adversaries in the future. Policymakers must exercise special caution in their dealings with adversaries over territorial questions, both to manage their confrontations short of escalation to war and to avoid becoming trapped in lengthy strings of recurrent confrontations.

As suggested earlier, territory is an important element of states' identity and cohesion. For this reason, leaders may see territorial issues as a useful way to try to rally domestic support in times of political or economic trouble. Nonetheless, the high salience of territorial issues to both participants in a territorial dispute makes this is a very dangerous path to tread. As noted earlier, Argentine President Galtieri attempted to use the Malvinas Islands to increase support for his leadership and for the military regime as a whole. Argentina's invasion of the islands led to a costly defeat for its military, though, and quickly led to Galtieri's removal from power. Similarly, Bolivian President Daniel Salamanca was overthrown by the Bolivian military as the Chaco War turned against Bolivia and Paraguay occupied most of the disputed Chaco Boreal.

Even where a territorial dispute does not lead to military defeat or the overthrow of a political leader, territorial disputes can create political obstacles to peace. Israel is now seeing the negative political consequences of three decades of occupation of the Golan Heights, which were captured from Syria in the 1967 Six Day War after being used for decades as a staging ground for Syrian attacks on Israel. Syria has refused to consider any peace settlement with Israel that would not return the entire Golan Heights to Syrian control, but large segments of Israeli society (encouraged by opposition political parties) oppose any attempt to trade "Israeli" land on the heights for peace. Before his 1995 assassination, Israeli Prime Minister Yitzhak Rabin had promised that any withdrawal from the heights would be preceded by a popular referendum—but even after Rabin and his advisors had apparently decided to negotiate over the future of the heights, a large majority of the Israeli public opposed evacuation, constraining the government's efforts to reach a lasting peace (see, for example, Economist 1995, 12). These examples demonstrate the risks inherent in pressing territorial demands, ranging from the outbreak of war (which can be costly even for the victors) to the growth of political opposition and perhaps the loss of political power.

On a more optimistic note, my findings reveal that territory and territorial issues alone do not determine the course or outcome of international relations. Territorial issues have been shown to increase the likelihood of recurrent conflict between the same adversaries, and Vasquez (1993) suggests that most pairs of enduring interstate rivals have clashed over territorial issues during their rivalries. Nonetheless, not every territorial dispute has been followed by the recurrence of militarized conflict, and not all adversaries that fought over territorial issues have ended up in an enduring rivalry. Similarly, territorial issues were shown to increase the likelihood of militarized response in interstate disputes and to increase the likelihood of escalation to full-scale war. Not every dispute over territorial issues escalated to war, though. Many territorial disputes have remained limited to low levels of severity, and some territorial issues have been resolved or managed without a single militarized confrontation between the involved states. Further research, along the lines of Huth (1996), should attempt to understand the factors that lead some territorial questions to violence while others are resolved peacefully.

Successful management of territorial issues may be a difficult proposition, as shown by the effects of territorial contention on escalation and conflict recurrence, but it is certainly possible. Vasquez (1993, 150–151) and Huth (1996, 189–192) offer some suggestions about how territorial disputes may be resolved or managed, ranging from the deterritorialization of disputes or the conclusion of explicitly defined diplomatic settlements of territorial questions to preventive diplomacy or intervention by external actors. As Vasquez (1993, 146–152) argues, territorial conflict need not continue for the entire relationship of two states, and former adversaries can learn to live with each other peacefully once their territorial concerns have been resolved. It is to be hoped that further scholarly research will increase our understanding of how territorial differences can be settled peacefully and that future policymakers will be able to apply this understanding when they deal with potentially explosive territorial issues.

The author wishes to thank Doug Lemke, Bill Reed, and John Vasquez for their comments and suggestions. Any opinions, findings, conclusions, or recommendations expressed herein are those of the author and do not necessarily reflect the views of these other individuals.

NOTES

1. Many of Holsti's specific issue types can be combined into similar categories, in order to simplify analysis. For example, territorial issues are directly involved in Holsti's issues of territory, strategic territory, and territory (boundary), as well as more indirectly in his issues of national unification–consolidation, secession–state creation, empire creation, commerce-navigation, commerce-resources, and perhaps others.

2. The militarized-dispute dataset, as currently distributed, is not organized dyadically; rather, it is organized by the entire dispute and by the individual actor in the dispute. To achieve the dyadic breakdown I matched up each actor on side A of each dispute with each actor on side B of the same dispute. I then discarded those dyadic adversaries that could not have confronted each other in the dispute because their dates of participation did not overlap or because they both had a level of hostility score of 1, which indicates that neither side initiated any militarized action in the dispute (and is thus a participant only because it was the target of another state's militarized action).

Further details about this dyadic breakdown procedure are available from the author.

3. I used version 2.10 of the militarized-dispute data for this analysis. Previous versions of this chapter employed an earlier version of the dataset, with a slightly different number of cases in each table, but none of the results or conclusions has changed.

4. Where several issues are at stake in the same militarized dispute, the issue that is most central to that particular dispute is coded as the primary issue.

5. My "decisive" category includes four of the eight COW outcome codings: victory for side A, victory for side B, yield by side A, and yield by side B. These four categories are essentially the same type of outcome, with a clear winner and loser in each, and I have no theoretical reason to separate them. Furthermore, the small number of cases in some of these categories would make separate analysis more difficult. For the purposes of this set of analyses, I have also removed several other categories of outcome codings, because of problems in interpretation. The removed categories include "released" outcomes, in which a seized individual or ship is released during the dispute, as well as "unclear" and "missing" outcomes. A total of 536 outcomes were removed from the 3,043 dyadic disputes, leaving 2,507 decisive, compromise, and stalemated outcomes.

6. Conflict occurring many years after the end of an earlier dispute may be unrelated to the first dispute, so limits must be set on the amount of time that may elapse between disputes for the second dispute to be considered recurrent conflict. Following Hensel (1996) and similar work on the gaps that may occur between disputes for a relationship to be considered a rivalry, I limit this analysis to the first fifteen years after the conclusion of a given dispute. It should be noted that disputes ending after 1977 have not yet had a full fifteen-year period in which conflict could recur; in statistical terms these cases are considered "right censored." Removing these censored cases from analysis did not change my results appreciably, though, suggesting that this censoring does not pose a major problem for these analyses.

7. The proportion of dyadic disputes involving territorial issues is slightly lower than the proportion of all disputes because of the multiparty disputes in the dataset. A number of disputes involved more than two participants, not all of which sought status quo alterations of the same issues. As long as at least one of the participants on either side of a dispute sought changes in the territorial status quo, the dispute is coded as involving territorial issues, but not every dyad involved in that dispute necessarily involved territorial issues as well.

8. Additional analysis reveals that this difference does not depend on the nature of my dyadic disaggregation of the militarized-dispute data. Using the

aggregated dispute-level data, 31.3 percent of disputes over territorial issues involve nonmilitarized responses by the target side of the dispute, whether this includes only one state or several. Nonmilitarized response remains more than twice as likely using this aggregated data, with 61.3 percent of all disputes over nonterritorial issues involving nonmilitarized responses; the difference also remains highly significant (X^2 = 150.78, 1 d.f., p < .001).

9. Using the dyadic data instead of the aggregated data presented in Table 3, 17.1 percent of all disputes involving territorial issues escalate to war, as compared with 9.2 percent of all nonterritorial disputes. The likelihood of escalation thus remains substantially higher when territorial issues are involved, and these results remain highly significant (X^2 = 36.64, 1 d.f., p < .001).

10. Postdispute stability is the time (in years) elapsed between the end of one dispute and the outbreak of the next dispute between the same two adversaries (Maoz 1984; Hensel 1994). As in my analysis of dispute recurrence, I limit this analysis to a maximum stability period of fifteen years. For those right-censored cases in which the temporal domain ends (at the conclusion of 1992) without the outbreak of renewed conflict but with fewer than fifteen years of stability, postdispute stability is measured as lasting through 1992. I ran separate analyses leaving out these cases, in order to see whether these cases affected the overall results, but there was no appreciable change in the results without them.

REFERENCES

Boulding, Kenneth. 1962. *Conflict and Defense: A General Theory.* New York: Harper and Row.

Bowman, Isaiah. 1946. "The Strategy of Territorial Decisions." *Foreign Affairs* 24: 177–194.

Brecher, Michael. 1993. *Crises in World Politics: Theory and Reality.* New York: Pergamon Press.

Bremer, Stuart A. 1992. "Dangerous Dyads: Conditions Affecting the Likelihood of Interstate War, 1816–1965." *Journal of Conflict Resolution* 36: 309–341.

Diehl, Paul F. 1985. "Contiguity and Escalation in Major Power Rivalries, 1816–1980." *Journal of Politics* 47: 1203–1211.

———. 1991. "Geography and War: A Review and Assessment of the Empirical Literature." *International Interactions* 17: 1–27.

———. 1992. "What Are They Fighting For? The Importance of Issues in International Conflict Research." *Journal of Peace Research* 29: 333–344.

Economist. 1995. "Opening the Road to Damascus." *Economist,* June 3, 12.

Fearon, James. 1994. "Signaling versus the Balance of Power and Interests: An Empirical Test of a Crisis Bargaining Model." *Journal of Conflict Resolution* 38: 236–269.

Finot, Enrique. 1934. *The Chaco War and the United States.* New York: L and S Printing.

Gochman, Charles S., and Russell J. Leng. 1983. "Realpolitik and the Road to War: An Analysis of Attributes and Behavior." *International Studies Quarterly* 27: 97–120.

Gochman, Charles S., and Zeev Maoz. 1984. "Militarized Interstate Disputes, 1816–1976." *Journal of Conflict Resolution* 28: 585–616.

Goertz, Gary, and Paul F. Diehl. 1992. *Territorial Changes and International Conflict.* London: Routledge.

Hastings, Max, and Simon Jenkins. 1983. *The Battle for the Falklands.* New York: W. W. Norton.

Hensel, Paul R. 1994. "One Thing Leads to Another: Recurrent Militarized Disputes in Latin America, 1816–1986." *Journal of Peace Research* 31: 281–298.

———. 1996. "The Evolution of Interstate Rivalry." Ph.D. diss., University of Illinois.

Hensel, Paul R., and Paul F. Diehl. 1994. "It Takes Two to Tango: Non-Militarized Response in Interstate Disputes." *Journal of Conflict Resolution* 38: 479–506.

Hill, Norman. 1945. *Claims to Territory in International Relations.* New York: Oxford University Press.

Holsti, Kalevi J. 1991. *Peace and War: Armed Conflicts and International Order, 1648–1989.* New York: Cambridge University Press.

Huth, Paul K. 1988. *Extended Deterrence and the Prevention of War.* New Haven, Conn.: Yale University Press.

———. 1996. *Standing Your Ground: Territorial Disputes and International Conflict.* Ann Arbor: University of Michigan Press.

Kocs, Stephen. 1995. "Territorial Disputes and Interstate War, 1945–1987." *Journal of Politics* 57: 159–175.

Lebow, Richard Ned. 1981. *Between Peace and War: The Nature of International Crisis.* Baltimore, Md.: Johns Hopkins University Press.

———. 1985. "Miscalculation in the South Atlantic: The Origins of the Falklands War." In *Psychology and Deterrence,* edited by Robert Jervis, Richard Ned Lebow, and Janice Gross Stein. Baltimore, Md.: Johns Hopkins University Press.

Lemke, Douglas. 1995. "The Tyranny of Distance: Redefining Relevant Dyads." *International Interactions* 21: 23–38.

Levy, Jack S., and Lily I. Vakili. 1992. "Diversionary Action by Authoritarian Regimes: Argentina in the Falklands / Malvinas Case." In *The Internationalization of Communal Strife*, edited by Manus I. Midlarsky. London: Routledge.

Luard, Evan. 1970. *The International Regulation of Frontier Disputes.* New York: Praeger.

———. 1986. *War in International Society.* London: I. B. Tauris.

Mann, Golo. 1968. *The History of Germany since 1789*, translated by Marian Jackson. New York: Frederick A. Praeger.

Mansbach, Richard, and John Vasquez. 1981. *In Search of Theory: A New Paradigm for Global Politics.* New York: Columbia University Press.

Maoz, Zeev. 1984. "Peace by Empire? Conflict Outcomes and International Stability, 1816–1976." *Journal of Peace Research* 21: 227–241.

Morgenthau, Hans J. 1978. *Politics among Nations.* 5th ed. New York: Alfred A. Knopf.

Most, Benjamin, and Harvey Starr. 1980. "Diffusion, Reinforcement, Geopolitics, and the Spread of War." *American Political Science Review* 74: 932–946.

Murphy, Alexander. 1990. "Historical Justifications for Territorial Claims." *Annals of the Association of American Geographers* 80: 531–548.

Reynolds, H. T. 1984. *Analysis of Nominal Data.* 2d ed. Newbury Park, Calif.: Sage Publications.

Rout, Leslie B., Jr. 1970. *Politics of the Chaco Peace Conference, 1935–1939.* Austin: University of Texas Press.

Senese, Paul D. 1996. "Geographical Proximity and Issue Salience: Their Effects on the Escalation of Militarized Interstate Conflict." *Conflict Management and Peace Science* 15: 133–161.

Siverson, Randolph, and Paul Diehl. 1989. "Arms Races, the Conflict Spiral, and the Onset of War." In *Handbook of War Studies,* edited by Manus I. Midlarsky. Boston: Unwin Hyman.

Small, Melvin, and J. David Singer. 1982. *Resort to Arms: International and Civil Wars, 1816–1980.* Beverly Hills, Calif.: Sage Publications.

Snyder, Glenn H., and Paul Diesing. 1977. *Conflict among Nations: Bargaining, Decision Making, and System Structure in International Crises.* Princeton, N.J.: Princeton University Press.

Vasquez, John. 1993. *The War Puzzle.* Cambridge, U.K., and New York: Cambridge University Press.

———. 1995. "Why Do Neighbors Fight? Proximity, Interaction or Territoriality." *Journal of Peace Research* 32: 277–293.

Warren, Harris Gaylord. 1949. *Paraguay.* Norman: University of Oklahoma Press.

5

Geographical Proximity and Issue Salience: Their Effects on the Escalation of Militarized Interstate Conflict

Paul D. Senese

One of the most well-supported notions in international politics is the observation that neighbors fight. More specifically, the empirical literature shows strong support for the conflict engendering influence of geographical proximity on interstate relations (e.g., Bremer 1992; Diehl 1985; Gochman 1991; Huth 1996; Vasquez 1993; Wallensteen 1981). The opportunity for conflict between states, and its escalation to war once begun, seems to be enhanced when the (potential) combatants are within close proximity of one another.

While contiguity appears to provide a heightened opportunity for conflict, the actual motivation for engagement can frequently be traced to the issues of contention between possible foes. Principle among these issues is the salience of a territorial disagreement and its ability to stimulate militarized entanglements between states (e.g., Diehl 1992; Goertz and Diehl 1988, 1992; Holsti 1991; Vasquez 1995). Territorial issues appear to increase leaders' willingness to press their claims to the point of military confrontation, and beyond. This dimension of willingness appears to tap into the propensity for state actors to act in a more bellicose fashion when the salience of the issue being contested is central to the integrity of the contesting parties. The analyses that follow develop and test propositions for the influence of both geographical proximity and issue salience on interstate conflict escalation. In an effort to go beyond previous work in this area, the examination below probes the individual impacts of these two factors, rather than assuming that one can be used as a surrogate for the other.

CONFLICT ESCALATION

Disputes between states break out for many and varied reasons. The mere occurrence of disputes is not my focus in this study; the evolution of disputes is. Why do some interstate disputes quickly fade away, to be remembered solely as small blips in history, while others escalate to levels of hostility and fatality that mark them as important events in the history of humankind? Also of interest are those disputes that end up somewhere in between, escalating beyond low levels of intensity but not quite reaching the status of war. An analysis of these midlevel disputes is especially interesting because the literature has largely focused on the dispute-to-war issue, not concerning itself greatly with the analysis of more finely grained escalation patterns.

Recent scholarly work has attempted to uncover the characteristic profile of conflict-prone states and groups of states (see, for example, Bremer 1992, 1993; Maoz and Abdolali 1989; Maoz and Russett 1993). Deriving expectations for their results from the literature of international relations, these studies have focused on several attributes associated with pairs of states that may increase (or decrease) their likelihood for becoming embroiled in various forms of conflict. The analyses that follow pick up on these previous efforts, with an express focus on geographical proximity and issue salience, in an attempt to enhance our knowledge of why some interstate disputes are resolved or end with little loss of life but others escalate in severity and hostility.

Lower-level conflict erupts quite frequently around the globe. States often come into conflict with one another over a plethora of issues, ranging from territorial disagreements to fundamental ideological differences. Whatever the specific reason for the initial spark of discord, the fact remains that states are not always benevolent to one another. Pairs of states will become embroiled in disputes over time, but the question of interest in this paper lies in clarifying the traits associated with the continued escalation of these disputes, not in looking at their causes. The domain of inquiry will be limited to those pairs of states that have already passed a low-level threshold into conflict, with the potential to evolve to still-greater levels of strife.

PREDICTORS OF ESCALATION:
ISSUE-TYPES AND GEOGRAPHICAL PROXIMITY

What is it that conditions certain disputes to be resolved—or simply end—quickly, whereas others evolve into large-scale confrontations? In an effort to make inroads into an answer to this query, the analyses below limit their attention primarily to the effect of issue-type and geographical proximity on militarized interstate dispute escalation.[1]

Interstate disputes are fought for a wide range of reasons. The Soviet-American rivalry in the post–World War II period was based largely on issues of ideology, although individual disputes varied by specific issue. Other disputes revolve around issues of personality, policy, and reputation, to name a few. Probably the most salient issue that has been contested since the inception of the modern state system—and before, as well—has been that of territory. Disagreements between states for territorial reasons have occurred frequently (Holsti 1991; Vasquez 1993, 1995).[2]

By definition, nation-states comprise well-defined and controlled areas of land. When this basic element of a state's makeup is at issue, it should follow that the conflict will be given high priority. Disagreements over ideology and policy may be important, but fighting for one's own territory is paramount (Diehl 1992). Escalation of disputes is, of course, more likely when both sides have a high willingness to stay the course. Relating this to the territory dimension, it follows that territorial disputes, where both sides care a great deal about the stakes involved, will escalate with a higher probability.[3] These types of disputes over territory, in which both sides are highly concerned about the stakes, are often fought by contiguous states.

Feuding over one's own or bordering territory is raised to an even higher level. The importance of such disputes between neighbors may have lessened over time,[4] but their occurrence is still notable in such examples as the Iran-Iraq conflict over the Shatt-al-Arab waterway, Somalia's war with Ethiopia over the Ogaden region, and Iraq's war to possess Kuwait. Losing such a conflict would do more than hurt the reputation or prestige of a participating state; it could serve to displace large numbers of indigenous populations and submit the loser to partial occupation by the victor. Such concerns are related to the tangible, zero-sum effects that may result directly from defeat in a dispute fought over bordering land. These increased stakes, associated with territorial conflicts between neighbors, raise the likelihood that both sides will not back down at successively higher levels of dispute intensity.

The geographical location of a state, not taking into consideration the issue dimension, has frequently been cited as an important influence on propensity for conflict. Bremer (1992) finds that contiguous states (generally, neighbors) are much more prone to fight one another than are noncontiguous ones. This relationship is in evidence for both disputes and wars. Diehl (1985) finds a statistically significant relationship between contiguous borders and the escalation of Great Power disputes into war. Although his study was limited to Great Powers, there is no reason to believe that this subset of cases should behave differently from the entire population. Contiguous disputes between lesser powers are more common than are noncontiguous ones, due to the relative difficulty these states encounter when attempting to project their limited capabilities across great distances. Furthermore, the stakes and issues involved in such disputes, though they may seem rather trivial in comparison with those connecting Great Power disputants, are of utmost importance to those involved.

Siverson and Starr (1991) conceptualize contiguity as a factor that furnishes possible combatants with the opportunity to fight because of their proximity. States may choose not to fight, or may escalate the conflict once hostilities have begun, but the proximity of contiguous states provides a setting that is attractive to conflict. Higher levels of conflict require increasing levels of participant commitment. It is plausible to expect that great distances between disputants will quell their propensity for engaging in increasingly bloody conflicts. The mobilization of troops and equipment, along with the development of strategy on unfamiliar terrain, serves to deter noncontiguous disputes from evolving to higher levels. Simply put, war costs tend to be lower with contiguity, so states are more inclined to participate when the venue of combat is geographically proximate.

Combined with the opportunity component supplied by contiguity, the territorial dimension supplies actors with a component of willingness. Domestic populations are more concerned with maintaining the integrity of land and will be more willing to fight in defense of it than in defense of some more distant ideological or policy issue. This intangible importance attached to territory can be differentiated from the more tangible, zero-sum elements mentioned above.[5] In the United States, the snowballing of discontent over involvement in Vietnam in the late 1960s and early 1970s is evidence that the far-flung defense of democracy against communism was not sufficient to rally the domestic population for a long and difficult conflict.

John Vasquez (1996) argues that disputes among enduring rival contiguous dyads over issues of territory are more likely to escalate to war than are disputes among noncontiguous rivals. His analysis uses contiguity as a surrogate for territory: he assumes that disputes between contiguous dyads will usually be over territorial issues and thus will escalate to war more frequently than will other types. His results, though admittedly preliminary, support his contentions.

The proposition developed here moves beyond the use of contiguity as a surrogate for classifying disputes as fought over territorial issues. The updated COW Project's Militarized Interstate Dispute (MID) dataset provides information about the issues over which disputants contend. Thus, I can directly tap into the issue-type of a dispute without resorting to surrogate measures. The first proposition to be tested can be stated as follows:

Hypothesis 1: Territorial disputes are more likely to escalate in severity and hostility than are nonterritorial disputes.

Beyond this initial proposition, I also expect contiguity to interact with the territory dimension, providing an even stronger impetus for escalation. Although a large proportion of disputes between contiguous states are fought over territory—and vice versa—not all are. Territorial disputes between contiguous dyads should be more important, more threatening, more urgent, more closely related to vital national interests, and therefore more worth risking war over than should disputes concerning distant lands and issues. From this flow the following hypotheses:

Hypothesis 2: Contiguous dyads are more likely to escalate the severity and hostility of their disputes than are noncontiguous dyads.

Hypothesis 3: Disputes fought over territorial issues by contiguous states are more likely to escalate in severity and hostility than are other types of disputes.

Hypothesis 1 is an attempt to tap into the importance of the willingness component posited for territory as an issue in disputes; hypothesis 2 tests the opportunity stature of contiguity; and hypothesis 3 draws on the interactive power of the two propositions in increasing the likelihood of disputes for escalation. Vasquez (1996) draws attention to the need for testing the importance of territorial conflict and contiguity separately. The testing of hypotheses 1 and 2 are an attempt to do just this, and hypothesis 3 delves into the potent possibilities that the interaction of the two hypotheses should have. By testing these hypotheses, I will attempt to separate the effects of territorial issues and geographical proximity as well as explore their joint influence. In sorting out these impacts, the examination that follows is the logical next empirical step in piecing together a significant section of the conflict puzzle; namely, that portion which is concerned with the influence of both issue salience and geography.

OPERATIONALIZATION AND MEASUREMENT

Interstate disputes are, fundamentally, concerned with the interactions of—at least—pairs of states. The important perceptions held by each side about the other lead me to use the interstate dyad as the appropriate level of analysis. The dependent variable, escalation, measures the level that interactions between pairs of states reach. An interstate dyad is defined as any pair of states that are members of the interstate system, where system membership is defined by the rules of the COW Project (Small and Singer 1982, 38–43).[6]

The interstate-dispute dyad is the observational unit employed in the analyses that follow. The results reported are for those disputes that begin and end as one-on-one confrontations. Disputes with multiple original members on one or both sides introduce additional concerns. It is difficult to discern the exact importance and commitment of each state in multiple-actor episodes.[7] The observations are taken from the updated MID dataset. For a disagreement between states to be considered an interstate dispute, at least one of the following events of military confrontation must occur: an explicit threat to resort to military force; the mobilization, deployment, or other display of military force; or the actual use military force. For these acts to be included, they "must be explicit, overt, nonaccidental, and government sanctioned" (Gochman and Maoz 1984, 586).[8]

The updated MID set contains 2,034 cases between 1816 and 1992. Observations were eliminated for three reasons. First, disputes that did not begin as one-on-one confrontations were excluded because of the difficulty in assessing several of the predictor variables in such cases. Second, disputes that did not remain one-on-one episodes were eliminated from consideration.[9] Third, if missing data for any of the variables of interest plagued a dispute, it was not included. After these exclusion rules were imposed, the sample size was reduced to 1,130.

The Dependent Variable: Dispute Escalation

The movement from the initial spark of discord to higher levels of conflict is the phenomenon to be explained in this research. This phenomenon has routinely been referred to as escalation, with only cursory attention paid to the exact empirical meaning of the concept. When one thinks of escalation, an obvious first thought is one associated with an upward spiral of relations between two opponents. But beyond this, the meaning of the concept can take on subtle differences depending on the theoretical concerns of the researcher.

Leaders' perceptions of escalation can differ over time and among states. Tapping into the exact intentions and perceptions of decision makers is a daunting task, especially in studies that examine a large number of cases. Short of being able to measure accurately whether state leaders intend certain actions to be escalatory, I must fall back to empirical approximations of escalation. The analyses conducted in this paper rely on two indicators of escalation: hostility and severity.

Hostility Levels
The first measure of dispute escalation revolves around the level of hostility associated with the actions of states. Some actions are, by their very nature, more hostile than others. For example, a show of

ships is more hostile than a threat to blockade, and an actual blockade is more hostile than both a threat to blockade and a show of ships. Many times, however, the policy of a blockade is preceded first by the threat to blockade and next by the show of ships. The blockade is, then, a more hostile policy than the ones preceding it. The movement from a threat to an actual use of force represents escalation in the hostility between the two sides in a dispute. Policymakers often have a range of options to choose from for their next action in a conflict. In general, they can choose to back down, negotiate, do nothing, continue the current level of hostility, or increase the hostility level. Disputes that reach the level of hostility at which actual military force is used are considered more hostile than are disputes that include only threats and displays of force.

The MID dataset codes the actions of disputants into one of twenty-two categories:

1 = Nonmilitary act

---

2 = Threat to use force
3 = Threat to blockade
4 = Threat to occupy territory
5 = Threat to declare war
6 = Threat to use nuclear weapons

---

7 = Show of troops
8 = Show of ships
9 = Show of planes
10 = Alert
11 = Nuclear alert
12 = Mobilization
13 = Fortify border
14 = Border violation

---

15 = Blockade
16 = Occupation of territory
17 = Seizure
18 = Clash
19 = Other use of force

20 = Declaration of war

21 = Use of chemical, biological, or nuclear weapons

---

22 = Interstate war

For the purposes of this analysis, the twenty-two actions have been collapsed into five categories. Actions 2–6 are lumped into the category of threat to use force; action 7–14, into the category of display of force; and actions 15–21, into the category of use of force.[10] Action 22, interstate war, is characterized by an act of war and at least 1,000 battle-associated deaths. The sequence of hostility escalation that a dispute can go through, then, is threat to display to use to war.

Of the 1,130 disputes examined in the hostility tests below, the majority (1,041, or 92 percent) fall into the display and use categories, with the use category being the most common (751, or 66 percent). The threat (65, or 6 percent) and war (24, or 2 percent) groupings comprise the remaining cases. Disputes are grouped into these categories based on the highest level of hostility reached by any one disputant. All of the disputes in the sample are characterized by at least one act that is more hostile than no militarized action (action type 1), leading to the absence of this category in the hostility analyses below.[11]

Not all disputes that reach levels of hostility above a threat are preceded by recorded acts at lower levels. For instance, some disputes that end at the use of force level do not have recorded threat and display acts. In other words, some disputes begin with uses of force. These disputes do not fit the classic conception of spiraling conflict so common in the literature and typified by the events leading up to the outbreak of World War I. Instead, the preceding acts in such episodes may be diplomatic or vague (somewhere below the level of a threat to use military force), so that the first recordable action is already at the point at which force is used. The statistical tests I used do not assume that recordable threats and displays of force precede disputes ending at the use level; they only assume that uses of force are more intense forms of conflict than are threats and displays. The MID hostility scale is certainly a valid ordinal indicator of increasingly hostile disputes, because threats to use force are less hostile than are displays of force, which, in turn, are less hostile than are actual uses of force. Because I am interested primarily in examining the influence of geographical proximity and/or issue salience on the propensity of disputants to engage in more or less intense forms of conflict, the MID hostility indicator is an appropriate measure for the empirical tests that follow.[12]

Severity Levels

The severity of interstate disputes is measured by the number of battle deaths incurred by both sides. Some conflicts end short of any fatalities, whereas others evolve to levels that reach into the thousands. An increase in severity is usually associated with an increase in the intensity of actions taken by combatants, in terms of uses of force. For a dispute to end up with 1,000 battle deaths it must, at one time, have gone through the lower levels of severity. In other words, there must have been a time when 100 and 400 deaths were recorded.

The analyses that follow are not interested in those dyads that have not passed the initial threshold into dispute. What I am interested in is explaining why some disputes pass through the lower rungs of severity, whereas others end without great losses of life. The MID dataset includes seven levels of fatalities in its coding procedures: 0, 1–25, 26–100, 101–250, 251–500, 501–999, and more than 999. Of the 775 disputes that reached the use-of-force hostility level,[13] 75 percent (579) ended with no fatalities; the remaining 25 percent (196) ended up with some battle deaths.

A closer inspection of the variation within and across categories of each dependent variable (hostility and severity) provides a better picture of why analysis of both is superior to an examination of only one or the other. All cases in which a threat is the highest level of hostility are characterized by no battle deaths. Similarly, all display-of-force cases have no battle deaths. The interstate-war categories are identical. The variation in the severity measure is entirely captured within the subset of cases characterized by uses of force on the hostility scale. Included within this use-of-force category are disputes with fatalities ranging from 0 to 999.

It seems intuitively plausible that the variance in severity within the use-of-force category can be traced to the amount of control that decision makers have on each measure. Leaders make decisions as to whether they want policies of threats, displays, or uses of force implemented, and the resultant hostility level is a direct result of those decisions. However, leaders have less control over the number of battle deaths incurred in a dispute. When an order is given for a blockade or a clash with an enemy, the number of lives lost is only partially controlled by those decision makers. The unraveling of such policy choices can take on many varied turns during implementation. In this way, it appears that the severity scale represents a dimension of escalation over which leaders have only partial control, whereas the hostility scale is directly determined by the choices of leaders.

In trying to capture how leaders perceive the actions of the opponent in a dispute, both measures are necessary. The leaders in a target state do not only care that they incurred no deaths as a result of an act by the opponent; they are also closely concerned about the intended hostility of that act. The ordinal differentiation between threats and displays of force captures this additional information pertaining to the perception of the target, as well as the intention of the initiator. In much the same way, targets perceive the importance of uses of force differently based on the number of deaths incurred. An occupation of territory completed without any bloodshed is surely perceived differently from one associated with significant losses of life. These important dimensions of escalation, in which state leaders act and to which they react, can only be captured using both severity and hostility as dependent variables.

The Explanatory Variables

Issue-Type

The MID dataset specifies the particular aspect of the status quo that the revisionist state was seeking to change in the dispute. The issues at stake fall into one of four categories: territory; policy; regime/government orientation; and other alterations, a catchall category for the few cases that do not fall into one of the other three. The theoretical expectations derived in the previous section link the importance of territorial issues to an increased likelihood that disputes will escalate. Because my hypotheses differentiate issues on the basis of whether disputes were fought over territory, the policy, regime/government, and other alteration categories are lumped together. They represent disputes in which territory was not the primary issue at stake. The result is a binary indicator of issue-type, with 348 cases coded territorial and 782 as nonterritorial.

Contiguity

To determine whether dispute antagonists are geographically proximate, I used the COW contiguity dataset.[14] The dataset includes five types of state-to-state contiguity: contiguous by land, or separated by fewer than 12, 24, 150, or 400 miles of water. The analyses below use a simplified version of this set, classifying dyads that are contiguous by land or separated by 150 miles or less of water as contiguous and all other dyads as not contiguous.[15] Thus, the dispute dyads are classified into one of two groups: contiguous by land or by fewer than 150 miles of sea (699); and not contiguous (431).

Another dimension of contiguity that has received some attention in recent studies taps into facets of colonialism and dependency.[16] These relationships are important and valuable information for studies that deal with questions regarding these topics. Because my theoretical expectations about the influence of contiguity tap mainly into that dimension of the concept dealing with the geographical proximity and importance of quarrels with noncolonial neighbors, I do not use those data to represent contiguity. I am concerned primarily with the importance attached to disputes fought against enemies that are geographically proximate to the homeland, not colonial possessions. The territory and contiguity variables exhibit a .30 (simple) correlation, little evidence of overlap in what they are measuring.

The (simple) correlation between Contiguous and the interactive term (Contig-Terr) is .46; between Territory and the interactive term, .88. This high correlation between the interactive term and Territory suggests that a territorial variable alone should capture the effects that the interactive term was constructed to measure, for it appears that most territorial disputes are fought by neighbors. Because of their collinearity, the interactive and territory variables are not included in the models that are tested and reported below. Instead, separate analyses are conducted with the inclusion of the interactive term.[17]

Alternative Predictors

Also incorporated into the analyses that follow are six conditioning factors that are commonly discussed in the international relations literature. These variables are included for two reasons: they provide a more detailed picture of the escalation puzzle associated with interstate disputes; and they are routinely cited for their notable influence on conflict dynamics. A very brief description of these potential controls will suffice for the purposes of this paper.[18]

The first of these additional explanatory variables is relative power. The importance of power in the study of international relations has been repeated often.[19] Frequently mentioned in discussions about the effects of power on conflict is the preponderance-versus-parity debate.[20] Advocates of power preponderance argue that disputes between relatively equal states are more likely to escalate than are those between relatively unequal antagonists. This is in direct contrast to the reasoning forwarded by proponents of the power-parity model, who assert that when two states are relatively equal in capabilities, neither can be confident of victory, and they therefore deter each other from taking such chances. The merits of the preponderance argument seem to find more support in recent research (Sullivan 1990, for example), and it is this side of the debate from which my expectations derive. To assess the degree of power equality between disputants, I use the COW Composite Index of National Capabilities (CINC).[21] The Preponderant variable, a relative power measure, is coded 1 if one state in a dyad is more than ten times as powerful as the other; 0 if it is not.

In recent years, the joint-democracy-produces-peace postulate has received substantial attention. The bulk of the evidence appears to favor the conclusion that democracies rarely, if ever, go to war with one another (see, for example, Maoz and Russett 1993; Russett 1993; Ray 1995).[22] In addition, democracies tend to engage in militarized disputes with each other less frequently than do other types of dyads (Bremer 1992). With these observations at the dispute and war-initiation points as a backdrop, I expect dispute dyads constituting two democracies to escalate with a lower likelihood than those dyads consisting of either one or no democratic states. The coding of states as democratic or not, here, is based on the Polity II (Gurr, Jaggers, and Moore 1989) dataset's democracy rating for states from 1800 to 1986. The Polity II democracy indicator is an additive eleven-point (0–10) scale, based on assessments of the competitiveness of political participation, openness of executive recruitment, and constraints on chief executives.[23] The scale is dichotomized in the following manner: polities with scores from 0 to 5 are coded nondemocratic, and polities with scores from 6 to 10 are coded democratic. The Both

Democratic variable is coded 1 if both disputants are democracies; 0 if they are not.

The importance of alliances in interstate relations has been repeated many times. A traditional notion of alliances leads one to believe that aligned states will escalate their conflicts less frequently than will nonaligned pairs.[24] In order to distinguish dispute dyads that are allied from those that are not, I use the COW formal-alliance data (Small and Singer 1969).[25] The separation of alliances into the categories of mutual-defense pacts, neutrality agreements, and ententes is not utilized below. Instead, all three are lumped into a general alliance category.[26] This coding decision accurately captures whether pairs of states are committed to mutual agreements with one another. Each dispute dyad is coded as to whether the two states were linked in an alliance in the year prior to the onset of the dispute. The Allied term is coded 1 if disputing parties are aligned; 0 if they are not.

Young polities often act quite differently than do older ones. The political maturity—and stability—of a state can operate as an important conditioner of leaders' propensities to engage in intense conflict. I expect disputes between two relatively mature states to be resolved more quickly than those between one or no mature actors. More mature states will recognize the costs of increasing conflict severity and hostility, relative to timely resolution of grievances, and call on their experience in interstate relations to avoid higher levels of conflict. To test for the possibility that the maturity—or stability—of a state's internal political apparatus affects conflict behavior, I include two dummy variables for polity maturity. The measure for polity maturity is taken from the Polity II dataset, which includes a measure of polity persistence in years. It represents the number of years since the last fundamental, abrupt polity change in a state (1800–1986). For polities that were formed before 1800, the appropriate number of years was added to the score for 1800. The polity persistence variable is dichotomized into mature and not mature groups based on a twenty-five-year threshold. If the polities have persisted at least twenty-five years, they are considered mature; otherwise they are considered not mature. This threshold is arbitrary, although it does seem plausible that twenty-five years is a valid amount of time for a polity to be considered mature.[27] Dispute dyads are then assigned to one of three groups: both mature; one mature; or both not mature. Two dummy variables are constructed from this grouping. One Mature and No Mature are coded 1 if the condition is present or 0 if it is not, with dyads constituting two relatively mature states resulting in a 0 coding on both variables.

Most research on polarity and conflict attempts to connect the propensities of state actors to the number of major powers present in the system. The correlates of Power Transition, Hegemonic Stability, and Long Cycle theory are all in line with this notion (see, respectively, Organski and Kugler 1980; Gilpin 1981; Thompson 1988). Periods characterized by a single dominant state are noted for their stable qualities; stable in the sense that they are characterized by a relatively low amount of escalating conflict. The conclusions of these perspectives are not, however, universally agreed on within the literature of international relations (see, for example, Deutsch and Singer 1964; Wright 1965; Morgenthau 1973; Waltz 1979). My tests assess the likelihood of interstate-dispute escalation in unipolar, bipolar, and multipolar system structures. These analyses use the classification of polarity included in Thompson (1988, 213–214), with slight modifications. Years listed by Thompson as near unipolar are coded either unipolar or bipolar, depending on the codings of the years immediately surrounding them.[28] Bipolar and Multipolar are dummy variables coded 1 when a dispute occurs during appropriate years or 0 when it does not, with periods of unipolarity characterized by a 0 coding on both polarity variables.

Maoz and Russett (1993), after finding support for a normative model of democratic conflict avoidance at the dyadic level, speculate in their conclusion that an increase in the proportion of (mature) democracies in the international system may serve to lessen the frequency of conflict in the future. The literature speaking to this type of global democratic effect takes on several varying interpretations of the issue. Whether posed in the guise of institutions, conventions, or regimes, this literature traditionally leans heavily on the pacific effects of certain systemic norms—in this case, democracy. Keohane's (1989) conceptualization of conventions as informal institutions, constituting implicit rules and understandings that shape the expectations of actors, approximates the conceptualization of the democratic-system norm forwarded here. Straying from the norm of seeking a quick and just solution to lower-level conflict may serve to label a state as an outcast in a more democratic system. Thus, I expect to find a negative association between systemic democracy and the likelihood that disputes will escalate in hostility and severity. System Democracy is a continuous indicator of the proportion of states in the system each year that are democratic (>5 on the Gurr scale).

DATA ANALYSIS

My primary analyses used ordered logit techniques to determine the effects of contiguity and territorial issues on the ordinal dependent variables of dispute escalation.[29] The use of regression analysis in such instances is not appropriate, due to the introduction of bias by the necessary—and strong—assumption of equal intervals among categories of the dependent variable.[30]

Hostility Escalation

The first set of analyses examined the influence of contiguity and territorial issues on dispute-hostility patterns. It was posited that disputes fought over territorial issues and/or between contiguous foes would be significantly more likely to escalate than would those without these characteristics. This expectation is derived, theoretically, from the literature of international relations and, empirically, from the results of analyses examining related dimensions of conflict in the past.

The results for the multivariate ordered logit model are presented in Table 1. A chi-square significance test shows the log-likelihood value of the full model to be a significant improvement (p < .001) over that of the restricted (null) version.

Numerous studies have confirmed the conflict-engendering impact of contiguity. The results reported in Table 1, however, do not support these contentions in regard to the escalation of hostility between contiguous disputants in one-on-one affairs. The coefficient for the Contiguous variable is negative and insignificant. Evidently, contiguity has no important influence on the likelihood that hostility will escalate once the initial threat threshold has been passed and combatants are engaged in a dispute. It was posited that disputes fought primarily over territory escalate more frequently than those fought over other issues. Such expectations are clearly not supported by the results. The Territory variable is insignificant and negative, indicating no difference in hostility-escalation probabilities when disputes under way are fought over territory. Geographical proximity and issue-type appear to have no important escalatory impact on the level of hostility that interstate disputes reach.[31] In fact, they show insignificantly negative effects. The variation of the analysis—not shown in Table 1—employing an interactive indicator for contiguous-territorial disputes also reveals an insignificant estimate.[32]

The results for the relative power and alliance variables are not significant in the posited direction. Power balances and alliances appear

TABLE 5.1
Multivariate Ordered Logit Results for Dispute Hostility Escalation

Maximum Likelihood Estimates[a]

Log-likelihood	-963.89
Restricted (slopes = 0) log-l.	-979.32
Chi-squared (10)	30.866
Significance level	.0006

Cell Frequencies for Outcomes:

Outcome	Frequency	Proportion
Threat	65	.0575
Display	290	.2566
Use	751	.6646
War	24	.0212

Variable	Coefficient	Std. Error	Prob$|t| \geq x$
CONSTANT	2.7278	.3282	.0000
CONTIGUOUS	-.0717	.1523	.6812
TERRITORY	-.0972	.1476	.7691
PREPONDERANT	-.1232	.1449	.1978
BOTH DEMOCRATIC	.3725	.2302	.9502[b]
ALLIED	-.0052	.1687	.4877
BIPOLAR	-.2431	.1405	.0418[b]
MULTIPOLAR	-.7979	.2352	.0003[c]
ONE MATURE	.5483	.1880	.0018[c]
NO MATURE	.5421	.2032	.0038[c]
SYSTEM DEMOCRACY	-.1591	.7822	.4194

[a]Significance levels in all tables are calculated for one-tailed tests.
[b]p < .05; [c]p < .01

to have no important impact on hostility-escalation likelihoods for adversaries that have already passed the initial threshold into a dispute. Dyadic maturity reveals itself as a strong pacifying condition in interstate disputes, for the presence of one (One Mature) or two (No Mature) immature disputants significantly increases the probability of hostility escalation. The similar magnitude of the coefficients for the two maturity dummy variables suggests that the effect is interactive, not additive, in nature. The number of Great Powers in the international system has a significant influence on hostility levels. The magnitude of the significant coefficients reported for the Bipolar and Multipolar variables suggests that the escalation proneness of the system goes up in an additive fashion as the number of great powers increases. No evidence is found in support of a pacifying norm based on an increasing proportion of democratic states, for the System Democracy variable is insignificant and negative. Lastly, joint democracy has a positive effect on the likelihood that disputes will escalate, for the Both Democratic variable is positive and significant ($p < .05$). This result is contrary to my expectations.[33]

The patterns of escalation present between each hostility level were the next target of investigation: specifically, how the individual predictor variables influence dispute escalation at each stage between threat and war. Such information may help in sorting out the unexpected insignificant finding reported for geographical proximity and territorial issues in Table 1. In order to probe such phenomena, a series of three multivariate probit equations were estimated. The first coded disputes ending at the threat level as 0 and all others as 1; the second coded those ending at the level of display or lower as 0 and all others as 1; and the third coded those short of war as 0 and those escalating to war as 1.

The results, which should provide vital insights into the importance of the display, use, and war thresholds, are reported in Tables 2–4. Of the three, only Table 3 (display to use) is a significant improvement over the null version ($\chi = 40.9$). This is the first indication that the decision to use force is the one that drives many of the ordered logit results.

Geographical proximity plays no meaningful role in each of the three binary probit models. These findings are consistent with those reviewed earlier for the Contiguous variable in Table 1. Disputes fought over territorial issues are significantly more likely to escalate

Table 5.2
Multivariate Probit Results for Threat-Display Threshold

Maximum Likelihood Estimates

Log-likelihood	-241.27
Restricted (slopes = 0) log-l.	-248.71
Chi-squared (10)	14.868
Significance level	.1369

Cell Frequencies for Outcomes

Outcome	Frequency	Proportion
Threat	65	.0575
>Threat	1065	.9425

Variable	Coefficient	Std. Error	Prob|t| ≥ x
CONSTANT	1.2112	.2735	.0000
CONTIGUOUS	.0524	.1406	.3547
TERRITORY	.2591	.1609	.0498[a]
PREPONDERANT	-.1858	.1334	.0820
BOTH DEMOCRATIC	-.0141	.2115	.4735
ALLIED	.2917	.1833	.9504[a]
BIPOLAR	-.0907	.1371	.2542
MULTIPOLAR	-.4093	.2264	.0353[a]
ONE MATURE	.0056	.1840	.4878
NO MATURE	-.0952	.1982	.6845
SYSTEM DEMOCRACY	.3685	.7779	.6822

[a]$p < .05$; [b]$p < .01$

from threats to higher levels than are disputes fought over other issues. The same is true for the probability that short-of-war cases will escalate to war. These results are consistent with my posited expectations. States are more willing to press their concerns by displaying force and going to war when those concerns are primarily territorial in nature. Interestingly, though, Territory has an insignificant negative impact at the display-use threshold. The findings at the use-of-force threshold appear to be driving the ordered logit outcome shown in Table 1. The interactive term (Contig-Terr) reveals the same influence as Territory, so the results are not reported here.

The analyses conducted to this point do not support my posited expectations for the impact of contiguity on the escalation of disputes. In addition, the results are mixed as to their support for the primacy

Table 5.3
Multivariate Probit Results for Display-Use Threshold

Maximum Likelihood Estimates

Log-likelihood	-682.85
Restricted (slopes = 0) log-l.	-703.30
Chi-squared (10)	40.895
Significance level	.0000

Cell Frequencies for Outcomes

Outcome	Frequency	Proportion
<Use	355	.3142
>Display	775	.6858

Variable	Coefficient	Std. Error	Prob|t| ≥ x
CONSTANT	.3971	.2015	.0244
CONTIGUOUS	-.0864	.0943	.8200
TERRITORY	-.1355	.0924	.9287
PREPONDERANT	-.0559	.0907	.2688
BOTH DEMOCRATIC	.2627	.1407	.9690[a]
ALLIED	-.0204	.1021	.4209
BIPOLAR	-.1764	.0869	.0211[a]
MULTIPOLAR	-.5647	.1528	.0001[b]
ONE MATURE	.3755	.1190	.0008[b]
NO MATURE	.4174	.1261	.0005[b]
SYSTEM DEMOCRACY	-.0008	.5004	.4994

[a]$p < .05$; [b]$p < .01$

of territorial issues in pushing disputes to higher levels of intensity. Specifically, for the issue variable, the disputes that reach the use-of-force level—but that end short of war—are not in line with my expectations and appear to be influencing the ordinally based results.

With this in mind, I narrowed my focus to the use-of-force category. Within this hostility category are seven levels of severity, ranging from 0 to 1,000 or more battle deaths. Confining my attention to the 775 disputes that escalated beyond the display-of-force, I investigated another indicator of escalation, severity. As I mentioned above, state leaders are quite sensitive to the amount of human carnage produced by conflict. A closer inspection of disputes in which force is used can help clarify some of the important questions raised above.

Table 5.4
Multivariate Probit Results for Use-War Threshold

Maximum Likelihood Estimates

Log-likelihood	-110.27
Restricted (slopes =0) log-l.	-116.19
Chi-squared (10)	11.843
Significance level	.2957

Cell Frequencies for Outcomes

Outcome	Frequency	Proportion
<War	1106	.9788
War	24	.0212

Variable	Coefficient	Std. Error	Prob|t| ≥ x
CONSTANT	-2.0849	.4183	.0000
CONTIGUOUS	.3092	.2147	.0749
TERRITORY	.3418	.1899	.0360[a]
PREPONDERANT	-.0452	.2089	.4144
BOTH DEMOCRATIC	-.0562	.3148	.4291
ALLIED	-.1145	.2355	.3134
BIPOLAR	.1777	.2038	.8083
MULTIPOLAR	.4271	.3027	.9209
ONE MATURE	.0974	.2547	.3512
NO MATURE	-.1954	.2847	.7537
SYSTEM DEMOCRACY	-1.1398	1.0687	.1431

[a]p < .05

Severity Escalation

Table 5 shows the results of the multivariate analysis of severity escalation. The information provided by the predictor variables does significantly improve the predictive power of the model (based on the improved log-likelihood value of the full over the restricted version; (χ^2 = 102.81). Beyond this, the posited conflict engendering impact of contiguity is in evidence when analyzing severity escalation. The coefficient for the Contiguous variable is positive and significant. It appears that one of the opportunities that geographical proximity endows disputants is a deadly one, namely, the propensity to inflict significantly greater amounts of human destruction on one another.

Table 5.5
Table 5.5
Multivariate Ordered Logit Results for Dispute Severity Escalation

Maximum Likelihood Estimates

Log-likelihood	-648.48
Restricted (slopes = 0)	-699.89
Chi-squared (10)	102.81
Significance level	0000

Cell Frequencies for Outcomes:

Outcome	Frequency	Proportion
0	579	.7471
1–25	99	.1277
26–100	40	.0516
101–250	26	.0335
251–500	5	.0065
501–999	2	.0026
>999	24	.0310

Variable	Coefficient	Std. Error	Prob|t|≥x
CONSTANT	-3.2725	.5674	.0000
CONTIGUOUS	.5389	.2304	.0097[a]
TERRITORY	1.1054	.1900	.0000[a]
PREPONDERANT	-.3677	.2265	.0492[b]
BOTH DEMOCRATIC	.2665	.2919	.8194
ALLIED	.2944	.2211	.9085
BIPOLAR	.2658	.1939	.9147
MULTIPOLAR	.2549	.3713	.7538
ONE MATURE	.8562	.3861	.0133[b]
NO MATURE	.9905	.3951	.0061[a]
SYSTEM DEMOCRACY	1.2078	1.1944	.8440

[a]p<.01; [b]p<.05

While the earlier analyses reveal contiguity as imparting no significant influence on the level of hostility ordered by decision makers, the present examination clearly points out the elevated stakes involved when force is used between geographically proximate combatants.[34]

The result reported for the effect of territory on escalation also clearly supports my expectations. It was posited that disputes fought primarily over territory escalate more frequently than do those fought over other issues. The Territory variable is positive and significant, indicating a marked difference in severity-escalation probabilities when disputes are fought over territory. This result differs from the insignificant Territory effect reported for hostility escalation. A possible explanation for such a disparity may stem from the observation that states are less likely to press their demands to the point at which fatalities are incurred over issues that are not territorial in nature. The willingness to press demands through threats and displays of force is equally likely, regardless of the issues at stake. But when the imposition of dispute-level demands reaches the stage at which uses of force begin to entail loss of life, those disputes over territorial stakes appear to be the ones deemed most worthy of continuation.

The impacts of joint democracy, alliances, different numbers of Great Powers, and systemic democratic norms on severity levels are all insignificant. In line with my expectations, disputes fought between relatively unequal combatants are significantly less likely to escalate in severity than are those between relative equals. Also in line with my expectations, the absence of two mature antagonists increases the probability that quarrels result in more battle deaths. Similar to the hostility findings, the maturity effect appears to be dyadic, for the magnitudes of the One Mature and No Mature coefficients are fairly equal.

In order to facilitate a comparison, I computed the predicted probabilities that use-of-force disputes will escalate to war (more than 999 battle deaths) based on the presence or absence of contiguity and territorial issues. These predicted probabilities were calculated by setting the values of each dichotomous predictor variable equal to 0, whereas the continuous-systemic-democracy indicator was set to its mean of .325.[35] The predicted escalatory impact of territory is stronger than that of contiguity, as territorial—use of force—disputes are expected to escalate to war (more than 999 battle deaths) more than three times (.013–.004) more frequently than are nonterritorial ones. Contiguous disputes are expected to reach the war level two times (.008–.004) more often than are noncontiguous entanglements. This provides a rough indication of the power of territorial issues to push combatants up the escalation scale, once lives begin to be lost, as compared with disputes fought over other concerns. Recent work by Vasquez (1993, 1995) traces out a theoretical explanation for just such a finding, and the results reported here certainly fall nicely into line with his expectations for the importance of territorial issues on conflict intensity.

CONCLUSIONS

My expectations for the influence of contiguity and territorial issues were simple—namely, that both would impart a meaningful, positive impact on the likelihood that militarized disputes would escalate. Not surprisingly, the analyses of severity patterns show that contiguous disputes are significantly more likely to escalate than are noncontiguous ones. Similarly, the salience of territorial issues is prominent in pushing conflict to higher levels of human carnage. What is somewhat surprising, however, is that neither of these factors affects hostility escalation. A possible explanation for these findings may not be quite as difficult to formulate as first impressions might indicate.

A state leader is no more likely to escalate his or her commitment to conflict through displays and uses of force when the opponent is a neighbor. The results summarized above, especially in Table 1, reveal this lack of escalatory influence on hostility. If force is used, however, greater losses of life are incurred when the antagonists are geographically proximate and/or fighting over territorial issues (see Table 5).

The combination of these findings has two implications. First, geographical proximity and territory have no effect on the decisions leaders make at lower levels of engagement, specifically their propensity to display and use force (with no casualties);[36] saber rattling is equally likely between neighbors and long-distance foes. Second, contiguity and territory have a positive impact on the severity of disputes that do pass through these lower levels of strife. It appears that contiguity may supply the opportunity for more lives to be lost, simply because it is easier to conduct more potentially severe operations when an enemy is nearby. The willingness component, however, may be attributed to the issues at stake, with territorial disagreements appearing to be more salient and, thus, more worthy of risking lives over.

Lastly, the dispute-severity patterns reveal the power of territorial issues relative to geographical proximity. Vasquez (1993) posits that proximity may simply be a weaker measure of territory and, hence, less significant in its effect. One could also make the argument that the opportunity for conflict supplied by contiguity was, in a way, controlled for in my analyses, because I only looked at cases in which conflict had already begun. It is possible that the most profound impact for geographical proximity is in evidence at the point at which a dispute actually begins, not at those levels of increasingly hostile conflict that occur at later stages.

These findings certainly open the door for future efforts to develop a more sophisticated theoretical rationale for encompassing their implications. Critical tests devised to ferret out the particular nuances of the linkage between geographical proximity, territory, and escalating conflict are a logical next step toward isolating more precise explanations. There is little doubt that both contiguity and territory are central to the puzzle of interstate-conflict dynamics. The magnitude and significance of their influence, however, cannot be assumed as a constant. Although their role in the onset of disputes and war has been isolated, their influence between these two popular "firebreak" points is certainly more complex and particular than previously assumed.

The author is grateful to Stuart Bremer, Paul Diehl, Gary Goertz, Glenn Palmer, and John Vasquez for comments on the earlier version.

NOTES

1. In an earlier study, Senese (1995) constructs and tests a more complex formulation of the factors that may have an important effect on the escalation of interstate disputes.

2. Holsti (1991) concludes that the importance of territorial issues in disagreements between states has declined over time. This conclusion itself, however, is open to contention (see Vasquez 1993).

3. Hensel (1995) finds evidence supporting this claim in the context of recurrent conflict patterns between democratic states, suggesting the saliency of territorial issues even between pairs of states that are relatively pacific; that is, democracies.

4. This suggestion is prompted by the belief that distance between possible antagonists plays a lesser role as technological advances improve the ability of states to project their power. Gochman (1991), however, reports findings that do not support such an argument.

5. Issues that are tangible and zero-sum are commonly related to states' being more hostile. However, a contending argument posits that tangible issues

are more easily divisible and, therefore, less prone to conflict (Vasquez 1983). Assessing the relative importance of the tangible and intangible conceptualizations is a project worthy of serious consideration, though I do not directly examine it here.

6. The states examined here and their qualifying years are the same as those given in Table 2.1 in Small and Singer (1982), except for a few modifications that have been made since that time.

7. Tests were also conducted for cases that begin as one-on-ones but attract other states after the first day of conflict. These analyses revealed no important differences from those reported below. The role that joiners play in the escalation and resolution of disputes is admittedly important and deserving of scholarly attention. The present research is concerned, for the most part, with the escalation patterns of disputes with single participants on each side.

8. For a complete explanation of the original MID dataset, see Gochman and Maoz (1984). For a discussion of the updated set, see Jones, Bremer, and Singer (1996).

9. For analyses of cases characterized by joining behavior, and for assessments of the impact of joiners, see Senese (1995).

10. The inclusion of seizures in the use-of-force category may be, and has been, considered questionable by some of us involved in assembling the updated MID set. The results on which I report include the seizure cases. To check the robustness of these findings, however, I also conducted analyses from which these cases had been omitted. The results of those tests were not meaningfully different from those reported here.

11. This makes sense, for only state interactions that include a military component—at least a threat by at least one side—are included in the MID data.

12. A number of excellent works in the area of conflict have utilized the same COW hostility scale (from earlier versions of the MID data) as an indicator of conflict intensity and/or escalation propensities. See, for example, Bueno de Mesquita and Lalman (1992); Maoz and Abdolali (1989); Maoz and Russett (1993); and Russett (1993).

13. The focus in the severity analyses on the use-of-force hostility category was driven by two factors. First, all disputes ending at the threat and display levels experienced no battle-associated deaths, whereas the use and war groupings are characterized by the entire range of severity. Second, the hostility analyses suggest the importance of the use category, leading me to examine severity patterns within this crucial set of cases. The severity tests were subsequently conducted with the entire sample of 1,130 disputes, as well. The results were almost identical and are not reported here.

14. Stuart Bremer, to whom I express my thanks, supplied these data to me. For more information on them, see Gochman (1991).

15. An earlier study (Bremer 1992) shows the major effect of proximity on conflict to be captured by a "contiguous by land or sea" versus "not contiguous" distinction.

16. For more information on the contiguity data, including colonial border cases, see Siverson and Starr (1991).

17. Numerous scholars point to the multicollinearity problem that is inherent in the use of a multiplicative term; see, for example, Althauser (1971); Johnston (1972); Jackman (1974); Blalock (1979); Smith and Sasaki (1979); and Lewis-Beck (1980). A few (including Friedrich 1982) argue for the inclusion of an interactive variable, nonetheless. The implications of including the multiplicative version of contiguity and territorial issues in the same statistical model as the individual variables may be theoretically and, possibly, methodologically important, but I have chosen to delay their examination for a later effort that can focus on them more extensively.

18. For a detailed operationalization and discussion of these alternative predictors, see Senese (1995).

19. For empirical work at the dyadic level, see Garnham (1976); Weede (1976); Baldwin (1979); Bueno de Mesquita (1981); Siverson and Sullivan (1983); Gochman (1991); and Bremer (1992).

20. Traditional support for the preponderance side can be found in Organski (1958); Blainey (1973); and Gilpin (1981). Support for power parity, in the balance-of-power tradition, can be found in Claude (1962).

21. For a more detailed discussion of the measure, see Singer, Bremer, and Stuckey (1972).

22. For dissenting opinions on the democratic peace postulate, see Cohen (1994); Layne (1994); Spiro (1994); James, Solberg, and Wolfson (1995); and Mansfield and Snyder (1995).

23. Another index of democracy commonly used is that which is utilized in Chan (1984). Overall, the Chan and Gurr measures stand in substantial agreement, for they are correlated at +0.86 (Yule's Q), as reported in Bremer (1993).

24. For a dissenting argument on this point from the perspective of expected-utility theory, see Bueno de Mesquita (1980, 1981). An empirical answer to this challenge is presented in Bremer (1992).

25. These data were amended and modified by Alan Sabrosky and supplied to me by Stuart Bremer, to whom I express my thanks.

26. Bremer (1992) finds evidence that the type of alliance characterizing a dyad has some importance, but the major effect of alliance on conflict can be captured by a simple allied–not allied dichotomy.

27. To make sure that the results are not dependent on the selection of the twenty-five-year threshold, the tests were also undertaken using twenty and thirty-year separations. These alternative coding rules produced nearly identical results, and I have not reported on them here.

28. Thompson (1988, 214), himself, suggests the need for such adjustments in his note following Table 9.4.

29. McElvey and Zavoina (1975) developed the ordered probit model, using the standard normal distribution. The ordered logit variant is estimated in the same fashion, but using the standard logistic distribution instead of the standard normal.

30. For a good discussion of the advantages of the ordered probit or logit model over regression in the presence of an ordinally ranked dependent variable, as well as the derivation of the model, see McElvey and Zavoina (1975); Maddala (1983, 46–49); King (1989, 113–115); and Greene (1993, 672–676).

31. I also conducted three separate bivariate analyses to examine the individual effects of contiguity, territory, or their interaction on dispute hostility levels. The coefficients for Contiguous, Territory, and Contig-Terr were insignificant in each of these tests.

32. A statistical model including the individual predictors (Contiguous and Territory), as well as their interaction (Contig-Terr), was also tested. The inclusion of the interaction term only lowered the log-likelihood value of the full model by a small amount, while it introduced the problem of multicollinearity into its interpretation. For these reasons, the results are not reported here, and their implications should be treated with caution.

33. For a more detailed examination of the effect of joint democracy on the escalation of disputes, see Senese (1997).

34. Three separate bivariate analyses were also conducted, examining the individual effects of contiguity, territory, or their interaction on dispute severity levels. The coefficients for Contiguous, Territory, and Contig-Terr were positive and significant ($p < .05$) in each of these tests.

35. Greene (1993, 675) suggests this convention.

36. Remember, all of the cases included in these analyses have at least reached the point at which the threat to use force has been imposed.

REFERENCES

Althauser, Robert P. 1971. "Multicollinearity and Non-Additive Regression Models." In *Causal Models in the Social Sciences*, edited by Hubert M. Blalock Jr. Chicago: Aldine-Atherton.

Baldwin, David. 1979. "Power Analysis and World Politics." *World Politics* 31: 161–194.

Blainey, Geoffrey. 1975. *The Causes of War.* New York: Free Press.

Blalock, Hubert M., Jr. 1979. *Social Statistics.* Rev. 2d ed. New York: Mc-Graw-Hill.

Bremer, Stuart A. 1992. "Dangerous Dyads: Conditions Affecting the Likelihood of Interstate War, 1816–1965." *Journal of Conflict Resolution* 36: 309–341.

———. 1993. "Democracy and Militarized Interstate Conflict." *International Interactions* 18: 231–250.

Bueno de Mesquita, Bruce. 1980. "An Expected Utility Theory of International Conflict." *American Political Science Review* 74: 917–931.

———. 1981. *The War Trap.* New Haven, Conn.: Yale University Press.

Bueno de Mesquita, Bruce, and David Lalman. 1992. *War and Reason: Domestic and International Imperatives.* New Haven: Yale University Press.

Chan, Steve. 1984. "Mirror, Mirror on the Wall...Are the Freer Countries More Pacific?" *Journal of Conflict Resolution* 33: 617–648.

Claude, Inis. 1962. *Power and International Relations.* New York: Random House.

Cohen, Raymond. 1994. "A Pacific Union: A Reappraisal of the Theory That Democracies Do Not Go to War with Each Other." *Review of International Studies* 20: 207–223.

Deutsch, Karl W., and J. David Singer. 1964. "Multipolar Power Systems and International Stability." *World Politics* 16: 390–406.

Diehl, Paul F. 1985. "Contiguity and Military Escalation in Major Power Rivalries, 1816–1980." *Journal of Politics* 47: 1203–1211.

———. 1992. "What Are They Fighting For? The Importance of Issues in International Conflict Research." *Journal of Peace Research* 29: 333–344.

Diehl, Paul F., and Gary Goertz. 1988. "No Trespassing! Territorial Changes and Militarized Conflict." *Journal of Conflict Resolution* 32: 103–122.

Friedrich, Robert J. 1982. "In Defense of Multiplicative Terms in Multiple Regression Equations." *American Journal of Political Science* 26: 797–833.

Garnham, David. 1976. "Dyadic International War, 1816–1965: The Role of Power Parity and Geographical Proximity." *Western Political Quarterly* 29: 231–242.

Gilpin, Robert. 1981. *War and Change in World Politics.* New York: Cambridge University Press.

Gochman, Charles S. 1991. "Interstate Metrics: Conceptualizing, Operationalizing, and Measuring the Geographic Proximity of States since the Congress of Vienna." *International Interactions* 17: 93–112.

Gochman, Charles S., and Zeev Maoz. 1984. "Militarized Interstate Disputes, 1816–1976: Procedures, Patterns, and Insights." *Journal of Conflict Resolution* 28: 586–615.

Goertz, Gary, and Paul F. Diehl. 1988. "A Territorial History of the International System." *International Interactions* 15: 81–93.

———. 1992. *Territorial Changes and International Conflict.* London: Routledge.

Greene, William H. 1993. *Econometric Analysis.* 2d ed. New York: Macmillan.

Gurr, Ted R., Keith Jaggers, and Will H. Moore. 1989. "Polity II." *DDIR Update* 3: 1–7.

Hensel, Paul R. 1995. "Political Democracy and Militarized Conflict in Evolving Interstate Rivalries." Paper presented at the annual meeting of the American Political Science Association, Chicago, Ill.

Holsti, Kalevi J. 1991. *Peace and War: Armed Conflicts and International Order, 1648–1989.* Cambridge, U.K.: Cambridge University Press.

Huth, Paul K. 1996. *Standing Your Ground: Territorial Disputes and International Conflict.* Ann Arbor: University of Michigan Press.

Jackman, Robert W. 1974. "Political Democracy and Social Equality: A Comparative Analysis." *American Sociological Review* 39: 20–45.

James, Patrick, Eric Solberg, and Murray Wolfson. 1995. "An Identified Systemic Test of the Democracy-Peace Nexus." Paper presented at the annual meeting of the Peace Science Society (International), Columbus, Ohio.

Johnston, J. 1972. *Econometric Methods.* 2d ed. New York: McGraw-Hill.

Jones, Daniel M., Stuart A. Bremer, and J. David Singer. 1996. "Militarized Interstate Disputes, 1816–1992: Rationale, Coding Rules, and Empirical Patterns." *Conflict Management and Peace Science* 15: 163–213.

Keohane, Robert O. 1989. *International Institutions and State Power: Essays in International Relations Theory.* Boulder, Colo.: Westview Press.

King, Gary. 1989. *Unifying Political Methodology: The Likelihood Theory of Statistical Inference.* New York: Cambridge University Press.

Kocs, Stephen. 1995. "Territorial Disputes and Interstate War, 1945–1987." *Journal of Politics* 57: 159–175.

Layne, Christopher. 1994. "Kant or Cant: The Myth of Democratic Peace." *International Security* 19: 5–49.

Lewis-Beck, Michael S. 1980. *Applied Regression: An Introduction.* Beverly Hills, Calif.: Sage Publications.

Maddala, G. S. 1983. *Limited-Dependent and Qualitative Variables in Econometrics.* Cambridge, U.K.: Cambridge University Press.

Mansfield, Edward, and Jack Snyder. 1995. "Democratization and War." *Foreign Affairs* 74: 79–98.

Maoz, Zeev, and Nasrin Abdolali. 1989. "Regime Types and International Conflict, 1816–1976." *Journal of Conflict Resolution* 33: 3–35.

Maoz, Zeev, and Bruce Russett. 1993. "Normative and Structural Causes of Democratic Peace, 1946–1986." *American Political Science Review* 87: 624–638.

McElvey, W., and R. Zavoina. 1975. "A Statistical Model for the Analysis of Ordinal Level Dependent Variables." *Journal of Mathematical Sociology* 5 (Summer): 103–120.

Morgenthau, Hans J. 1973. *Politics among Nations.* 5th ed. New York: Alfred A. Knopf.

Organski, A. F. K. 1958. *World Politics.* New York: Alfred A. Knopf.

Organski, A. F. K., and Jacek Kugler. 1980. *The War Ledger.* Chicago: University of Chicago Press.

Ray, James Lee. 1995. *Democracy and International Conflict.* Columbia: University of South Carolina Press.

Russett, Bruce. 1993. *Grasping the Democratic Peace: Principles for a Post–Cold War World.* Princeton, N.J.: Princeton University Press.

Senese, Paul D. 1995. "Dispute to War: Patterns and Processes in the Escalation of Militarized Interstate Conflict." Ph.D. diss., Binghamton University.

———. 1997. "Between Dispute and War: The Effect of Joint Democracy on Interstate Conflict Escalation." *Journal of Politics* 59: 1–27.

Singer, J. David, Stuart A. Bremer, and John Stuckey. 1972. "Capability Distribution, Uncertainty, and Major Power War, 1820–1965." In *Peace, War and Numbers,* edited by Bruce M. Russett. New York: Free Press.

Siverson, Randolph M., and Harvey Starr. 1991. *The Diffusion of War: A Study of Opportunity and Willingness.* Ann Arbor: University of Michigan Press.

Siverson, Randolph M., and Michael P. Sullivan. 1983. "The Distribution of Power and the Onset of War." *Journal of Conflict Resolution* 27: 473–494.

Small, Melvin, and J. David Singer. 1969. "Formal Alliances, 1816–1965: An Extension of the Basic Data." *Journal of Peace Research* 6: 257–282.

———. 1982. *Resort to Arms: International and Civil Wars, 1816–1980.* Beverly Hills, Calif.: Sage Publications.

Smith, Kent W., and M. S. Sasaki. 1979. "Decreasing Multicollinearity: A Method for Models with Multiplicative Functions." *Sociological Methods and Research* 8: 35–56.

Spiro, David E. 1994. "The Insignificance of Liberal Peace." *International Security* 19: 50–86.

Sullivan, Michael P. 1990. *Power in Contemporary International Politics.* Columbia: University of South Carolina Press.

Thompson, William R. 1988. *On Global War: Historical-Structural Approaches to World Politics.* Columbia: University of South Carolina Press.

Vasquez, John A. 1983. "The Tangibility of Issues and Global Conflict: A Test of Rosenau's Issue Area Typology." *Journal of Peace Research* 20: 179–192.

————. 1993. *The War Puzzle.* Cambridge, U.K.: Cambridge University Press.

————. 1994. "Crisis Escalation and Intervention in Ongoing War." Unpublished paper, Department of Political Science, Vanderbilt University.

————. 1995. "Why Do Neighbors Fight? Proximity, Interaction, or Territoriality." *Journal of Peace Research* 32: 277–293.

————. 1996. "Distinguishing Rivalries That Go to War from Those That Do Not: A Quantitative Comparative Case Study of the Two Paths to War." *International Studies Quarterly* 40: 531–558.

Wallenstein, Peter. 1981. "Incompatibility, Confrontation, and War: Four Models and Three Historical Systems, 1816–1976." *Journal of Peace Research* 18: 57–90.

Waltz, Kenneth N. 1979. *Theory of International Politics* New York: Random House.

Weede, Erich. 1976. "Overwhelming Preponderance as a Pacifying Condition among Contiguous Asian Dyads, 1959–1969." *Journal of Conflict Resolution* 20: 395–412.

————. 1984. "Democracy and War Involvement." *Journal of Conflict Resolution* 28: 649–664.

Wright, Quincy. 1965. *A Study of War.* 2d ed. Chicago: University of Chicago Press.

PART IV

Territory and the Resolution of Conflict

6
Alliances That Never Balance: The Territorial-Settlement Treaty

Douglas M. Gibler

INTRODUCTION

On August 20 and 21, 1939, the National Socialist government in Germany successfully negotiated a nonaggression pact with the Soviet Union. Both parties agreed not to attack the other or become involved in alliances or commitments targeting the other, and both the Soviet Union and Germany pledged to remain neutral if either state were attacked by a third state. The announcement of the pact shocked the future allied states, and plans for including Russia in a "peace front" were dropped (Langer 1972, 1132). By September 17, 1939, Germany had secured its eastern front by removing the Soviet Union as an immediate threat, and Poland was officially partitioned when Russian troops met the Germans near Brest-Litovsk. World War II had begun.

More than one hundred years earlier, in November 1815, representatives of England, Austria-Hungary, Russia, and Prussia had signed the Quadruple Alliance, which established the terms of the peace settlement that was to follow the Napoleonic Wars. Dedicated to preventing the return of Napoleon or a possible Napoleonic dynasty, the four states secured guarantees of cooperation from the other alliance members should another revolutionary state threaten the new system. More importantly, the four states agreed formally to the preservation of the then current distributions of territory in Europe and informally to a congress system dedicated to resolving serious disputes between alliance members. By 1818, the restored French Bourbons had added their consent to the territorial settlement, and the congress system was well on its way to establishing one of the most peaceful periods in modern history (Langer 1972, 652–653, 715–717; Wallensteen 1984).

Although these two cases provided for dramatically different forms of alliance commitments and affected the war-proneness of member states in radically different ways, they have been treated as equal units in most empirical studies on alliance formation.[1] Perhaps overly enamored with realist conceptions of alliance behavior, which argue that alliances are formed to balance power between states, current research has ignored the multifaceted nature of alliances. Despite early calls for reconceptualizing the alliance variable (Bueno de Mesquita and Singer 1973, 272–273; Ward 1973, 58) and recent acknowledgments of the need for a typology of alliances (Vasquez 1993, 171; Gibler 1997) few studies have examined the variegated effects alliances have had on the war-proneness of states, and most of this work has been dedicated to the somewhat narrow topic of alliance reliability (Sabrosky 1980; Bueno de Mesquita 1981; Ray 1990).

The lack of consensus about the theoretical linkages between alliances and war—or peace—has led some scholars to argue for a reexamination of the method used to investigate the alliance-war process (Smith 1995, 405–406). However, it is not at all clear whether the methods currently in use are to blame for the theoretical confusion. Indeed, in spite of the lack of conceptual clarity, an extensive body of evidence has been accumulated showing that alliances are followed more often by war than by peace (Singer and Small 1966b; Levy 1981). It has also been convincingly demonstrated that alliances are associated with the expansion of war (Siverson and King 1979, 1980; Siverson and Starr 1990) and that alliance polarization and the buildup of alliances in the system are associated with world wars (Midlarsky 1983, 1986; Wayman 1984; Kegley 1994).

These impressive findings are tempered, however, by the inability to explain a large number of anomalous, peaceful alliances. Levy (1981), for example, has demonstrated that 44 percent of neutrality and defense pacts in the seventeenth century, 33 percent in the eighteenth century, 72 percent in the nineteenth century, and 13 percent in the twentieth century were not followed within five years by a war involving an ally. The variation across centuries, especially the large percentage of peaceful nineteenth-century alliances, suggests that not all alliances are created equal.

Generally, alliances are used by states as a method of preparing for war, but a significant minority of them attempt to avoid war by removing contentious issues from the system. Instead of trying to establish peace through realist prescriptions of deterrence, these territorial-settlement treaties are alliances that resolve territorial disputes between alliance members in addition to forming traditional alliance commitments.[2] In this chapter I identify and catalog these peaceful alliances.

THEORY AND MEASUREMENT

According to the territorial explanation of war, the single most important factor that escalates a dispute to the point of war is the presence of a territorial issue which actors try to resolve through the use of power politics (Vasquez 1993, chap. 4). Building on the recent emphasis on territory as a source of conflict (Goertz and Diehl 1988, 1992) and the growing evidence that contiguity increases the chances of war in a dyad (Diehl 1985a, 1985b; Bremer 1992), the territorial explanation of war argues that how states handle the sensitive issue of territorial control with their neighbors greatly affects the chances of war between those states. States that pursue alliances, military buildups, and other power-politics measures in response to territorial issues tend to increase their chances of going to war. However, if states are capable of resolving or removing these territorial issues from their agenda, it is argued that they will be capable of avoiding war for prolonged periods of time, even if other contentious issues arise (Vasquez 1993, 146–147, 151–152).

One of the ways in which states resolve territorial issues is through the use of alliances (Gibler and Vasquez 1995). For the past two centuries there have been at least twenty-seven incidents in which states have either exchanged territory or agreed to the status quo settlement of territory and have then cemented their new relationship with the signing of an alliance. The twenty-seven territorial-settlement treaties are listed in Table 1.

Table 6.1.
List of Territorial Settlement Treaties

Alliance	Alliance Member	Source[a]	Date of Inception	Date of Termination	Type of Pact[b]	Settlement Type; Disputed Territory
COW1	Austria, Baden, Bavaria, Hanover, Hesse-Electoral, Hesse-Grand Ducal, Mecklenburg-Schwerin, Prussia, Württemberg	Parry 1978, 64: 444–452 (in French)	June 18, 1815	Dec. 1848	Defense	Status quo: German Confederation
COW2	Austria, England, France, Prussia, Russia	Parry 1978, 65: 301–322	Nov. 20, 1815	Dec. 1823	Defense	Status quo: France
COW4	Russia	Parry 1978, 84: 2–6	June 26, 1833 (Sept. 7, 1833)	Dec. 1840	Defense	Status quo: Dardanelles
COW7	Austria, England, Prussia, Russia, Turkey	Parry 1978, 90: 286–292 (in French)	July 15, 1840	Dec. 1840	Defense	Exchange: Crete, Syria, Mecca, Medina, Egypt
COW32	England, Turkey	Parry 1978, 153: 68–74	June 4, 1878	Dec. 1880	Defense	Exchange: Cyprus
COW34	Austria, Germany, Russia	Pribram 1967, 1: 37–49	June 18, 1881	Dec. 1887	Neutrality or nonaggression	Status quo: Turkey, Balkans
COW36	Austria, England, Italy	Pribram 1967, 1: 124–133	Dec. 12, 1887	Dec. 1895	Entente	Status quo: Turkey, Dardanelles
COW37	Austria, Italy, Spain	Pribram 1967, 1: 116–123	May 4, 1887	Dec. 1895	Neutrality or nonaggression	Status quo: Mediterranean Agreement
COW38	Germany, Russia	Pribram 1967, 1: 274–278	June 18, 1887	Dec. 1890	Neutrality or nonaggression	Status quo: Balkans, Dardanelles
COW40	China, Russia	Parry 1978, 153: 425	May 1896	Dec. 1902	Defense	Exchange: Trans-Siberian Railroad

Alliance	Alliance Member	Source[a]	Date of Inception	Date of Termination	Type of Pact[b]	Settlement Type; Disputed Territory
COW42	Austria-Hungary, Russia	Pribram 1967, 1: 184–195	May 8, 1897	Dec. 1908	Entente	Status quo: Balkans
COW43	England, Portugal	Gooch 1927, 1: 93–94	Oct. 14, 1899	Dec. 1949	Defense	Status quo: Portugal
COW46	England, France	Parry 1978, 195: 198–216	April 8, 1904	Dec. 1918	Entente	Status quo: Morocco, Egypt
COW47	England, France, Spain	Parry 1978, 196: 353–356 (in French)	Oct. 3, 1904	Dec. 1918	Entente	Status quo: Morocco
COW50	England, Russia	Parry 1978, 204: 404–409 (in French)	Aug. 31, 1907	Dec. 1918	Entente	Status quo: Persia, Afghanistan, Tibet
COW67	Afghanistan, Turkey	BFS, 118: 10	March 1, 1921		Defense	Status quo: Khiva, Afghanistan, Bokhara
COW72	Estonia, Latvia	League of Nations 17 LTS: 189	Oct. 19, 1923 (Nov. 1923)	Dec. 1940	Defense	Status quo: border agreement
COW74	Italy, Yugoslavia	League of Nations 24 LTS: 33	Jan. 27, 1924	Dec. 1927	Neutrality or nonaggression	Exchange: Fiume, Porto Barros
COW85	Persia, Russia	BFS, 126: 943	Jan. 31, 1927	Dec. 1945	Neutrality or nonaggression	Status quo: border agreement
COW97	England, Iraq	BFS, 132: 280	Jan. 26, 1931 (1932)	Dec. 1956	Defense	Status quo: Iraq
COW154	China, Russia	BFS, 149: 346	Aug. 14, 1945	1947	Defense	Exchange: Mongolia, Manchurian Railroad, Dairen, Port Arthur
COW180	Burma, China	BFS, 164: 649	Jan. 28, 1960		Neutrality or nonaggression	Status quo: border agreement

Alliance	Alliance Member	Source[a]	Date of Inception	Date of Termination	Type of Pact[b]	Settlement Type; Disputed Territory
COW187	Cameroon, Central African Republic, Chad, Congo (B), Dahomey, Gabon, Ivory Coast, Malagasy, Mauritania, Niger, Senegal, Upper Volta, Rwanda, Togo	BFS, 166: 440 (in French)	May 12, 1961 (Sept. 1961)	Dec. 1964	Defense	Status quo: affirmation of all existing (colonial) borders
COW188	Algeria, Burundi, Cameroon, Central African Republic, Chad, Democratic Republic of Congo (B), Democratic Republic of Congo (K), Dahomey, Ethiopia, Gabon, Ghana, Guinea, Ivory Coast, Liberia, Libya, Malagasy, Mali, Mauritania, Morocco, Niger, Rwanda, Senegal, Sierra Leone, Somalia, Sudan, Tanzania, Togo, Tunisia, Uganda, United Arab Republic, Upper Volta, Malawi (1964), Zambia (1964), Gambia (1965)	BFS, 167: 225	May 25, 1963		Entente	Status quo: border agreement
COW190	Gambia, Senegal	Rohn 1983, no. 53609	February 18, 1965		Defense	Status quo: border agreement
COW198	Bangladesh, India	Rohn 1983, no. 570048	May 16, 1972		Neutrality or nonaggression	Status quo: border agreement
COW203	Panama, United States	*United States Treaty Series*, 33 UST 10029: 2–29	Sept. 7, 1977		Defense	Exchange: Panama Canal

[a] The "source listing" gives the bibliographic reference for the entire treaty text. Only one source is listed. Abbreviations for the sources are as follows:

BFS is	British and Foreign State Papers
League is	League of Nations Treaty Series
UST is	United States Treaty Series

Rohn 1983 is listed when the entire treaty text cannot be located, along with a reference number for the treaty. Rohn lists state archives in which the texts of the numbered treaties can be found.

[b] Singer and Small (1966, 5) used these three major forms of commitments to delineate their alliance types:

    I. Defense pact: intervene militarily on the side of any treaty partner that is attacked militarily.

    II. Neutrality or nonaggression pact: remain militarily neutral if any cosignatory is attacked. The neutrality pact is usually more specific than the nonaggression pact.

    III. Entente: consult and/or cooperate in a crisis, including armed attack.

The text of these alliances can be found in most major compilations of international treaties. The *League of Nations Treaty Series* is an excellent source for the interwar period, and the *United Nations Treaty Series* contains the texts of most post-1945 alliances. Parry's (1978) *Consolidated Treaty Series* is a wonderful source for alliances made between 1648 and 1920. Using Martens (1889) as a principal source, Parry gives English translations for most of the alliances; he also notes the lack of translations. Pribram's (1967) two-volume set is very helpful for treaties made by Austria-Hungary before World War I. Rohn's (1983) index of alliances is a monumental source for the alliance researcher. However, it contains only cursory descriptions of each alliance and sometimes leads the researcher to obscure references—even when more readily available texts print the treaty text.

Exchange Settlements

Territorial settlements are divided into two categories. The "exchange" category represents cases in which alliance members have actually exchanged territory through an alliance. To qualify as an exchange settlement, the treaty text has to explicitly describe the terms of the exchange and the territory to be transferred. Exchanges that occur outside the text of the treaty are not considered. Six of the twenty-seven cases described here are exchange settlements.[3]

An example of this type of commitment is the 1924 alliance between Mussolini's Italy and the Kingdom of Yugoslavia. Rights to the city of Fiume were transferred to Italy, and control of Porto Barros was given to Yugoslavia as a supplementary convention to the "pact of friendship" between the two states. The treaty resolved the boundary between the two states. It also contained numerous stipulations regarding the disposition of roads, aqueducts, port rights, railways, and bridges (League of Nations 1924, 33–49).

Similarly, the United States began the transfer of the Panama Canal to Panama in 1977. In exchange for Panama's guaranteeing the permanent neutrality and continued operation of the canal, the United States made assurances regarding the territorial sovereignty of the isthmus nation. Although the United States received little compensation for the transfer of the canal, the alliance does meet the criteria for an exchange settlement because territorial control was exchanged.

The other four exchange settlements took place in two different geographical areas. First, the 1840 alliance dedicated to pacifying the Levant and the 1878 alliance between Great Britain and Turkey tried to settle the very difficult question of control over the Dardanelles and the eastern Mediterranean Sea. Imposed on Mohammed Ali by Austria, Great Britain, Prussia, and Russia, the 1840 alliance with Turkey guaranteed Ali hereditary possession of Egypt in exchange for his relinquishing control over Crete, northern Syria, Mecca and Medina, and the Turkish fleet (Parry 1978, 65: 301–322), thus protecting that region from political instability. The defensive alliance between Great Britain and Turkey in 1878 provided for the defense of Turkey by Great Britain in the advent of a rise of "Russian aggression" in Asia. However, the alliance also transferred control of Crete to Great Britain in exchange for this protection. Guaranteeing fair treatment of the Muslim population, Great Britain also agreed to pay Turkey "whatever is the excess of revenue over expenditure in the island" (Parry 1978, 153: 71).

The last two exchange settlements involve Russia–Soviet Union and China. The 1896 secret alliance between these two countries was reported fourteen years later in the *London Daily Telegraph*, which also carried the French text and the English translation of the treaty. Fearing the growing Japanese aggression toward both states, the alliance called for shared military operations in case of attack. It also contained two articles (Articles IV and V) dedicated to the establishment of a Russian railway through China. The railway would be most useful for moving troops in wartime, but the alliance also stipulated that Russia could operate the railway during peaceful periods even though it ran through a significant segment of the Chinese northern territories (Parry 1978, 153: 425).

Almost fifty years later the same two states made further arrangements for the maintenance of railway operations. The 1945 alliance laid the groundwork for relations between the Soviet Union and China after the defeat of Japan. In addition to a treaty of friendship, it stipulated that the railway from Harbin to Dairen and Port Arthur would "become the common property of the U.S.S.R. and the Chinese Republic and [would] be operated by them jointly" (BFS 149: 349). All railways spurs and lands would also be commonly owned. Two additional protocols were signed allowing for joint use of Port Arthur as a naval base and proclaiming Dairen a "free Port open to the trade and shipping of all countries" (pp. 353–356).

Status Quo Settlements

"Status quo" settlements are much more numerous—twenty-one of the twenty-seven cases—than the exchange settlements. They are cases in which two or more states agreed to settle a disputed territory by formally accepting the status quo distribution of control in the region. Representing formal contracts between states, these treaties gave some guarantee that valuable territories would not be used in ways that affected the security of the alliance members. A large number of these agreements were aimed at pacifying the highly contested Balkan region during the nineteenth century and the colonies and former colonies of Europe during the early and middle twentieth century. Also included in this category are treaties that provide for the demarcation of current borders. The border agreements generally occurred after World War II.

The Quadruple Alliance is an example of this form of settlement. The victorious powers carefully delimited the boundaries of the French state following the war. For example, Article I of the treaty gives a detailed listing of the de facto French border, of which the following is only a small portion:

The Frontiers of France shall be the same as they were in the year One thousand seven hundred and ninety, save and except the modifications on one side and on the other which are detailed in the present Article. First, on the

Northern Frontiers, the Line of Demarcation shall remain as it was fixed by the Treaty of Paris, as far as opposite to Quiverain, from thence it shall follow the ancient limits of the Belgian Provinces. . . . From Villers near Orval upon the confines of the Department Des Ardennes, and of the Grand Duchy of Luxembourg as far as Perle. . . . From Perle it shall pass. (Parry 1978, 65: 301–322)

The treaty text never details military commitments for the alliance signatories; it only contains provisions for the settlement of France.

Although the post-Napoleonic alliance is an obvious case of the status quo settlement of a disputed territory, it is unusual because it is a peace settlement. Only four of the territorial settlements—COW1, COW2, COW4, and COW198—were clearly peace settlements. In addition to the peace settlement with France, 1815 also saw Prussia initiate an alliance with the majority of German states, including Austria's German provinces, to form the Germanic Confederation. Its purpose was to guarantee external and internal peace in Germany and to protect it from possible foreign foes (Russia and France) and the rise of domestic liberalism. The alliance also provided for clear demarcation and acceptance of the current borders of the confederated states, qualifying it as a status quo settlement (Langer 1972, 715; Parry 1978, 64: 444–452).

The Treaty of Hunkiar-Iskelesi between Russia and Turkey in 1833 resolved many of the issues that had been disputed during the Russo-Turkish War (1828–1829). This peace settlement, in effect for eight years, committed each party to come to the other's aid in case of attack. However, a secret article of the treaty relieved the Turks of this obligation in exchange for keeping the Dardanelles closed to foreign traffic:

[A]s His Majesty the Emperor of all the Russians, wishing to spare the Sublime Ottoman Porte the expense and inconvenience which might be occasioned to it, by affording substantial aid, will not ask for that aid if circumstances should place the Sublime Porte under the obligation of furnishing it, the Sublime Ottoman Porte, in the place of the aid which is bound to furnish in case of need, according to the principle of reciprocity of the Patent Treaty, shall confine its action in favour of the Imperial Court of Russia, to closing the Strait of the Dardanelles, that is to say, to not allowing any Foreign Vessel of War to enter therein under any pretext whatsoever. (Parry 1978, 84: 6)

The last peace settlement was signed by India and Bangladesh in 1972, after the 1971 Bangladesh War between India and Pakistan. Recognizing the independence of Bangladesh, India guaranteed acceptance of the sovereignty of the Bangladesh state and provided for demarcation of the border between the two countries (Zaheer 1994, 426–433). Rohn's (1983, alliance 570048) treaty profile confirms the border demarcation, but the index states that the treaty text is available only through the Indian archives, which are not available in most American libraries.

The status quo settlements of the late nineteenth and early twentieth centuries were usually dedicated to resolving territorial issues in the Balkans and the Mediterranean. From 1881 to 1897, four agreements were signed confirming acceptance of territorial boundaries in the Balkans, and from 1887 to 1904, four other agreements detailed various positions around the Mediterranean (mostly Morocco). The Balkan agreements[4] mostly attempted to resolve disputed claims between Russia and Austria but also provided for the resolution of various claims to The Straits, a contested issue for most maritime powers, especially England. For example, the first Balkan agreement, the League of the Three Emperors (1881), stipulated that: "The three Courts, desirous of avoiding all discord between them, engage to take account of their respective interests in the Balkan Peninsula. They further promise one another that any new modifications in the territorial status quo of Turkey in Europe can be accomplished only in virtue of a common agreement between them" (Pribram 1967, 1: 39).

Similarly, the second agreement regarding the Balkans, an exchange of notes in 1887, confirmed the current boundaries and sovereignties of Turkey and the Balkan states in four of its first five points:

2. The maintenance of the status quo in the Orient, based on the treaties, to the exclusion of all policy of compensation.

3. The maintenance of the local autonomies established by these same treaties.

4. The independence of Turkey, as guardian of important European interests (independence of the Caliphate, the freedom of the Straits, etc.), of all foreign preponderating influence.

5. Consequently, Turkey can neither cede nor delegate her suzerain rights over Bulgaria to any other Power, nor intervene in order to establish a foreign

administration there, nor tolerate acts of coercion with this latter object, under the form of either of a military occupation or of the dispatch of volunteers. Likewise, Turkey, constituted by the treaties guardian of the Straits, can neither cede any portion of her sovereign rights, nor delegate her authority to any other Power in Asia Minor. (Pribram 1967, 1: 125–127)

The question of The Straits also dominated the last two Balkan treaties. However, the principle of the freedom of The Straits was rejected in both cases in deference to Russian claims. For example, in the Reinsurance Treaty of 1887 (signed six months before the treaty among Austria, England, and Italy) Germany recognized "the rights historically acquired by Russia in the Balkan Peninsula, and particularly the legitimacy of her preponderant and decisive influence in Bulgaria and in Eastern Rumelia," and both countries also agreed "to admit no modification of the territorial status quo without a previous agreement between them" (Pribram 1967, 1: 277). However, Bismarck, in an effort to keep Russia from France, went further in this attempt to buy Russia's friendship, promising Russia rights he knew could never be guaranteed because of the opposition of Great Britain and Austria (Langer 1972, 785): "The two Courts recognize the European and mutually obligatory character of the principle of the closing of the Straits of the Bosphorus [sic] and of the Dardanelles, founded on international law, confirmed by treaties, and summed up in the declaration of the second Plenipotentiary of Russia at the session of July 12 of the Congress of Berlin" (Pribram 1967, 1: 277).

The somewhat contradictory character of these three Balkan agreements may indicate that the process of resolving territorial disputes is at least as important as their actual resolution. Russian claims often conflicted with the claims of Austria and Great Britain, especially concerning The Straits, but these conflicting claims did not result in war as long as all parties were trying to formally resolve the contentious issues. An indication of the importance of this process is manifested in the last agreement concerning the Balkans, the 1897 accord between Austria and Russia.

In this agreement both countries relinquished their ambitions for conquest of the Balkans, and Russia recognized the territorial acquisitions of Austria-Hungary in the Treaty of Berlin (Bosnia, Herzegovina, and so forth). The principle of Albanian independence was also admitted by both states. However, despite relative agreement on the territorial status quo in the Balkans, Russia was unable "to admit of concession" on the principle of freedom of the Straits. An Austrian note attached to the agreement showed that Austria realized that the cause of Russian refusal was "a principle of legitimate security, a principle the recognition of which was accorded us from the outset" (Pribram 1967, 1: 189).

The ability of both states to overcome disagreements over the status of the Straits and still manufacture an agreement lends some credence to the argument that process is at least as important as consequence. In other words, settling territorial claims is most important for bringing about peace between two countries, but, short of that, attempting to resolve disputed territorial claims can be just as necessary.

The turn-of-the-century Mediterranean agreements were generally attempts to resolve claims over disputed colonial rights. The first agreement, between Austria, Italy, and Spain in 1887, began the process of communication among concerned states. The agreement proclaimed that, "for the principal purpose of maintaining there the present status quo, Spain and Italy will keep in communication with one another . . . by conveying to each other all information of a kind to enlighten each other concerning their respective dispositions, as well as those of other Powers" (Pribram 1967, 1: 117). This principle of communication was maintained until the settlements of 1904. These agreements, reached by Great Britain, France, and Spain, recognized British rights to Egypt in exchange for British recognition of French rights to a *zone d'influence* in Morocco. Both treaties detailed accepted actions each country could take concerning their respective colonial interests and provided for the common usage of certain territories—the Suez and the Moroccan ports, mostly (Parry 1978, 195: 198–216, 196: 353–356). The other Mediterranean agreement was a recognition of Portuguese colonial interests by Great Britain in 1899. This relatively obscure treaty is not contained in most treaty compilations but is printed in Gooch (1927, 93–94).

The mid- and late-twentieth-century status quo agreements, the remainder of the territorial-settlement treaties, detail border agreements reached by newly emerging states. For example, Turkey recognized the territorial sovereignty and boundaries of Afghanistan, including the regions of Bokhara and Khiva, in 1921. Similarly, Estonia and Latvia, in an agreement signed at Riga, recognized demarcation lines between the two countries and established a commission to oversee disputed border areas. The agreement was similar to the French peace settlement of 1815 in the amount of detail it contained:

The frontier line between the two Republics shall be traced on the spot by a Mixed Frontier Commission, composed of three members of each Party and shall be shown by them on two maps. . . . The frontier line shall be marked on the spot by visible signs. Independently of this both Parties by mutual agreement or each Party separately may put obstacles to impede the crossing of the frontier all along the line or at some given part thereof, as deemed necessary. (League of Nations 1917: 198–199)

In another form similar to the 1815 French settlement, no provisions were made regarding potential hostilities or the neutrality or friendship of the two contracting states.

Although border agreements generally took place on the dyadic level—the two agreements mentioned above as well as China and Burma in 1960 and Gambia and Senegal in 1965—two African agreements were unique in that they settled boundaries for an entire region. The 1963 OAU Charter was an attempt by member states to consolidate their postcolonial victories. With a highly conservative charter that recognized the principles of member-state equality, sovereignty, and territorial integrity developed in the 1961 accords, the OAU positioned itself as a mediator for conflict resolution and tried to downplay issues of territory. At its outset, the OAU was comprised of relatively weak political coalitions that could not survive an African balkanization; boundaries became less important than effective political control.

The boundaries of the newly independent states were those that had delimited the largest unit of effective colonial administration and thus the largest unit of effective nationalist political organization. These boundaries usually had more juridical and administrative reality than social or economic content, but they sufficed to permit political coalitions to be formed and to allow the leaders of those coalitions to take advantage of the times to negotiate a transfer of sovereignty (Foltz 1991, 348).

This process of accepting the colonial administration's demarcation lines, culminating with the Cairo Conference Agreement in 1964 (not included in the COW dataset), has led to an incredible stability among African boundaries. Believing that "once one border had been changed, clamors would arise for changes everywhere, which would put all states at risk," African states largely traded traditional, tribal regions for the manufactured, colonial boundaries (Foltz 1991, 348–355).

WAR BEHAVIOR AND OTHER CHARACTERISTICS OF THE TERRITORIAL-SETTLEMENT TREATIES

Table 2 examines the effect of territorial settlements on the conditional probability of two different types of war, wars involving one ally and wars involving more than one ally.[5] Leavy (1981) used these two dependent variables to examine the war-proneness of alliance involvement. "War involving an ally" measures whether an alliance is followed within five years (excluding the first three months after alliance formation) by a war involving one or more of the alliance members. "War involving more than one ally" measures whether alliances are followed by wars involving two or more alliance members within the same time frame. The average alliance is followed by war involving at least one of its members 35 percent of the time; it is followed by wars involving more than one of its members less than 15 percent of the time.

For this analysis, an alliance is considered to be war prone if it is followed by a war of each type within five years after the date of inception, excluding the first three months immediately following inception. This time period has been generally accepted (Singer and Small 1966a, 1966b, 1968; Levy 1981), although there has been experimentation with different temporal ranges (Ostrom and Hoole 1979). Only four of the twenty-seven territorial settlements were followed by wars involving an ally within five years after formation. This is an average rate of 15 percent versus an average rate of 39 percent for all other alliances. None of the territorial settlements was followed by wars involving two or more allies within five years, whereas the average war involvement for all other alliances is 17 percent.[6]

Table 6.2.
Conditional Probabilities of
War for Territorial-Settlement Treaties and Other Alliances

	Number of Wars Observed	Number of Counts Expected	Conditional Probability of War	Z^a	pr(Z)
Territorial Settlement Treaties (N = 27)					
War involving an ally	4	(9.60)	0.15	-5.91*	<0.0001
War involving two or more allies	0	(4.10)	0	-5.84*	<0.0001
All Other Alliances (N = 167)					
War involving an ally	64	(58.40)	0.38	0.96	0.1685
War involving two or more allies	29	(24.90)	0.17	0.94	0.1736

* p<0.01
[a] In a method similar to Bremer's (1992, 325–327, Table 1), this table also calculates a difference of proportions test that measures the statistical likelihood of obtaining the given conditional probability. Positive Z scores indicate more war was observed than expected; negative Z scores indicate less war was observed than expected. The pr(Z) value reflects the statistical significance of the Z score.

The very low Z scores for territorial-settlement treaties reflect the pacific nature of these alliances. In each case far fewer war onsets followed these alliances than had been statistically expected. Slightly more wars than were expected followed the other alliances once the control for territorial settlements was used. However, neither of these scores was significant.

Further examination of the four deviant cases—the alliances that were followed by wars involving an ally—sheds even more light on the irenic nature of these settlements. The 1899 settlement between Great Britain and Portugal was followed by the Boxer Rebellion in 1900. The 1904 settlement between France, Spain, and Great Britain was followed by the Spanish-Moroccan war four years and nine months later. The 1927 settlement between the Soviet Union and Persia was followed by the four-month-long Sino-Soviet War of 1929. Lastly, the settlement between China and Burma in 1960 was followed by the one-month-long Sino-Indian War two years later. Each of these cases, with the possible exception of the Spanish-Moroccan War, was followed by wars not clearly related to the members of the alliance, but, because of the way wars involving an ally are measured, the alliances are considered war prone. The Spanish-Moroccan War occurred after the territorial settlement was reached concerning Morocco, but the settlement did pacify the region for almost the entire five-year period. Clearly, as the evidence presented here demonstrates, the territorial-settlement treaty represents a peaceful form of alliance behavior. After controlling for the wars that are actually fought, in only one case was one of these treaties followed by a war involving an ally, and, as stated previously, none of these treaties was followed by a war involving two or more allies.[7]

It is of equal theoretical interest to note that the probability of war does not increase for alliances that do not attempt to resolve territorial disputes (Gibler and Vasquez 1995, 11 and Table 1). The implication here is that resolving territorial issues decreases the chances of war for an alliance, but the probability of war for alliances that do not settle territorial issues is determined by other factors. These other alliances have generally been followed by war, except in the nineteenth century (Levy 1981).

The findings presented here also provide evidence of the debate over why neighbors fight—whether because of territoriality, proximity, or interactions (Vasquez 1995). If neighbors fight because of their proximity to each other or because of the interactions of the two states, the territorial settlements listed here should have little impact on the probability that war will follow an alliance. However, the evidence clearly suggests that resolving territorial issues does decrease the chances of war between dyads, which supports the territorial explanation of war (Vasquez 1993, chap. 4).

Given the dramatic results presented in Table 2, one might speculate that another independent variable is responsible for the pacific nature of these treaties. However, as can be seen from a close examination of the territorial settlements, very few characteristics are shared by these treaties except for their efforts to resolve territorial disputes. The treaties are evenly dispersed throughout both the nineteenth and twentieth centuries (44 percent and 56 percent, respectively) and are formed by and among both major and minor states. These two factors are important because the nineteenth century was generally more peaceful than the twentieth century, even for alliance formation (Singer, Bremer, and Stuckey 1972; Bueno de Mesquita 1981; Levy 1981), and major states are most likely to become involved in wars and serious disputes (Bremer 1980; Eberwein 1982; Gochman and Maoz 1984, 606–609).

More than half of the territorial settlements listed in Table 1 were defensive alliances, but it is unclear why these alliance types would be associated with territorial settlements. Most studies assume that the defensive alliance is one of the most war-prone alliance types (for example, see Levy 1981, 588–589), and there is no theoretical connection between these alliances and territorial issues.

The fact that these settlements are pacifying even the most dangerous types of alliance commitments is further evidence of the unique nature of the territorial treaty. Table 3 ranks the states that join territorial settlements most often; all states that are in more than two treaties are listed.

The Soviet Union and Great Britain are present in more than one-third of the territorial settlements; and Austria, Germany and Turkey are also frequent territorial-settlement members. Because many of the territorial settlements resolve issues related to the Balkans, it is no surprise that these states would rank high on territorial-settlement

TABLE 6.3:
Ranking of States in Territorial Settlements

State	N	%
Russia/USSR	10	37
Great Britain	9	33
Austria	7	26
Prussia/Germany	5	19
Turkey	4	15
China	3	11
France	3	11
Italy	3	11

membership. Nevertheless, it is clear from Table 3 that the territorial settlements are not a product of any specific region or any specific subset of states. Territorial-settlement behavior seems to apply to all regions and all types of states.

ASSESSMENT

In sum, alliances that resolve territorial issues, either through the exchange of territory or through the acceptance of status quo distributions of territory, are rarely followed by war involving alliance members. In fact, in only four instances was one of these treaties followed by a war involving an ally (and only one of the four cases is directly related to the treaty). Removing the highly contentious issue of territory from the agenda of alliance members creates a sustained peace between even the most traditionally belligerent states in the system.

Identifying this one type of peaceful alliance is an important step toward reconceptualizing the alliance variable. Territorial-settlement treaties behave very differently from what realist theories would predict. Instead of trying to balance power in a region or in the system, these alliances exhibit the robust and multifaceted nature of diplomacy, demonstrating that a common practice having the same form— joining an alliance—can have very different motivations.[8] Therefore, it is strongly recommended that researchers remove these alliances from their data analyses—or, at the very least, control for them—if they are investigating the paths to or correlates of war. The presence of these irenic alliances would tend to mute most findings.

Scholars interested in the correlates of peaceful eras, however, should scrutinize these alliances for their implications for building peace. The presence of several peace settlements in these alliances could give indications of the structure of peaceful systems after major wars. Similarly, the border agreements and exchange settlements in the data provide examples of the peaceful resolution of dyadic conflict. In either case, the pacific nature of the territorial-settlement treaties listed here should be further analyzed.

My thanks to Gary Goertz and John Vasquez for their comments on earlier drafts of this chapter. All errors are, of course, my own.

NOTES

1. The Hitler-Stalin nonaggression pact is alliance number 126 in the COW dataset; the Quadruple Alliance is number 2.

2. Most realists would argue that a peaceful alliance is the product of successful deterrence. However, because these alliances target no other states in the system, it is difficult to argue that states involved in these settlements are making deterrence attempts. Instead, states involve themselves in territorial settlements to remove an exceedingly dangerous issue from their agenda and produce peace through conflict resolution rather than power-politics brinkmanship.

3. Not included in this category, or even in the broader category of territorial settlements, are treaties that promise future distributions of territory. Rather than removing issues of territory from the agendas of states, these future distributions of territory would likely only exacerbate territorial disputes, because war has always been one of the principal methods of altering territorial boundaries. The Hitler-Stalin nonaggression pact, with its future stipulations about the division of territory, is the classic example of this alliance type.

4. Austria, Germany, and Russia (1881); Austria, Great Britain, and Italy (1887); Germany and Russia (1887); Austria-Hungary and Russia (1897).

5. Seventeen alliances were excluded from this entire analysis because at least one of their members was at war. The focus of this study is on the onset of war, not its expansion.

6. Multivariate tests have also been performed on these treaties with controls for Singer and Small type, number of alliance members, status of alliance members, and success in previous wars of alliance members. In all cases the findings have remained robust and significant (Gibler and Vasquez 1995).

7. This last finding also means that the territorial-settlement treaty is one of the most reliable alliance types. Because no wars involving two or more alliance members followed these treaties, no wars followed where "friend" became "foe" (Sabrosky 1980; Bueno de Mesquita 1981; Ray 1990).

8. This is another example of a situation in which the "same" indicator can "mean" very different things. Goertz (1994) elaborates on this point and shows the importance of understanding the context from which these indicators are drawn.

REFERENCES

Bremer, Stuart. 1980. "National Capabilities and War Proneness." In *The Correlates of War II: Testing Some Realpolitik Models*, edited by J. David Singer. New York: Free Press.

———. 1992. "Dangerous Dyads: Conditions Affecting the Likelihood of Interstate War, 1816–1965." *Journal of Conflict Resolution* 36: 309–341.

BFS [*British and Foreign State Papers*]. 1812–1954. London: James Ridgway, H. M. Stationery Office.

Bueno de Mesquita, Bruce. 1975. "Measuring Systemic Polarity." *Journal of Conflict Resolution* 19: 77–96.

———. 1978. "Systemic Polarization and the Occurrence and Duration of War." *Journal of Conflict Resolution* 22: 241–267.

———. 1981. *The War Trap*. New Haven, Conn.: Yale University Press.

Bueno de Mesquita, Bruce, and J. David Singer. 1973. "Alliances, Capabilities, and War: A Review and Synthesis." *Political Science Annual* 1973: 237–281.

Diehl, Paul. 1985a. "Arms Races to War: Testing Some Empirical Linkages." *Sociological Quarterly* 26: 331–349.

———. 1985b. "Contiguity and Military Escalation in Major Power Rivalries, 1816–1980." *Journal of Politics* 47: 1203–1211.

Diehl, Paul, and Gary Goertz. 1988. "Territorial Changes and Militarized Conflict." *Journal of Conflict Resolution* 32: 103–122.

Eberwein, Wolf-Dieter. 1982. "The Seduction of Power: Serious International Disputes and the Power Status of Nations, 1900–1976." *International Interactions* 9: 57–74.

Foltz, William. 1991. "The Organization of African Unity." In *Conflict Resolution in Africa*, edited by Francis Deng and I. William Zartman. Washington, D.C.: Brookings Institution.

Gibler, Douglas M. 1997. *Reconceptualizing the Alliance Variable: An Empirical Typology of Alliances*. Ph.D. diss., Vanderbilt University.

Gibler, Douglas M., and John A. Vasquez. 1998 (forthcoming). "Uncovering the Dangerous Alliances, 1495–1980." *International Studies Quarterly* 42.

Gochman, Charles S., and Zeev Maoz. 1984. "Militarized Interstate Disputes, 1816–1976: Procedures, Patterns, and Insights." *Journal of Conflict Resolution* 28: 585–616.

Goertz, Gary. 1994. *Contexts of International Politics*. Cambridge, U.K.: Cambridge University Press.

Goertz, Gary, and Paul Diehl. 1988. "A Territorial History of the International System." *International Interactions* 15: 81–93.

————. 1992. *Territorial Changes and International Conflict*. London: Routledge.

Gooch, G. P., ed. 1927. *British Documents on the Origins of the War, 1898–1914*. London: H. M. Stationery Office.

Kegley, Charles W., Jr. 1994. *A Multipolar Peace? Great-Power Politics in the Twenty-First Century*. New York: St. Martin's.

Langer, William, ed. 1972. *An Encyclopedia of World History*. Boston: Houghton Mifflin.

League of Nations. 1920–1946. *League of Nations Treaty Series*. Geneva.

Levy, Jack. 1981. "Alliance Formation and War Behavior: An Analysis of the Great Powers, 1495–1975." *Journal of Conflict Resolution* 25: 581–613.

————. 1983. *War in the Modern Great Power System, 1495–1975*. Lexington: University Press of Kentucky.

Martens, Fedor F. ed. 1889. *Recueil des principaux traités d'alliance*. Paris.

Midlarsky, Manus. 1983. "Alliance Behavior and the Approach of World War I: The Use of Bivariate Negative Binomial Distributions." In *Conflict Processes and the Breakdown of International Systems*, edited by Dina Zinnes. Denver: University of Denver Monograph Series in World Affairs, no. 20.

————. 1986. "A Hierarchical Equilibrium Theory of Systemic War." *International Studies Quarterly* 30: 77–105.

Moul, William. 1988. "Great Power Nondefense Alliances and the Escalation to War of Conflicts between Unequals, 1815–1939." *International Interactions* 15: 25–43.

Ostrom, Charles W., Jr., and Francis W. Hoole. 1978. "Alliances and War Revisited: A Research Note." *International Studies Quarterly* 22 (June): 215–236.

Parry, Clive. 1978. *The Consolidated Treaty Series*. Dobbs Ferry, N.Y.: Oceana.

Pribram, E. F. 1967. *The Secret Treaties of Austria-Hungary, 1879–1914*. 2 vols. New York: Howard Fertig.

Ray, James Lee. 1990. "Friends as Foes: International Conflict and Wars between Formal Allies." In *Prisoners of War?: Nation-States in the Modern Era*, edited by Charles S. Gochman and Alan Ned Sabrosky. Lexington, Mass.: Lexington Books.

Rohn, Peter. 1983. *World Treaty Index*. Santa Barbara, Calif.: ABC-Clio.

Sabrosky, Alan Ned. 1980. "Interstate Alliances: Their Reliability and the Expansion of War." In *The Correlates of War II: Testing Some Realpolitik Models*, edited by J. David Singer. New York: Free Press.

Schroeder, Paul. 1976. "Alliances, 1815–1945: Weapons of Power and Tools of Management." In *Historical Dimensions of National Security Problems,* edited by Klaus Knorr. Lawrence: University Press of Kansas.

Singer, J. David, and Melvin Small. 1966a. "Formal Alliances, 1815–1939: A Quantitative Description." *Journal of Peace Research* 3: 1–32.

———. 1966b. "National Alliance Commitments and War Involvement, 1815–1945." *Peace Research Society (International) Papers* 5: 404–422.

———. 1968. "Alliance Aggregation and the Onset of War, 1815–1945." In *Quantitative International Politics: Insights and Evidence,* edited by J. David Singer. New York: Free Press: 247–286.

Singer, J. David, Stuart Bremer, and John Stuckey. 1972. "Capability Distribution, Uncertainty, and Major Power War, 1820–1965." In *Peace, War, and Numbers,* edited by Bruce M. Russett. Beverly Hills, Calif.: Sage Publications.

Siverson, Randolph, and Joel King. 1979. "Alliances and the Expansion of War." In *To Augur Well: Early Warning Indicators in World Politics,* edited by J. David Singer and M. Wallace. Beverly Hills, Calif.: Sage Publications.

———. "Attributes of National Alliance Membership and War Participation, 1815–1965." *American Journal of Political Science* 24 (February): 1–15.

Siverson, Randolph, and Harvey Starr. 1990. "Opportunity, Willingness, and the Diffusion of War." *American Political Science Review* 84: 47–67.

Smith, Alastair. 1995. "Alliance Formation and War." *International Studies Quarterly* 39: 405–426.

United States Treaty Series. Washington, D.C.

Vasquez, John. 1993. *The War Puzzle.* Cambridge, U.K.: Cambridge University Press.

———. 1995. "Why Do Neighbors Fight? Territoriality, Proximity, or Interactions." *Journal of Peace Research* 32: 277–293.

Wallace, Michael D. 1973. "Alliance Polarization, Cross-Cutting, and International War, 1815–1964." *Journal of Conflict Resolution* 17: 575–604.

Wallensteen, Peter. 1981. "Incompatibility, Confrontation, and War: Four Models and Three Historical Systems, 1816–1976." *Journal of Peace Research* 18: 57–90.

———. 1984. "Universalism vs. Paricularism: On the Limits of Major Power Order." *Journal of Peace Research* 21, no. 3: 243–257.

Ward, Michael D. 1973. *Research Gaps in Alliance Dynamics.* University of Denver Monograph Series in World Affairs, 19, book 1.

Wayman, Frank. 1984. "Alliances and War: A Time-Series Analysis." In *Prisoners of War? Nation-States in the Modern Era,* edited by Charles S. Gochman and Alan Ned Sabrosky. Lexington, Mass.: Lexington Books: 93–113.

Zaheer, Hasan. 1994. *The Separation of East Pakistan: The Rise and Realization of Bengal: Muslim Nationalism.* Oxford: Oxford University Press.

7

See You in "Court"?
The Appeal to Quasi-Judicial Legal Processes
in the Settlement of Territorial Disputes

Beth Simmons

Acentral theme in much recent international relations scholarship is the growing role of supranational authority in the resolution of disputes among sovereign states. Across a wide range of issues, legally binding forms of third-party dispute settlement have become important in resolving interstate agreements. The evolution of the dispute-settlement procedures embodied in the General Agreement on Tariffs and Trade into the more formal and less discretionary structure of the World Trade Organization has streamlined the legal settlement of a growing volume of trade disputes involving a broad array of complainants and respondents. The 1996 inauguration of the International Maritime Court in Hamburg to handle disputes arising from the United Nations' Law of the Sea provides a forum in which questions of ocean management, fisheries, pollution control, sea bed mining, shipping lanes, and maritime territorial disputes may be resolved through legally binding processes (Clark 1996). Regionally, the European Court of Justice has acted, within limits but to an astonishing degree, to expand supranational authority over member states (Burley and Mattli 1993). There is even growing enthusiasm for the use of the once virtually moribund International Court of Justice (ICJ): during the cold war, the court decided only one contentious case a year, on average; in 1995, however, it had a record number of thirteen cases before it, and attention turned to the problem of overload rather than underutilization (Boutros-Ghali 1995). Nor is the appeal to supranational authority limited to the arena of "low politics." Countries as diverse as Eritrea and Yemen, Qatar and Bahrain, and Malaysia and Indonesia have recently made a commitment or expressed an interest in territorial arbitration or adjudication.[1] Whether looking to the positive example of Chad and Libya's use of the ICJ to settle their territorial dispute or the disastrous example of Iraq's unilateralism regarding Kuwaiti territory, willingness to consider a legal commitment to review by a judicial or quasi-judicial body seems to be growing.

This chapter examines the role of international legal approaches to the settlement of territorial disputes. What are the conditions that make resort to negotiations inadequate for the settlement of a territorial dispute? Why do governments make legal commitments that bind their future behavior with respect to how a territorial agreement is to be resolved? That is, what conditions make a formal legal commitment to arbitrate a dispute an attractive alternative? And, finally, why do states sometimes actually go through with such commitments to submit to third-party review of their territorial claims?

Motivating this study is the question of the role that international quasi-judicial processes can play in the resolution of territorial disputes among states. Previous research suggests that international law may play an important role in reducing the incidence of territorial disputes. Paul Huth (1996), for example, has found that clear legal agreements reduce the probability that a dispute will arise in the first place. By his estimate, some 142 border agreements were concluded between 1816 and 1990, and 126 of these were still in force and honored by both states in 1995 (Huth 1996, 92; see also Kocs 1995). If supranational authoritative rulings contribute to such agreements, then there are good reasons to expect them to make a positive contribution to settling the dispute peacefully.

However, in much mainline theorizing in international relations, states are viewed as making commitments—especially formal, legal commitments—either cautiously or cynically and are overwhelmingly reluctant to delegate decision making to supranational bodies of any kind.[2] Dominant international relations paradigms have not to date provided clear hypotheses about why states choose to make legally binding agreements and why they sometimes go even farther and choose to renounce their sovereign right to be the sole judge of what constitutes acceptable behavior.

In the first section of this chapter I review three strands of international relations theory and cull from them expectations regarding the role that international legal commitments play in resolving territorial disputes. Next I describe the scope of my empirical analysis and the methods I used to evaluate the data on territorial disputes in Latin America. Third, I present findings that link domestic political conditions with difficulties in resolving disputes, that link previous ratification difficulties with the commitment to third-party arbitration, and that suggest that a commitment to arbitrate significantly raises the probability of actually concluding the quasi-judicial procedure leading to a binding decision. In the final section I conclude that international law and institutions can be, and probably have been, used strategically by states with domestic political conditions that prevent resolution of potentially costly international disputes.

INTERNATIONAL RELATIONS THEORY AND THE ROLE OF LAW IN SETTLING TERRITORIAL DISPUTES

The role of international legal processes has hardly been central to the study of international relations in general, and it certainly has been a minor avenue of inquiry with respect to such crucial national interests as territory. This is due in part to the dominance of realist thought that emphasizes power, rather than law, as the major influence on interstate disputes. Most realists—theoreticians and practitioners—tend to be highly skeptical that law influences state actions in any important way (Boyle 1980; Bork 1989–1990). Even though Hans Morgenthau (1985, 295) was ready to admit that "during the four hundred years of its existence international law ha[d] in most instances been scrupulously observed," he concluded that this could be attributed either to convergent interests or prevailing power relations. Governments, he thought, make legal commitments cynically and "are always anxious to shake off the restraining influence that international law might have upon their foreign policies, to use international law instead for the promotion of their national interests" (Morgenthau 1985).[3] As Stanley Hoffmann has written (1956, 364), the national state is "a legally sovereign unit in a tenuous net of breakable obligations." Raymond Aron (1981) put it succinctly: "International law can merely ratify the fate of arms and the arbitration of force."

For realists, the essential flaw in international law is its decentralization. Because the decisions of third parties are highly unlikely to be enforced, states have little incentive to turn to quasi-judicial processes—and little reason to comply. Why an international dispute ought ever be referred to a third party is virtually inexplicable in realist terms; any controversies that are submitted to third-party rulings are likely to be those in which the stakes are very low. Thus, Aron and other realists were prepared to admit that "the domain of legalized interstate relations is increasingly large" but argued that "one does not judge international law by peaceful periods and secondary problems" (Aron 1981, 733). Furthermore, major powers are highly unlikely to use supranational legal processes, for they are typically well equipped to use other forms of unilateral persuasion (Bilder 1989, 478). Since territorial disputes have historically contributed to violent interstate conflict (Goertz and Diehl 1992; Vasquez 1993; Kocs 1995; Huth 1996) and continue to be one of the primary causes of the kinds of regional instability that has manifested itself in the post–cold war period (Kolodziej and Kanet 1996, 9–11), one might expect realist approaches to explaining their resolution to be highly persuasive.

A different set of expectations is suggested by a more functional approach to the study of international institutions. Most basically, functionalists view international agreements as a way to address a perceived need: international legal agreements are made because states want to solve common problems that they have difficulties solving any other way, for example, unilaterally or through political means alone (Bilder 1989, 492). Rational functionalists share realists' concern with the incentives states face to make or break international agreements, but rather than starting from the assumption that states cynically manipulate their legal environment, they engineer it in what are taken to be generally sincere efforts to address an otherwise suboptimal outcome. Both realism and rational functionalism are interest-driven approaches in which incentives play a crucial role.[4] The latter has, however, been far more willing to view the particular agreements and even the international legal system in toto as a collective good, from which states collectively can benefit, but to which none wants to contribute disproportionately and by which none wants to consistently be disadvantaged. The focus of analysis in this approach has been on the perceived benefits of a system of rule-based behavior and on the individual incentives states face to contribute to, or detract from, such a system. Because they are often crucial to arriving at solutions, agreements are taken seriously. In the absence of severe, unresolved, collective-action problems or overwhelming incentives to defect that have not been addressed, obligations are therefore likely to be met.

Rational functionalism and traditional realism look on territorial settlements from somewhat different perspectives. Realists often model the dispute as one over resources—whether tangible or intangible—the division of which is viewed by states as zero-sum and crucial to their national interests—hence potentially worth a violent confrontation. Rational functionalism is more likely to view a territorial settlement as itself a valuable international institution. No doubt agreement on such an institution involves distributional issues, but it also involves joint gains that accrue to both parties. The expected size of these joint gains is an important variable to be weighed in the decision of how to settle the dispute. Jurisdictional certainty, for example, especially when accepted within a framework of a well-defined and mutually accepted rule of law, is something polities are likely to value very highly. In the absence of such institutions, states pay a high opportunity cost—lost trade, investment, social-development costs due to high military expenditures—which increase the anticipated value of settlement.

The starting point for functionalist explanations of international agreements relates to the incapacity of states to solve a problem without the institutional device. Like realists, most functionalist approaches to international politics begin with the premise that states delegate sovereignty begrudgingly. Certainly, there is a strong preference for resolving international controversies through political means, even unilaterally if necessary. However, functional theories recognize that, for a number of reasons, this may not be possible. Most functional theorizing has been systemic, focusing largely on international market failure and on problems of collective action (Keohane 1984). Relatively little attention has been given to the domestic political reasons why international cooperation may not be possible in the absence of an international institution, but increasingly researchers recognize that domestic institutions can at times be a barrier to the realization of outcomes that might benefit society as a whole: preference outliers can capture domestic institutions and thus hold policies hostage to their demands; well-organized interests can exert particularistic influences on policy, decreasing overall welfare; decision makers can have time-inconsistent preferences that cause them to pursue short-term interests at the expense of longer-term gains; political polarization can lead to suboptimal outcomes or decisional paralysis at the domestic level. Clearly, in principle, the source of the suboptimality in functional theory can be domestic or systemic in nature.

International legal processes, to the extent that they are effective in this literature, may operate through a number of mechanisms that affect a government's willingness to comply. Unlike realist theory, however, centralized enforcement is rarely one of these mechanisms. Rather, the reason states make and then keep agreements is related to reputation: because states anticipate that they will pay a higher cost in the long run for breaking commitments, they are reluctant to do so (Schachter 1991, 7). To enhance the reputational consequences of noncompliant behavior, international agreements often provide mechanisms that increase transparency and therefore improve information regarding other states' behavior (Keohane 1984; Milgrom, North, and Weingast 1990; Mitchell 1994).

The rational functionalist literature suggests that international legal institutions potentially play a crucial role in the settlement of contentious interstate issues. One way they do this is by providing a clear focal point for acceptable behavior (Garrett and Weingast 1993). Some scholars point out that such focal points can actually gain a high degree of legitimacy both internationally and domestically (Franck 1990; Peck 1996, 237). This legitimacy, in turn, has important political consequences (Claude 1966, 367). For example, those who have examined bargaining in the context of legal-dispute settlement have argued that concessions tend to be easier to make, from a domestic political point of view, when they are legally required by an authoritative third party (Merrills 1969; Fischer 1982).[5] Overall, explicit international agreements make it more costly to renege on a commitment than would be the case in their absence. In this formulation, the search for a legitimate rule is a rational response to the need to find a stable solution to a problem or dispute that otherwise is difficult to resolve.

Another approach that has recently received some attention in the study of interstate disputes and more recently in legal circles may be termed "democratic legalism."[6] In this formulation, regime type is crucial to understanding the role of law in interstate relations (Slaughter 1995). Applied to the central questions of my analysis, this approach would hold that liberal democracies are more likely to comply with international legal obligations, and two lines of reasoning are advanced to sustain this argument. One suggests that because liberal democratic regimes share an affinity with prevalent international legal processes and institutions, they tend to be more willing to depend on the rule of law for their external affairs. The argument depends on the notion that norms regarding limited government, respect for judicial processes, and regard for constitutional constraints carry over into the realm of international politics. One way to think about this affinity argument is that governments in search of solutions to particular disputes are boundedly rational. As such they tend to search the domain of available mechanisms and processes not randomly but as conditioned by their domestic legal and constitutional experience. Thus, countries with independent judiciaries are more likely to trust and respect international judicial processes than are those that have no domestic experience with such institutions. Political leaders who are accustomed to respecting constitutional constraints on their power in a domestic context are more likely to accept principled legal limits on their international behavior.[7] These arguments dovetail nicely with a growing agenda in political science which argues that liberal democracies are more likely than are other regime types to revere law, promote compromise, and respect processes of adjudication (Doyle 1986; Raymond 1994; Dixon 1993).

A second, distinct mechanism has also been used to back expectations of the importance of democracy for legal approaches to dispute settlement. This rests on the observation that leaders in liberal democracies may be constrained by the influence that international legal obligations have on domestic groups, who are likely to cite such obligations in order to influence their own government's policy. In one version of this argument, the mechanism through which democratic constraints come into play is through domestic interest groups, which may have an interest in or preference for settling a dispute or abiding by a particular agreement (Young 1979; Schachter 1991, 7). In another rendition, the effect of international law works through the separation of powers, most especially through an independent judiciary but also through the legislative branch (Forsythe 1990). The weight of an international obligation or authoritative legal forum may be crucial in convincing various domestic audiences to oppose a government's policy of continued disputation, especially in the face of a clear rule or authoritative decision (Fisher 1981, 134). There is an affinity between this line of argument and various strands of functional reasoning that view international institutions as crucial in influencing the domestic political debate surrounding a controversial foreign-policy choice. The distinctive contribution of democratic legalism is its expectation of systematic differences between liberal democracies and nondemocracies in this regard: domestic political constraints encouraging law-abiding behavior are assumed to be much stronger in the former than the latter. For these reasons, more democratic countries are expected to be more willing to turn to legal processes to settle disputes and to comply more readily with these decisions once they are made.

These theoretical orientations provide varying expectations with regard to key variables for understanding the desire that states may or may not have to go the quasi-judicial route to settlement of their territorial disputes. Realism expects large states, presumably in possession of a broad array of political resources, to pursue their interests, especially important national interests, through political rather than legal procedures. Rational functionalism would associate the use of legal approaches with expected benefits that cannot be achieved through political negotiations alone; the greater these perceived benefits and the more difficult they are to achieve through negotiations, the more incentives governments face to turn to legal institutions for their resolution. Finally, democratic legalism posits a greater willingness on the part of democratic regimes to submit their disputes to legal processes. The domestic commitment to the rule of law is expected to have implications for the willingness of governments to accept limitations on their international political behavior.

SCOPE AND METHODS

In the remainder of this chapter I assess several hypotheses suggested by these three theoretical orientations regarding why states make legally binding commitments and the conditions under which they turn to third parties to help settle their territorial disputes through quasi-judicial means. Arbitration and adjudication are both considered here as examples of such quasi-judicial procedures. Although important differences exist between the two legal procedures, these differences do not seem severe enough to exclude one at the expense of reducing the sample. Not surprisingly, arbitration is much preferred to adjudication, because the former allows specific ground rules to be spelled out in detail by the parties themselves, including the identity of the arbitrators and the boundaries of the issues to be decided, in a "compromis" prior to the procedures. Adjudication, on the other hand, invokes an existing legal framework and institution.[8] It is hardly surprising that states have more frequently chosen a form of third-party decision making over which they have more control. However, the result in each case is a legally binding ruling, carrying similar obligations with respect to subsequent behavior. Given my concern regarding the acceptance of authoritative supranational authority, combining these forms of legal ruling is justified.

The cases presented here are limited to Latin America (Central and South America).[9] This region provides an interesting opportunity to study legal processes with respect to territorial issues. Over the course of their independent histories (dating back in most cases at least to the 1830s), most, though by no means all, borders in this region have been contested, though to varying degrees, for widely varying periods and with differing propensities for the use of violence. Importantly for my project, the region provides a range of attempts to use legal solutions to address territorial issues. A number of multilateral agreements commit the Latin American countries to the peaceful resolution of their disputes, including territorial disputes, and these provide an opportunity to examine whether such agreements have figured significantly in actual territorial settlements. Third-party involvement has featured a range of personalities and organizations, from high representatives of the United States, to the Pope; from the Organization of American States to the United Nations, and from the short-lived Central American Court of Justice to today's ICJ. Indeed, one of the most interesting aspects of territorial-dispute resolution in this region is the unusual propensity of independent countries to submit to authoritative third-party legal rulings. With one small exception,[10] there has never been a legally constituted third- party ruling on a land border in continental Europe, there have been two between independent countries in Africa, two in the Middle East, three in Asia, the Far East and the Pacific, and twenty in Latin America! In fact, one country, Honduras, has sought third-party legal rulings four times on all three of its international borders, twice turning to the ICJ (regarding the border with Nicaragua in 1960 and with El Salvador in 1992).

On the other hand, restricting cases to Latin America does introduce some limitations into the analysis. First, our measure of liberal democracy is more compressed than would be ideal given my interest in testing the relationship between liberal democratic regimes and the propensity to use legal solutions to territorial conflicts. Furthermore, the linguistic, religious, and, to a lesser extent, ethnic homogeneity of the region limit somewhat the ability to control for ethnic or cultural variables sometimes featured in other studies. Overall, however, this is one region in which there is a rich variance on many of the variables of substantive interest to this study, even though one should remain cautious about generalizing to other regions.

It is well known that the study of legal approaches to dispute resolution raises severe selection-bias issues that are not easily dealt with (Downs, Rocke, and Barsoom 1996). To try to ameliorate this problem, my analysis includes control cases involving no disputes as well as disputed borders; cases in which a third-party ruling was rendered in addition to cases in which one was not; and cases of compliance as well as cases of noncompliance (see Appendix 1 for the list of cases). The control cases were generated by including all cases of shared borders within the region regardless of whether adjacent territory was ever the subject of dispute. One reason for including the control cases is to test the possibility that cases in which the parties turned to legal procedures are not significantly different from the cases of no conflict. If ruled cases look a great deal like no-dispute cases, then it would be fair to maintain that third-party involvement is marginal in its effect; the door would then be open for skeptics to argue that the dispute likely would have been solved anyway.

In fact, territorial disputes do differ systematically from cases of shared borders that are never disputed: disputed cases tend to involve countries that are much more evenly matched by several measures of military capabilities than do cases of no dispute. A simple difference of means test indicates that the nondisputed control cases had much higher ratios (more powerful: less powerful) for various measures of capabilities than did the disputed border cases.[11] Perhaps such asymmetries deter disputes, as smaller countries readily concede territory to larger ones. Thus, in examining only cases of disputes, we are likely to be dealing with cases that are more evenly matched in terms of military capabilities than would be a random sample of all borders. The differences are far less significant, however, between cases that were disputed but not ruled on and those in which authoritative rulings were made. In short, whenever we look at border disputes, we are probably excluding the most extreme cases of power differences between the countries involved. Because of the bias introduced by dealing with somewhat more evenly matched (disputing) cases, we should expect power asymmetry to have a much smaller impact on the decision to seek legal solutions to territorial disputes. This does not mean that power does not matter in the decision to employ legal approaches, for it has systematically shaped the pool of disputes under investigation.

For this reason, tests have been conducted on the entire set of cases (including controls), as well as on specified subsets. Results are reported only where these differ substantially. The results presented below were obtained using logistic regression analysis, with each border pair as a case.

FINDINGS

Realist theory does not offer a good explanation for the decision by states to commit themselves to use authoritative third parties to render an arbitral award regarding territory. To the extent that some explanation must be found within the realist paradigm, however, third-party arbitration is likely to take place only over matters that do not involve a vital national interest. The more significant the matter at stake for a state's power, the less likely is the decision to be made to cede sovereign control over the right to self-judge. Functionalism, on the other hand, would suggest that states commit themselves to arbitration whenever what is perceived as a potentially valuable solution eludes a more unilateral or explicitly political approach. The use of quasi-judicial processes can be seen as a substitute for a state's ability to settle a dispute or solve a problem through negotiation. If the basic functional logic holds, states with low political capacity tend to commit themselves to use third parties resolve the conflict. Finally, democratic legalism would predict that democratic regimes are more willing to submit to the rule of law and thus are more trusting of a neutral third party and quasi-judicial procedures at the international level.

Table 1 presents some evidence to consider in addressing these hypotheses (see Appendix 2 for definitions and for sources of the dependent and explanatory variables). The dependent variable is a dichotomous indicator of whether the country pair has agreed to a bilateral arbitration agreement regarding the particular territorial claim in question. Here I use "ratification failure"—the number of times a signed border treaty failed to be ratified in one or both of the signatory countries—as an indicator of lack of domestic political capacity for purposes of testing a domestically based functionalist argument. The functionalist argument suggests that where governments have been unable historically to secure domestic ratification on a desired agreement, they are more likely to commit the country to accept arbitration to legitimate an international settlement. I also include a measure of border length as an imperfect measure of the importance the two countries are likely to attach to any given border settlement. From a functional point of view, if settled borders are highly valued international institutions, a long shared border—such as that between Chile and Argentina, for example—is especially important for the establishment of jurisdictional certainty. In this case, a functionalist argument might suggest that the longer the border the greater the benefit of having a legal framework for its definitive settlement.

Whether the pair of countries concerned was more or less democratic was used to test democratic legalism, with the expectation that democratic pairs would be more likely to commit themselves to have the dispute arbitrated. "Past violence" and "resources"[12] are used indicators of the importance the countries attach to the territory for purposes of testing the realist hypothesis. The idea behind the former indicator is that where countries have been willing to use violence to press their claims, one can infer that the claim itself is likely to be of greater national significance than in cases where violence has never been used. As a result, realists might expect a negative correlation between the past use of force and the willingness to agree to arbitration. Alternatively, a positive correlation could be interpreted to suggest that unsuccessful settlement through the use of violence increases the attractiveness of legal solutions as a last resort.[13] I also include the ratio of military personnel as a test of the argument that the more powerful nations do not commit themselves to arbitration, as most realist theorists would anticipate.

The clearest finding is that a history of ratification failures is associated with a higher probability that governments agree to treaties that commit the state to arbitration. Where a history of ratification failure is present, the likelihood of an arbitration treaty increases. According to Model 1, which focuses on disputed cases only,[14] ratification failure increased the predicted probability of a commitment to arbitrate by nearly 57 percent when border length was constrained to be short and all other variables were held at their means. These results suggest that unsuccessful efforts to solve the problem diplomatically are associated with a commitment to let a third party arbitrate

Table 7.1
Commitment to Arbitrate

Dependent variable: Presence of a bilateral arbitration treaty
Results of logistic regression analysis[a]
Coefficients (standard errors)

	Model 1 Disputed Cases:	Model 2 Disputed Cases:
Constant	-0.472 (1.534)	2.589 (4.681)
Ratification failure	2.881[c] (1.482)	3.603[b] (2.204)
Democratic pair	--	0.433 (2.468)
Past violence	--	-0.858 (1.545)
Resources	--	-0.538 (1.544)
Ratio of military personnel	-0.082 (0.106)	-0.158 (0.236)
Border length	10.359 (52.981)	11.778 (80.96)
# of observations	32	30
Chi squared	16.57[d]	15.87[d]
-2 log-likelihood	17.05	11.17
% of cases correctly predicted	90.6	93.3

[a] All significance levels based on one-tailed tests.
[b] $p < 0.10$; [c] $p < 0.05$; [d] $p < 0.01$

or adjudicate the border between states. This supports a functionalist argument that the inability to reach a mutual agreement that both domestic publics can accept is a reason to commit to arbitration.

There was virtually no support for the realist hypotheses or for democratic legalism in the analysis (Model 2). In this sample, the presence of a democratic pair did not significantly affect the probability of making an arbitration commitment, though the sample range is quite truncated due the region and time period. Surprisingly, there was no support for the realist hypothesis, that only in "unimportant" cases do states agree to arbitrate. We would have expected a strong negative effect for past violence and resources were this true. Neither past violence—presumably a subjective indicator of how important the territory is for the countries in question—nor extent of natural resources in the region—a somewhat more objective indicator of the intrinsic significance of the territory—increased the probability that border pairs would make an arbitration commitment. There is no evidence that high stakes strip states' desire to commit to arbitration.

It is possible, however, that ratification failure is endogenous to regime type, thus masking the effects of democratic regimes. It could be the case that ratification difficulties are associated with democracy—a statistical collinearity problem—which then indirectly accounts for the arbitration commitment. This does not appear to be the case. Table 2 suggests that, whether analyzing all cases or disputed cases only, if anything, the more democratic countries were associated with a lower probability of ratification failures. Although this seems counterintuitive at first, this relationship is not difficult to understand. After all, representatives of democratic states are expected to be sophisticated negotiators: they will only negotiate in the range of agreements that they know can be accepted by their domestic constituency. Nondemocratic representatives, on the other hand, face weaker peremptory constraints. They may take actions that are out of touch or even illegitimate by whatever body is involved in the ratification process. One interpretation of the finding that less democratic countries are associated with more ratification failures could be that they lack legitimacy in their international negotiations, once again supporting the notion that functionalist reasons exist for entering into arbitration agreements, especially for less democratic states.

Two other interesting results appear in Table 2. The first is that border length had a significant impact on the probability of ratification failure: countries sharing short borders were about 59 percent more likely to experience ratification failure than were those with long borders, according to Model 2. Furthermore, the greater the asymmetry in military capabilities, the less likely was ratification failure, most obviously in Model 1, in which these asymmetries are much greater. (The effects of such asymmetries are diluted when looking at disputed cases only.) Once again, there is evidence that the more evenly matched the countries, the more common were domestic ratification difficulties, which in turn was associated with the tendency to commit to arbitration. Weaker states may have little choice but to ratify agreements in the face of a stronger opponent, while stronger states have probably designed these agreements to suit their own interests. Both of these effects would explain why power asymmetries improve the probability of ratification.[15]

Table 7.2:
Ratification Failure

Dependent variable: Whether a boundary treaty has failed to be ratified in one or both
  countries
Results of logistic regression analysis[a]
Coefficients (standard errors)

	Model 1 All Cases:	Model 2: Disputed Cases:
Constant	2.295[b] (1.356)	3.761 (2.382)
Democracy country 1	0.529 (0.449)	0.281 (0.551)
Democracy country 2	-.837[c] (0.426)	-.782[b] (0.471)
Border length	-1.869[c] (0.943)	-3.028[c] (.1.218)
Ratio of military personnel	-0.178[c] (0.098)	-0.250 (0.163)
# of observations	37	33
Chi squared	18.90[d]	20.14[d]
-2 Log-likelihood	31.71	24.11
% of cases correctly predicted	81.1	87.9

[a] All significance levels based on one-tailed tests.
[b] $p < 0.10$; [c] $p < 0.05$; [d] $p < 0.01$

Overall, the evidence seems to suggest that the major influence on the probability of making an arbitration commitment is the inability to secure domestic ratification. Interestingly, the evidence is somewhat stronger that nondemocratic regimes are more likely to run into ratification difficulties than are democracies, which quite possibly are more likely to be able to anticipate the feasible set of border solutions that will garner support at home. In the background conditioning all these effects is the influence of power symmetry, which contributed to the willingness to commit to arbitration and contributes to domestic ratification failure. More equal states in search of a border solution would therefore seem most likely to break their political-military impasse by reaching for legal solutions to an otherwise intractable and potentially costly border dispute.

What is the significance of an arbitration treaty? Does it really represent a commitment to arbitrate? Realists do not spend their time coding the existence of arbitration treaties, because their approach to international politics would predict very little explanatory value added by looking at such commitments as distinct from interests. Such promises may be made for tactical reasons that have little to do with the genuine desire to fulfill the promise. Certainly, powerful states are not likely to go through legal channels to resolve their border disputes. Functionalist logic suggests that the expected benefits explain the agreement; there is therefore every reason to believe that, in the absence of a severe collective-action problem or drastically changed circumstances, that *pacta sunt servanda*. Like the utilitarian explanation for keeping one's promises, functionalist explanations provide clear reasons for treaties to be observed. Democratic legalism, on the other hand, probably would not deny that such treaties are a good predictor of the actual decision to arbitrate but would tend to emphasize that democracies are more likely than nondemocracies to agree to go through with arbitration.

Table 3 presents some evidence that may help sort out these contending claims. The dependent variable here is whether the border or any portion of it had actually been the subject of an international arbitral or adjudicative ruling. The clearest relationship seems once again to support a functionalist approach: the existence of bilateral arbitration treaties is a good predictor of the completion of the arbitration process—that is, that there will actually be a ruling. States commit themselves to a process for settlement; their behavior reflects this commitment. In fact, holding all other variables at their mean and varying the value of an ad hoc arbitration agreement from none to one increased the probability of completing a arbitration procedure from 41 percent to 72 percent where the democratic pair was 0 and from 16 percent to 41 percent where the democratic pair was 1 (Model 3).

Some very interesting patterns emerge with respect to the kinds of commitments that lead to an actual arbitration. In the first place, general multilateral treaties were inversely associated with achieving a ruling. When all other variables are held constant at their means,

Table 7.3:
The Decision to Arbitrate

Dependent variable: Whether a third-party ruling has been made in each case
Results of logistic regression analysis
Coefficients (standard errors)

	Model 1 All Cases:	Model 2: Disputed Cases:	Model 3: Disputed Cases:
Constant	-1.403[b] (0.593)	-0.536 (0.774)	-0.075 (0.749)
Ad hoc Arbitration treaty	1.650[c] (0.694)	1.442[c] (0.651)	1.334[c] (0.636)
Territorial/bilateral treaty	0.499 (0.319)	0.414 (0.327)	0.339 (0.315)
General multilateral treaty	-1.661[c] (0.801)	-1.700[c] (0.800)	-1.768[c] (0.770)
Ratio of military personnel	--	-0.015 (0.040)	--
Democratic pair	--	--	-1.282 (1.084)
# of observations	43	38	36
Chi squared	18.61[d]	13.87[d]	13.65[d]
-2 log-likelihood	40.98	38.38	35.2
% of cases correctly predicted	79.1	68.4	72.2

[a] All significance levels based on one-tailed tests.
[b] $p < 0.10$; [c] $p < 0.05$; [d] $p < 0.01$

having signed a general multilateral agreement to arbitrate any matter with any other signatory reduced the actual probability of doing so
from 81 percent to 43 percent where the democratic pair was 0 and
from 55 percent to 17 percent where the democratic pair was 1. This
suggests that general commitments may be of limited usefulness for
solving specific problems. Invoking the functional mechanism for
compliance, the breaking of more general commitments may carry
fewer negative reputational consequences than the breaking of more
specific commitments. Or perhaps it is easier to make clever legal arguments as to why the general commitment does not cover the specific case, providing a technical excuse for its nonexecution. In fact,
there may be some tendency for "sincere" states to make specific
commitments, while more "cynical" states may be more likely to
sign grand pronouncements to which they have no intention of being
held: there was a moderate negative correlation (−.38) between the
signing of an ad hoc arbitration commitment and a general multilateral arbitration treaty. In any event, grand pronouncements to take
any dispute involving any signatory that cannot be solved through negotiation to a third party for arbitration was associated with a dimin-
ished probability of actually doing so.

On the other hand, bilateral and especially ad hoc agreements to
arbitrate showed a strong positive correlation with actually reaching
a ruling. The more specific the commitment, the more likely it was to
be carried out. Certainly this is partially due to the fact that commitments are endogenous to political considerations: states that are serious about settling disputes draw up more explicit commitments to do
so.[16] Here I have distinguished two levels of specificity with respect to
bilateral commitments: where agreements were drawn up to arbitrate
a specific dispute—ad hoc arbitration agreements—the effects were
consistently strong and positive. Note, however, that it is not automatic: for example, a 1904 boundary-arbitration convention coded as
"ad hoc" naming the emperor of Germany or Mexico as arbitrator was
agreed between Colombia and Ecuador but was never carried out.) In
the presence of general bilateral treaties, or boundary treaties with
specific arbitration provisions to address dispute settlement should a
dispute arise, an actual ruling is likely, though the relationship is not
as strong as with ad hoc agreements.

Contrary to the expectation of democratic legalism, the degree of
democracy did not have much impact. Regime type (whether the pair

of countries involved is relatively democratic) is not associated with arbitration using these data (Model 3). Furthermore, none of the realist hypotheses had any explanatory power: asymmetrical power did not contribute to whether a case would be arbitrated (Model 2); nor did past violence or extent of natural resources (not reported here).

What this analysis does not tell us, of course, is exactly why states in some cases committed themselves to arbitration but have failed to follow through. Governments may resist following through with arbitral commitments for a number of reasons. One may be that the commitment was made cynically, in order to gain some other political or diplomatic advantage without serious consideration given to following through. A less sinister reason may be that committing to the prospect of international arbitration caused the parties to redouble efforts to settle diplomatically, in which case the dispute may have been resolved, or "settled out of court," without the rendering of a ruling. A third possibility is rather more technical: the parties may not have been able to agree on the parameters of the question to be decided by the arbitrator, the entity named in the agreement may have refused to perform the task, or there may be disagreement over whether conditions actually trigger applicability of the agreement at all. For a number of reasons, one can hardly expect a perfect correlation between a prior commitment to arbitrate and the rendering of an actual ruling. Nevertheless, the patterns that do emerge support the power of specific agreements to shape outcomes much more convincingly than do more traditional realist expectations or regime characteristics.

Still, there are a number of reasons for caution in drawing sweeping conclusion from this analysis. The number of cases is relatively small. The analysis has been limited to Latin America, which imposes certain limitations on their generalizability. In particular, so few cases of liberal democracy—by present-day European standards—are to be found in this sample that a fair test of democratic legalism may not be possible. The relative linguistic, religious, and ethnic homogeneity of the region—variables that are certain to influence the course of such disputes in the former Soviet Union, for example—does not permit serious testing of these kinds of variables in influencing territorial disputes. Despite a number of acknowledged limitations, my findings carry some important implications for thinking about the role of international legal processes in the settlement of territorial disputes. The picture that emerges suggests that more evenly matched, less democratic governments find it difficult to negotiate international boundary agreements that can be accepted at home. This kind of domestic political incapacity—reflected here as ratification failures—is associated with the negotiation of arbitration treaties, which, with the exception of general multilateral commitments, are a good predictor that the case will in fact go to court. States—especially nondemocratic ones that suffer from an incapacity to reach and ratify their own bilateral agreements—are likely to make and fulfill commitments to use arbitration to settle their boundary disputes.

DISCUSSION AND CONCLUSIONS

The primary message of this chapter has been that although governments have a broad range of nonviolent options for settling their territorial disputes, judicial or arbitral settings are especially useful for those governments wishing to settle disagreements but needing an international institution that raises the stakes to settle—possibly through reputational effects, as functional theory suggests—and lends legitimacy to a particular territorial arrangement. One of the most interesting findings is that governments—not necessarily the most democratic ones—that seem unable to secure domestic ratification of international territorial agreements choose to commit themselves to specific forms of dispute settlement in the future: specific agreements to submit the dispute to a legally constituted third party with the authority to make a binding legal decision about the appropriate border arrangement. Furthermore, the evidence suggests that making such an arbitration commitment greatly increases the probability that the governments in question will in fact go through with the process and that a ruling will be rendered.

The picture supports functional arguments most readily: where extreme power asymmetries have not deterred a dispute in the first place, states are willing to commit to processes of third-party review—to agree to submit to supranational legal authority—because they wish to solve disputes that have eluded unilateral or bilateral political resolution (Bilder 1989, 492). The reason appears to be closely tied to the inability to negotiate an international agreement that can be ratified at home. Ironically, the less democratic governments—perhaps less attuned to the nature of probable domestic opposition to the content of their international negotiations—seem to face ratification problems more often than do more democratic regimes. Once a bilateral arbitration commitment is made, this was the strongest correlate for actually obtaining a ruling—evidence that the commitment is meaningful for action.

These findings have broader implications for the way in which we think about borders and territorial disputes in general. In much of the conflict-resolution literature, the prevailing assumption has been that territorial conflicts can be analyzed exclusively in terms of distributional issues. Often, empirical models has analyzed the divisibility resources (tangible or intangible), for example, as a major contributor to territorial conflict and difficulties in settlement. But this research has underlined another aspect of territorial settlement: agreed-on international borders are valuable international institutions that provide certainty, reduce the need for high military expenditures, encourage welfare-improving investment and trade, and reduce opportunity costs that cut into social development in the affected regions. There are good reasons to make such institutions explicit and legal, for when this happens, research indicates, violence subsides (Huth 1996), and opportunities for mutually beneficial economic and diplomatic interaction open up. Nonetheless, the functional literature suggests that there are a number of reasons why valuable international institutions are difficult to arrange through bilateral political means alone. In this chapter I have focused on domestic incapacities, which further research may reveal to be associated with nationalistic preference outliers that have been able to capture the ratification process in some political systems. It suggests not only that more attention be paid to domestic political conditions but also that more weight be given to an interpretation of borders that views them as mutually beneficial institutions rather than as strictly zero-sum distributional conflicts.

The importance of legal approaches to the settlement of territorial conflicts, in this conception, lies in the role that binding legal decisions are expected to play in influencing domestic political forces to accept a particular legally binding ruling. To commit to arbitrate is to stake the government's, and by extension, the country's, reputation on following through. Though not explored here, reputational consequences may be even greater in the decision about whether to comply with such a decision. This is because "Once a court has resolved a dispute and decided what ought to happen, the compliance objective of the community is clear: it wants its members to comply with that decision" (Fisher 1981, 25). In fact, in about half the cases of a formal third-party ruling covered in this analysis, both sides agreed formally to comply with the ruling. Similarly Hensel and Turres' work (1997) suggests that arbitration and adjudication rank near or at the top in terms of effectively reducing violence and ending the dispute once and for all. It may be the most appropriate settlement means available for government leaders who see tremendous mutual and national benefits to settlement, whose relative power capabilities make military settlement unlikely, and who face domestic constraints to settlement through straightforward political negotiation. For while it may be true that only governments that are willing to make concessions are likely to submit to such legal processes (Coplin 1968), it is not at all obvious that such concessions would be possible in their absence. As such, authoritative third-party rulings have historically been, and remain, a useful tool in overcoming domestic objectors and securing settlement once and for all.

APPENDIX 1
List of Cases

Cases of no dispute:

Argentina/Uruguay
Belize/Mexico
Brazil/Venezuela
Brazil/Guyana
El Salvador/Guatemala

Disputed cases, no use of authoritative third party:

Argentina/ Bolivia	1872–1925
Argentina/Great Britain	1820–1995
Bolivia/Brazil	1837–1925
Bolivia/Chile	1858–1995
Bolivia/Paraguay	1825–1938
Brazil/Paraguay	1860s–1932
Brazil/Peru	1821–1913
Brazil/Uruguay	1825–1995
Colombia/Panama	1903–1924
Guyana/Suriname	1975–1995

Disputed cases in which third party ruling is suggested or initiated, but not concluded:

Belize/Guatemala	1939–present
Brazil/Colombia	1826–1937
Colombia/Ecuador	1830–1916
Colombia/Nicaragua	1890–present
Colombia/Peru	1822–1933
Dominican Rep/Haiti	1844–1936
Guatemala/Mexico	1840–1895

Cases of third-party ruling, no compliance:

Case	Dates (Ruling Date)	By	Rejecter	Comments
Argentina/Chile	1847–1984 (1977)	United Kingdom	Argentina	Region: Beagle Channel; settled in 1984
Argentina/Chile	1847–1994 (1977)	United Kingdom	Chile	Awards were made in four sectors; two of these were rejected
Bolivia/Peru	1825–1911 (1909)	Argentina	Bolivia	Dispute was resolved by Peru's concessions
Chile/Peru	1881–1929 (1924)	United States	Peru	Subject of arbitration: whether to hold a plebiscite
Costa Rica / Nicaragua	1842–1900s (1888)	United States	Nicaragua	
Costa Rica / Nicaragua	1842–1900s (1916)	Central American Court of Justice	Nicaragua	Subject of arbitration: validity of an earlier (1888) ruling
Costa Rica / Panama	1903–1944 (1900)	France	Costa Rica	Prior to Panama's independence, a dispute between Costa Rica / Colombia
Costa Rica / Panama	1903–1944 (1914)	United States	Panama	
Ecuador/Peru	1842–present	Brazil	Ecuador	Ecuador initially accepted then rejected the ruling in 1960
Guyana/Venezuela	1951–present	United States	Venezuela	Venezuela rejected an ealier arbitration with the UK
Honduras/Nicaragua	1858–1960 (1906)	Spain	Nicaragua	Nicaragua claimed the ruling "null and void"

Cases of third-party ruling, compliance:

Case	Dates (Ruling Date)	By	"Loser"	Comments
Argentina/Brazil	1858–1898 (1895)	United States	Argentina	
Argentina/Chile	1872–1903 (1899)	United States	Not clear	Region: Los Andes
Argentina/Chile	1847–1966 (1966)	United Kingdom	Chile	Region: Palena sector 70% awarded to Argentina
Argentina/Chile	1847–1994 (1994)	Regional	Chile	Region: Laguna del Desierto
Argentina/Paraguay	1840–1939 (1878)	United States	Argentina	
Colombia/Venezuela	1838–1932 (1891)	Spain	Venezuela	Venezuela delayed compliance for some 25 years
El Salvador / Honduras	1861–1992 (1992)	ICJ	El Salvador	80% of disputed territory awarded to Honduras
Guatemala/ Honduras	1842–1933 (1933)	Costa Rica / Guatemala / United States	Not clear	
Guyana (British Guiana) / Venezuela	1880–1899 (1899)	United States	Venezuela	Ruling gave 34,000 square miles the United Kingdom, 8,000 square miles to Venezuela
Honduras/Nicaragua	1858–1960 (1960)	ICJ	Nicaragua	

APPENDIX 2
Data: Definitions and Sources

Dependent Variables

Ratification Failure: The number of treaties regarding specification of the border that have failed to be ratified in one or both countries (range 0 to 5, with twenty cases coded 0; eleven, 1; five, 2; four, 3; one, 4; and two, 5). The data were then recorded dichotomously: 0 = 0; 1–5 = 1. *Sources:* Ireland (1938, 1941); Allcock et al. (1992).

Arbitration Treaty: The presence (1) or absence (0) of one or more bilateral treaties that have provided for the arbitration of a specific border or border region. This includes ad hoc arbitration treaties and provisions within specific border treaties which indicate that differences arising from the treaty should be referred to third-party arbitration. Fourteen cases were coded 0; twenty-seven, 1. *Sources:* Ireland (1938, 1941); Allcock et al. (1992); Biger (1995).

Arbitration: Whether the boundary or any portion thereof (1) has been, or (2) has not been the subject of international arbitration (seventeen cases) or adjudication (three cases). Twenty cases were coded 1; twenty-five, 0. *Sources:* Ireland (1938, 1941); Allcock et al. (1992); Biger (1995). One ambiguous case is that of the 1910 arbitration in process by the king of Spain between Ecuador and Peru, which I have not coded as a completed ruling, because Ecuador's imminent rejection of the ruling caused the king to withdraw as arbitrator without issuing his decision (Krieg 1986, 37–44). Had the ruling been made, the result would certainly have been noncompliance.

Additional Domain Variable

Dispute: Whether (1) or not (0) the border between states has disputed by one or both states. To qualify as a disputed border, there had to be evidence of disagreement over the location of the boundary as articulated by the central or national government. Out of forty-four cases, thirty-nine were coded as disputed at some point; in five cases—Argentina/Uruguay, Belize/Mexico, Brazil/Venezuela, Brazil/Guyana, and El Salvador/Guatemala—I found no evidence of any territorial dispute. *Sources:* Ireland (1938, 1941); Allcock et al. (1992); Biger (1995).

Explanatory Variables

Military Personnel: The ratio of total military personnel in the larger country compared with that in the smaller country, averaged for the duration of the dispute. Original data were expressed in thousands. *Source:* COW National Material Capabilities dataset.

Democracy Country 1: The average democracy score for the first country in the pair, calculated from the POLITY III dataset, for the period covered by the duration of the dispute. *Source:* POLITY III dataset. For a complete discussion of the conceptualization and coverage of this dataset and comparisons with other democracy measures, see Jaggers and Gurr (1995).

Democracy Country 2: The average democracy score for the second country in the pair, calculated from the POLITY III dataset, for the period covered by the duration of the dispute. *Source:* POLITY III dataset.

Democratic Pair: Whether (1) or not (0) both countries in a given pair were relatively democratic during the dispute. The cutoff to qualify as a democracy was placed at the sample mean (2.6). Even with this very low threshold for democracy, only eight pairs were considered to both be rather more democratic. *Source:* POLITY III dataset.

Violence: A three-level rating of the degree of violence relating specifically to territorial and border issues between the two countries. Cases were coded 1 if there was virtually no mention of border or border-related violence between the two countries—for example, Colombia and Venezuela. Cases were coded 2 if there were skirmishes, clashes, or isolated incidents between police, armed forces, or local inhabitants, and also if there was a substantial show of force at any point during the episode—for example, the shows of force by Argentina and Chile in 1895, 1978, and 1982 regarding the Beagle Channel and lower Patagonia. Cases were coded 3 if there was substantial military conflict up to and including full fledged-war—for example, the War of the Pacific, 1879–1881, between Chile and Peru for control over territory. *Sources:* Ireland (1938, 1941); Allcock et al. (1992).

Resources: A three-level rating of the importance of natural resources for the territory under dispute. Cases were coded 1 if the issue of resources and their control was apparently absent from the dispute—for example, if the issue of resources was never mentioned, as in the case of Argentina and Brazil, or if the territory is unusable jungle or dessert). Cases were coded 2 if the territory was of moderate value— examples include agricultural land, like the "plains of the Atlantic River valley in the case of Honduras and Nicaragua; water rights, as in the case of Argentina and Paraguay; or control of fishing resources, as in the case of Argentina and Chile with respect to the Beagle Channel). Cases were coded 3 if they involved significant mineral or oil deposits or significant commercial assets, such as ports or control of a canal—Chile and Peru, for example, disputed control over Pacific ports as well as territory containing significant nitrate deposits). Nineteen cases were coded 1; eighteen, 2; and seven, 3. *Sources:* Ireland (1938, 1941); Allcock et al. (1992).

Multilateral General Arbitration Treaty: The number of multilateral, general arbitration treaties that both parties have ratified. Treaties had to have been in effect during the period in which the territory was under dispute; they were excluded if countries ratified the treaty after a dispute had been arbitrated or otherwise settled. For the null cases, treaties simply had to be in effect at some point during the first one hundred years of independence. Where one treaty appears to be a successor for another—as in the case of the Treaty of Peace and Amity, signed at the Central American Peace Conference in 1907, in effect between 1907 and 1918, which appears to have been succeeded by the 1923 convention for the establishment of an International Central American Tribunal, in effect between 1923 and 1934—these were coded as one treaty. Treaties that simply called for commissions of inquiry—for example, the 1923 Gondra Treaty, negotiated at the Fifth International Conference of American States—or for the peaceful settlement of disputes—like the 1933 South American Anti- War Pact—were excluded. Twenty-four country pairs were coded 0; eleven, 1; and three, 2. *Sources:* Ireland (1938, 1941); Allcock et al. (1992); Biger (1995).

Territorial and Bilateral General Arbitration Treaty: The number of treaties that have committed states to arbitrate territorial disputes. Included are general obligations to arbitrate disputes arising from a specific territorial agreement or to a bilateral general agreement to arbitrate disputes. Treaties had to have been in effect during the period in which the territory was under dispute; they were excluded if countries ratified the treaty after a dispute had been arbitrated or otherwise settled. Twenty-seven cases were coded 0; eleven, 1; four, 2; none, 3; and one, 5. *Sources:* Ireland (1938, 1941); Allcock et al. (1992); Biger (1995).

Ad Hoc Arbitration Treaties: The number of specific agreements, ratified by both parties, to arbitrate a particular territorial dispute. To
count as an ad hoc arbitration treaty, the main purpose of the agreement had to be to commit to the arbitration of a specific territorial
dispute. Though these have usually been proximate in time to the actual carrying out of a ruling, they do not automatically imply a ruling
will be made. Where one ad hoc arbitration agreement was obviously
designed to succeed another, the agreements were coded as one treaty.
For example, in 1971 Chile and Argentina signed an agreement that
Great Britain should arbitrate the Beagle Channel dispute; and in 1972
another agreement was signed transferring authority from the United
Kingdom to adjudication by the ICJ; these were coded as one ad hoc
commitment. Twenty-one cases were coded 0; seventeen, 1; four, 3;
and one, 4. *Sources:* Ireland (1938, 1941); Allcock et al. (1992); Biger
(1995).

NOTES

1. On the growing tendency for non-Western countries to turn to judicial
forms of dispute settlement, specifically with reference to the ICJ, see
McWhinney (1991).

2. In fact, of course, the willingness of states to submit crucial policy decisions to authoritative supranational scrutiny is not a new phenomenon. The
use of arbitration panels to judge such important issues as the maintenance of
neutrality during wartime, various questions of state responsibility, and even
territorial sovereignty burgeoned around the turn of the last century (Simpson
and Fox 1959). For a listing of more than 175 cases and rulings by arbitral panels or international courts, see Bernhardt, 1981. But see Jenks (1964, 101), who
argues that since World War II remarkable advances have been made in virtually every sector of international organization except the judicial sector.

3. See also Aron (1981, 110): "juridical interpretation, even when it is concretely improbable . . . is utilized as a means of diplomatic pressure." See also
the general discussion in Goertz and Diehl (1994).

4. There are important differences between and within these approaches
regarding the role of sanctions versus the use of incentives to manage the
process of compliance. Chayes and Chayes (1995) emphasize that interna-

tional law essentially has an important persuasive function and that, to enhance compliance, scholars and practitioners should move away from an enforcement model that focuses on sanctions and punishments to a management model that emphasizes positive incentives and negotiation to achieve compliance. Critics respond that such a managerial approach to compliance will only go so far; that deep cooperation—agreements that proscribe behavior that is truly difficult to forswear or prescribe behavior that is costly in the short term—will require some form of enforcement (Downs, Rocke, and Barsoom 1996). The distinction between the enforcement and management approaches is often made in the context of domestic law enforcement (Hawkins and Thomas 1984; Snavely 1990).

5. An anecdote that underscores this argument was the 1903 proposal by the Peruvian Foreign Minister to the Ecuadoran minister in Lima that the two sides secretly agree on a boundary line, which would then be conveyed the arbitrator who would then issue it as his own. "This plan would, it was thought, ease the pressure of public opinion on both governments since they would be obligated to accept the arbiter's decision" (Krieg 1986, 37). Though this agreement ultimately fell apart due to misunderstanding over the verbally agreed-on boundary line, it does underscore the value arbitrators were viewed as having as binding government constraints to deflect domestic opposition.

6. This is not a term used by proponents of this approach, but it is a convenient appellation for the purposes of this article.

7. "International law is not unlike constitutional law in that it imposes legal obligations upon a government that in theory the government is not free to ignore or change" (Fisher 1981, 30). Constitutional constraints most often rest on their shared normative acceptance, rather than on the certainty of their physical enforcement, providing another parallel to the international setting.

8. The distinction has been eroded by the use of chambers in the ICJ, however: three out of four of the cases in the late 1980s that used chambers were territorial disputes, indicative of how sensitive states about submitting this kind of issue to standing courts (Rosenne 1989, 236).

9. My list of disputed territorial claims differs from that of Paul Hensel and John Turres (1997) in a number of respects. First, with the exception of the Falklands Islands, I did not include disputes over islands: my dataset concentrates on mainland territorial disputes. Second, I did not include cases that involved imperial powers: my dataset concentrates on cases involving two independent countries. On this basis, thirteen cases are included in their dataset that are excluded from mine. (Note that many of the cases involving imperial powers also involve islands.) I have also included Central American cases (fifteen), which Hensel and Turres do not. Furthermore, Hensel and

Turres analyze country years. The disputed case is the unit of analysis in this study.

10. In 1957 Belgium and the Netherlands agreed to submit to the ICJ the question as to which of the two states had sovereignty over two plots of land totaling thirty-four acres. In its judgment of June 1959, the court voted 10 to 4 in favor of Belgium. There have also been several island arbitrations or adjudications: the case of Eastern Greenland (Denmark and Norway), ruled on by the Permanent Court for International Justice in 1933, involving the most significant amount of territory; and the Minquiers and Ecrebos Case (France and the United Kingdom), involving small islands, resolved by the ICJ in 1953.

11. For example, the ratio of military personnel in the larger of the two countries was nearly fifty times greater than that in the smaller country for cases in which disputes never arose, while this ratio was significantly smaller ($p < .001$)—six times—for cases in which borders were actually disputed. Similar differences in the ratio of total population and military expenditures held, as well.

12. The resource variable, in keeping with a fairly narrow interpretation of realist theory, includes only tangible resources that could conceivably contribute to the power base of the state (see Appendix 2). Although contributors to this volume have attempted to measure the intangible value of the territory, tangible resources are both better suited to my theoretical concern and less susceptible to subjective interpretation on the part of the analyst. I have therefore chosen to limit my analysis to tangible resources.

13. Thanks to Paul Diehl for suggesting this possible interpretation.

14. Results were substantially the same whether all cases or only disputed cases were analyzed.

15. Resources and past violence were also tested and found to have no impact on ratification failure (not reported here).

16. Though the results are not reported in these tables, the evidence suggests that states with a high ratification failure rate do not choose general, multilateral treaties; they are more closely associated with specific, ad hoc agreements to arbitrate.

REFERENCES

Allcock, John et al. 1992. *Border and Territorial Disputes.* Essex, U.K.: Long Group.

Aron, Raymond. 1981. *Peace and War: A Theory of International Relations.* Malabar, Fla.: Krieger.

Biger, Gideon. 1995. *The Encyclopedia of International Boundaries.* Jerusalem: Jerusalem Publishing House.

Bilder, Richard B. 1989. "International Third Party Dispute Settlement." *Denver Journal of International Law and Policy* 17: 471–503.

Bork, Robert H. 1989–1990. "The Limits of 'International Law.'" *National Interest* 18: 3–10.

Boutros-Ghali, Boutros. 1995. *Report of the Secretary General on the Work of the Organization.* A/50/1. New York: United Nations.

Boyle, Francis A. 1980. "The Irrelevance of International Law." *California Western International Law Journal* 10.

Burley, Anne-Marie, and Walter Mattli. 1993. "Europe before the Court: A Political Theory of Legal Integration." *International Organization* 47: 41–76.

Chayes, Abram, and Antonia Handler Chayes. 1995. *The New Sovereignty: Compliance with International Regulatory Agreements.* Cambridge, Mass.: Harvard University Press.

Clark, Bruce. 1996. "UN in Search of Peaceful Waters." *Financial Times,* October 18.

Claude, Inis L. 1966. "Collective Legitimization as a Political Function of the United Nations." *International Organization* 20: 367–379.

Coplin, W. D. 1968. "The World Court in the International Bargaining Process." In *The United Nations System and Its Functions: Selected Readings,* edited by Robert W. Gregg and Michael Barkin. Princeton, N.J.: Princeton University Press.

Diehl. Paul. 1996. "The United Nations and Peacekeeping." In *Coping with Conflict after the Cold War,* edited by Edward Kolodziej and Roger Kanet. Baltimore, Md.: Johns Hopkins University Press.

Dixon, William J. 1993. "Democracy and the Management of International Conflict." *Journal of Conflict Resolution* 37: 42–68.

Downs, George, David M. Rocke, and Peter Barsoom. 1996. "Is the Good News about Compliance Good News about Cooperation?" *International Organization* 50: 379–406.

Doyle, Michael. 1986. "Liberalism and World Politics." *American Political Science Review* 80: 1151–1169.

Fischer, Dana D. 1982. "Decisions to Use the International Court of Justice: Four Recent Cases." *International Studies Quarterly* 26: 251–277.

Fisher, Roger. 1981. *Improving Compliance with International Law.* Charlottesville: University of Press of Virginia.

Forsythe, David P. 1990. *The Politics of International Law: U.S. Foreign Policy Reconsidered.* Boulder, Colo: Lynne Rienner.

Franck, Thomas. 1990. *The Power of Legitimacy among Nations.* New York: Oxford University Press.

Garrett, Geoffrey, and Weingast, Barry. 1993. "Ideas, Interests, and Institutions: Constructing the EC's Internal Market." In *Ideas and Foreign Policy: Beliefs, Institutions, and Political Change,* edited by Judith Goldstein and Robert Keohane. Ithaca, N.Y.: Cornell University Press.

Goertz, Gary, and Paul F. Diehl. 1992. *Territorial Changes and International Conflict.* New York: Routledge.

———. 1994. "International Norms and Power Politics." In *Reconstructing Realpolitik,* edited by Frank W. Wayman and Paul F. Diehl. Ann Arbor: University of Michigan Press.

Hawkins, Keith, and John M. Thomas, eds. 1984. *Enforcing Regulation.* The Hague: Kluwer Nijhoff.

Hensel, Paul R., and John Turres. 1997. "International Law and the Settlement of Territorial Claims in South America, 1816–1992." Paper presented at the annual meeting of the American Political Science Association, Washington, D.C.

Hoffmann, Stanley. 1956. "The Role of International Organization: Limits and Possibilities." *International Organization* 10: 357–372.

Huth, Paul. 1996. *Standing Your Ground: Territorial Disputes and International Conflict.* Ann Arbor: University of Michigan Press.

Ireland, Gordon. 1938. *Boundaries, Possessions, and Conflicts in South America.* Cambridge, Mass.: Harvard University Press.

———. 1941. *Boundaries, Possessions, and Conflicts in Central and North America and the Caribbean.* Cambridge, Mass.: Harvard University Press.

Jaggers, Keith, and Ted Robert Gurr. 1995. "Tracking Democracy's Third Wave with the Polity III Data." *Journal of Peace Research* 32: 469–482.

Jenks, Clarence Wilfred. 1964. *The Prospects for International Adjudication.* Dobbs Ferry, N.Y.: Oceana.

Keohane, Robert. 1984. *After Hegemony: Cooperation and Discord in the World Political Economy.* Princeton, N.J.: Princeton University Press.

Kocs, S. 1995. "Territorial Disputes and Interstate War, 1945–1987." *Journal of Politics* 51, no. 1: 159–175.

Kolodziej, Edward, and I. William Zartman. 1996. "Coping with Conflict: A Global Approach." In *Coping with Conflict after the Cold War,* edited by Edward Kolodziej and Roger Kanet. Baltimore, Md.: Johns Hopkins University Press.

Krieg, William L. 1986. *Ecuadorean-Peruvian Rivalry in the Upper Amazon.* 2d ed., enl. Washington, D.C.: Department of State External Research Program.

McWhinney, Edward. 1991. *Judicial Settlement of International Disputes: Jurisdiction, Justiciability, and Judicial Lawmaking on the Contemporary International Court.* Dordrecht, Netherlands: Martinus Nijhoff.

Merrills, J. G. 1969. "The Justiciability of International Disputes." *Canadian Bar Review* 47: 241–269.

Milgrom, Paul R., Douglas North, and Barry Weingast. 1990. "The Role of Institutions in the Revival of Trade: The Law Merchant, Private Judges, and the Champagne Fairs." *Economics and Politics* 2: 1–23.

Mitchell, Ronald B. 1994. "Regime Design Matters: Intentional Oil Pollution and Treaty Compliance." *International Organization* 48: 425–458.

Morgenthau, Hans J. 1985. *Politics among Nations: The Struggle for Power and Peace.* New York: Alfred A. Knopf.

Peck, Connie. 1996. *The United Nations as a Dispute Settlement System: Improving Mechanisms for the Prevention and Resolution of Conflict.* The Hague, Netherlands: Kluwer Law International.

Raymond, Gregory. 1994. "Democracies, Disputes, and Third-Party Intermediaries." *Journal of Conflict Resolution* 38: 24–42.

Rosenne, Shabtai. 1989. *The World Court: What It Is and How It Works.* 4th ed. Dordrecht, Netherlands: Martinus Nijhoff.

Schachter, Oscar. 1991. *International Law in Theory and Practice.* Dordrecht, Netherlands: Martinus Nijhoff.

Simpson, John Liddle, and Hazel Fox. 1959. *International Arbitration: Law and Practice.* New York: Praeger.

Slaughter, Anne-Marie. 1995. "International Law in a World of Liberal States." *European Journal of International Law* 6: 503–538.

Snavely, Keith. 1990. "Governmental Policies to Reduce Tax Evasion: Coerced Behavior versus Services and Value Development." *Policy Sciences* 23, no.1: 57–72.

Vasquez, John. 1993. *The War Puzzle.* Cambridge, U.K.: Cambridge University Press.

Young, Oran. 1979. *Compliance and Public Authority: A Theory with International Applications.* Baltimore, Md.: Johns Hopkins University Press.

8

Camp David: Was the Agreement Fair?

Steven J. Brams and Jeffrey M. Togman

INTRODUCTION

Two approaches to the study of dispute resolution in international relations can be distinguished. The first explores how actual disputes were—or, for that matter, were not—resolved by the participants. This approach, which may be called inductive, seeks to provide generalizations drawn from specific examples of attempts at conflict resolution that were or were not successful.

The second approach, which may be called deductive, has received less attention in international relations. It involves the construction of theoretical models, usually based in game theory, whose consequences are applicable to the study of dispute resolution. This work, known as negotiation analysis (Young 1991), has only rarely been applied to cases of real-world disputes in international relations, like that between Egypt and Israel at Camp David in 1978 (for an analysis of this case using game-theoretic models of bargaining, see Brams 1990).

We will illustrate the relevance of the deductive approach in this article by showing how a newly developed procedure for dividing up goods in a dispute, or resolving issues in a conflict, could have been applied to a real-world territorial dispute that involved sovereignty and security issues as well. The procedure is called Adjusted Winner

(AW), which heretofore has been applied to only one other international dispute—that between Panama and the United States over the Panama Canal, which, after prolonged negotiations (Raiffa 1982; Brams and Taylor 1996), culminated in a treaty signed and ratified by the two countries in 1979.

In this chapter we will apply AW to the Camp David Accords of 1978, comparing the resolution that AW hypothetically would have given with the agreement that was actually reached (practical considerations of applying AW to this case that are not discussed here are given in Brams and Togman 1998). This comparison will enable us to draw conclusions about the potential use of AW in aiding negotiators to resolve disputes fairly and expeditiously. Although AW is applicable to numerous types of disputes, the Camp David case allows us to illustrate how conflicts with a significant territorial component can be resolved—using this procedure—and how deductive analysis can serve normative as well as explanatory ends.

PROPORTIONALITY AND ENVY-FREENESS

There are several important criteria by which to judge fairness. One is that all parties to a dispute are entitled to a fair share of a heterogeneous good, like a cake, parts of which each party may value differently. For example, one party may like the cherry in the middle, whereas another party may like the nuts on the side. The simplest notion of a fair share is a proportional share. That is, each of the n parties in a dispute is entitled to at least $\frac{1}{n}$ of the cake, as he or she views it. Fair-division procedures that guarantee a proportional share are said to satisfy the property of *proportionality*.

Another criterion of fairness, and one that is more difficult to obtain, is what we label *envy-freeness*. An envy-free division is one in which each party believes he or she has received the most valuable portion of that division. One way of conceptualizing such a division is to imagine an allocation in which no party believes he or she could do better by trading his or her portion for someone else's portion.

To illustrate how fair-division procedures can ensure proportionality and envy-freeness, consider the well-known procedure, applicable to two people, of "one divides, the other chooses." Suppose that Bob and Carol wish to divide a heterogeneous cake between themselves. If

Bob cuts the cake into two pieces, and Carol is allowed to choose whichever piece she prefers, each party can ensure both proportionality and envy-freeness by adhering to the following strategies:

1. By cutting the cake into two pieces that he considers to be of equal value, Bob can guarantee himself what he believes to be half the cake, regardless of which piece Carol chooses. Similarly, by choosing first, Carol can guarantee herself what she believes to be at least half of the cake. Thus, this procedure, in conjunction with these strategies, guarantees proportionality.
2. When these strategies are followed, this procedure guarantees that neither Bob nor Carol will believe that the other person received a larger portion of the cake than what he or she actually did receive. Thus, this procedure produces an allocation that is envy-free.

Envy-freeness and proportionality are equivalent when there are only two players—that is, the existence of one property implies the existence of the other. However, there is no such equivalence when there are three or more players. For example, if each of three players thinks he or she received at least one-third of the cake, it may still be the case that one player thinks another received a larger piece—say, one-half—so proportionality does not imply envy-freeness. Envy-freeness, on the other hand, does imply proportionality, for if none of the players envies another, each must believe he or she received at least one-third of the cake. Thus, envy-freeness is the stronger notion of fairness.

ADJUSTED WINNER

Although the simplicity of "one divides, the other chooses" is appealing, some bundles of goods are not quite analogous to a cake. The AW procedure is designed for disputes in which there are two parties and a number of discrete goods (or issues), each of which is divisible. Under AW, each of the two players is given 100 points to distribute across the goods. The goods are then allocated to the two players on the basis of their point distributions. We illustrate the procedure for making an allocation with a simple example.

Suppose that Bob and Carol must divide three goods, G_1, G_2, and G_3, between themselves. Based on the importance they attribute to obtaining each good, assume they distribute their points in the following manner:

	G_1	G_2	G_3	Total
Bob's point distribution	6	67	27	100
Carol's point distribution	5	34	61	100

Initially, Bob and Carol receive all the goods they have assigned more points to than the other player has. Thus, G_1 and G_2 are awarded to Bob, giving him $6 + 67 = 73$ of his points; and G_3 is awarded to Carol, giving her 61 of her points. If Bob's total points were equal to Carol's at this juncture, the procedure would end. However, this is not the case: Bob receives more of his points than Carol receives of hers.

Because the initial allocation is unequal, the next step is to transfer from Bob to Carol as much of a certain good or goods as is needed to give both parties the same point totals. This is called an *equitability adjustment*. The first good to be transferred is that with the lowest ratio of Bob's points to Carol's. In this example, G_1 has a lower ratio $(\frac{6}{5} = 1.20)$ than does G_2 $(\frac{67}{34} \approx 1.97)$.

Even transferring all of G_1 to Carol leaves Bob with a slight advantage (67 of his points to $5 + 61 = 66$ of hers). Hence, we turn to the good with the second-lowest ratio, G_2, transferring only that fraction of G_2 necessary to give Bob and Carol the same number of points.

Let x denote the fraction of G_2 that Bob will retain, with the rest transferred from him to Carol. We choose x so that the resulting point totals are equal for Bob and Carol. The equation for the equitability adjustment is as follows:

$$67x = 5 + 61 + 34(1-x)$$

This equation yields $x = \frac{100}{101} \approx 0.99$. Consequently, Bob ends up with 99 percent of G_2, for a total of 66.3 of his points, whereas Carol ends up with all of G_1, all of G_3, and 1 percent of G_2, for the same total of 66.3 of her points.

This outcome can be shown to satisfy several important properties (Brams and Taylor 1996). First, AW guarantees proportionality, because both players are assured of receiving at least 50 percent of their points. Second, because it is a two-person procedure, AW also ensures an envy-free allocation: neither player would trade his or her portion for that of the other. Third, the resulting allocation is *efficient* in that there is no other allocation that would give one player more of his or her points without giving the other player less. Finally, the resulting division is *equitable:* Bob's valuation of his portion is exactly the same as Carol's valuation of her portion.

By comparison, "one divides, the other chooses" ensures neither efficiency—there may be an allocation that is better for both players—nor equitability—the chooser may do better (in her eyes) than the divider does (in his). These and other criteria of fairness, equity, and justice are discussed in, among other places, Young (1994), Zajac (1995), Brams and Taylor (1996), and Kolm (1996).

In order for AW to satisfy the properties we have just described, two important conditions must be met: linearity and additivity. *Linearity* means that the added value, or marginal utility, of obtaining more of a good is constant (instead of diminishing, as is usually assumed)—so, for example, $2x$ percent of G_1 is twice as good as x percent for each player.

Additivity means that the value of two or more goods is equal to the sum of their points. Put another way, obtaining one good does not affect the value of obtaining another, or winning on one issue is separable from winning on another. Thus, goods or issues can be treated independently of each other, with packages of goods no more—nor less—than the sum of their individual parts. We will return to the additivity of issues when we discuss Camp David.

We have illustrated how AW works to solve a hypothetical dispute and indicated the properties it satisfies. But how useful would it be in resolving actual conflicts? Short of having parties to real-world disputes utilize the procedure, perhaps the best way to evaluate its potential usefulness is to look at what, hypothetically, would have occurred had the parties to an actual conflict applied AW.

CAMP DAVID AND ADJUSTED WINNER

On September 17, 1978, after eighteen months of negotiation and after a thirteen-day summit meeting, President Anwar Sadat of Egypt and Prime Minister Menachem Begin of Israel signed the Camp David Accords. Six months later, these accords provided the framework for the peace treaty that the two nations signed on March 26, 1979. This epochal agreement shattered the view of many observers that the thirty-year-old Arab-Israeli conflict was probably irreconcilable.

A number of factors make the Camp David negotiations an excellent case for examining the potential usefulness of AW. First, the Egyptians and the Israelis disagreed over several issues. These issues can be considered goods to be divided fairly, in the sense that a win by one side or the other is analogous to obtaining a good. Second, most of the issues were to some degree divisible, rendering the equitability-adjustment mechanism of AW applicable should division be necessary. Third, there is now considerable documentation of the positions of the two sides on the issues, including detailed accounts of the negotiations by several of the participants at Camp David. This written record allows us to make reasonable point assignments to each issue, based on the expressed concerns of each side.

The Camp David Accords, of course, need to be seen in the context of the seemingly intractable conflict that has existed between Arab nations and Israel from the time of the latter's creation in 1948. The Arab states, including Egypt, did not recognize Israel's right to exist and continually sought to annihilate it. However, Israel was victorious in the 1948–1949 war, the 1956 Sinai conflict, and the Six Day War of 1967. As a result of the 1967 war, Israel conquered and laid claim to substantial portions of territory that had belonged to its Arab neighbors, including the Sinai Peninsula, the West Bank, the Gaza Strip, and the Golan Heights.

In 1973, Egypt and Syria attempted to recapture the Sinai Peninsula and the Golan Heights, respectively, in the Yom Kippur War. The shuttle diplomacy of Secretary of State Henry Kissinger in 1973–1974 helped bring about two disengagement agreements between the warring sides but no permanent resolution of their conflict.

When President Jimmy Carter took office in January 1977, he deemed the amelioration, if not the resolution, of the Middle East conflict one of his top priorities. This conflict had contributed to major increases in the world price of oil; the fallout of these increases had been inflation and slowed economic growth.

From Carter's perspective, stable oil prices required an end to the turmoil in the Middle East (Quandt 1986, 32). Furthermore, Carter believed that the current disengagement was unstable and that some sort of settlement was necessary to prevent still another Arab-Israeli war and the potential involvement of the United States (p. 36). Thus, after assuming the presidency, he began almost immediately to use his office to press for peace in the Middle East.

The original U.S. plan was to involve all of the major parties, including the Palestine Liberation Organization, in the negotiations. As the talks proceeded, however, it became clear that the most practicable resolution would be one between Egypt and Israel. Indeed, at one point Sadat sent the U.S. president a letter urging that "nothing be done to prevent Israel and Egypt from negotiating directly" (Carter 1982, 294). By the summer of 1978, it seemed to Carter that a summit meeting was necessary to bridge the gap between Egypt and Israel. He invited Sadat and Begin to meet with him at Camp David.

When the Egyptian and Israeli leaders convened at Camp David, the two sides still disagreed on several major issues. For the purposes of our analysis, we grouped these issues into six categories.

1. The Sinai Peninsula

This large tract of land was conquered by Israel during the Six Day War and remained under its control after the Yom Kippur War. In many ways it was the most important issue dividing the two sides in the negotiations. For Israel, the Sinai provided a military buffer that offered considerable warning in case of an Egyptian attack. Israel had set up military bases in the peninsula, including three modern airbases of which it was very protective.

Israel had also captured oil fields in the Sinai that were of significant economic importance. Moreover, Israel had established civilian settlements in the Sinai that it was loath to give up. At one point at Camp David, Begin told a member of the American negotiating team, "My right eye will fall out, my right hand will fall off before I ever agree to the dismantling of a single Jewish settlement" (Brzezinski 1983, 263).

For Egypt, the Sinai was of such great importance that no agreement could be achieved that did not include Egyptian control over this territory. Almost all observers of the negotiations agree that, among all his goals, Sadat "gave primacy to a full withdrawal of Israel's forces from the Sinai" (Stein 1993, 81). He let the United States know at the earliest stages of the negotiations that although he would allow some modifications of the pre-1967 borders, the Sinai must be returned in toto (Quandt 1986, 50).

Roughly midway through the eighteen months of negotiation that led up to Camp David, Sadat began to focus almost exclusively on the Sinai in his discussions with both the Israelis and the Americans (Quandt 1986, 177). From a material perspective, military issues and the oil fields made the return of the Sinai imperative for the Egyptians. But perhaps more important, Egypt prized the Sinai for symbolic reasons: "the return of the whole of Sinai was a matter of honor and prestige, especially since Sinai had been the scene of Egypt's 1967 humiliation" (Kacowicz 1994, 135).

2. Diplomatic Recognition of Israel

Since its creation in 1948, Israel had not been recognized as a legitimate and sovereign nation by its Arab neighbors. In fact, almost all Arab nations remained officially at war with Israel and, at least for propaganda purposes, called for its liquidation. For Israelis, diplomatic recognition by Egypt, its most powerful neighbor, was an overriding goal.

Israel wanted more than just formal recognition. Israeli leaders desired normal, peaceful relations with Egypt, including the exchange of ambassadors and open borders (Brzezinski 1983, 281). Such a breakthrough could help liberate Israel from its pariah status in the region.

Egypt balked at normalizing relations with Israel, in part because other Arab nations would oppose such measures. Sadat also believed that normal diplomatic relations would take a generation to develop because they would require such profound psychological adjustments (Telhami 1990, 130).

In the actual negotiations, Sadat asserted that questions of diplomatic relations, such as the exchange of ambassadors and open borders, involved Egyptian sovereignty and therefore could not be discussed (Quandt 1986, 51). Recognition of Israel became so contentious an issue that it presented one of the major obstacles to the signing of both the Camp David Accords in 1978 and the formal peace treaty in 1979.

3. The West Bank and the Gaza Strip

For most Israelis, these two territories were geographically and historically integral to their nation—at least more so than was the Sinai. Indeed, the Israeli negotiating team held retention of these areas to be one of its central goals (Brzezinski 1983, 236).

Begin, in particular, considered these territories to be part of Eretz Israel (the land of Israel), not occupied foreign land. As one observer put it, "Begin was as adamant in refusing to relinquish Judea and Samaria as Sadat was in refusing to give up any of Sinai" (Quandt 1986, 66). By contrast, if Begin were to give up the Sinai, he was intent on obtaining some recognition of Israel's right to the West Bank and the Gaza Strip in return (Kacowicz 1994, 139).

For Egypt, these two territories had little economic or geostrategic worth; Sadat did not focus much on them as the negotiations proceeded. However, Egypt did face pressure from other Arab nations not to abandon the Palestinian populations in these territories. Sadat told his aides that he would not leave Camp David without some commitment from the Israelis to withdraw from the West Bank and Gaza (Telhami 1990, 129). In fact, once he arrived at Camp David, Sadat informed Carter, "I will not sign a Sinai agreement before an agreement is also reached on the West Bank" (Carter 1982, 345).

4. Formal Linkage between the Accords and Palestinian Autonomy

One of the major issues of the negotiations was the extent to which an Egyptian-Israeli agreement should be tied to formal, substantive progress on the issue of Palestinian autonomy. Begin held that there should be no linkage. Even though Egypt and Israel might agree to some framework for the Palestinian question, Begin claimed that this matter must be separate from a treaty between the two states (Quandt 1986, 178).

Sadat seemed to be of two minds on the issue. On one hand, he pushed for Israeli recognition of the Palestinians' right to self-determination as part of the treaty, holding that a bilateral agreement could not be signed before an agreement on general principles concerning a Palestinian state had been reached. On the other hand, he pointed out that a truly substantive agreement on this issue could not be negotiated by the Egyptians alone. However, he opposed possible deferral on this issue to an Arab delegation, which, he knew, could sabotage the talks.

5. Israeli Recognition of Palestinian Rights

From the Israeli perspective, recognizing the rights of the Palestinian people was difficult because of competing sovereignty claims by the Israelis and the Palestinians. When President Carter declared at a meeting with Sadat in Aswan, Egypt, that any solution to the conflict "must recognize the legitimate rights of the Palestinian people," the Israelis reacted negatively (Quandt 1986, 161). But because this recognition was not attached to any substantive changes (see issue 4 above), it was not viewed as excessively harmful to Israeli interests. In fact, Israeli Foreign Minister Moshe Dayan at one point sent a letter to the American negotiating team, indicating that Israel would be willing to grant equal rights to Arabs in the West Bank (p. 106).

From the Egyptian point of view, some form of Israeli recognition of the rights of Palestinians was deemed necessary. Even if the formulation were vague and largely symbolic, Sadat felt strongly that he needed at least a fig leaf with which to cover himself in the eyes of other Arab nations (Brzezinski 1983, 236; Quandt 1986, 188). Rhetorically, such a declaration would allow Egypt to claim that it had forced Israel finally to recognize the rights of the Palestinian population, an accomplishment that no other Arab state had been able to achieve. Furthermore, this formulation was appealing to Sadat, because it would not require the participation of other Arab states.

6. Jerusalem

Control of Jerusalem had been a delicate issue since 1948. The United Nations demanded in 1949 that the city be internationalized because of competing religious and political claims. Until the Israelis captured and unified the city in 1967, it had been split between an eastern and a western section.

For Israelis, Jerusalem was the capital of their nation and could not be relinquished. At Camp David, Dayan told the Americans that it would take more than a U.N. resolution to take the city away from Israel: "They would also need to rewrite the Bible, and nullify three thousand years of our faith, our hopes, our yearnings and our prayers" (Dayan 1981, 177)

As was the case with other territorial claims, Egypt faced pressure from the Arab nations to force Israeli concessions on this issue. An Egyptian representative impressed on the Israelis that a constructive plan for Jerusalem would "lessen Arab anxiety and draw the sting from Arab hostility" (Dayan 1981, 49). However, Egypt did not push strenuously on this issue and, in fact, seemed willing to leave it for the future.

THE ISSUES AS GOODS

We consider these six issues as goods to be distributed between the two sides using the AW procedure. Assuming that both Egypt and Israel have 100 points to allocate across the goods, we offer a hypothetical point allocation in Table 1. This allocation, to be sure, is somewhat speculative: it is impossible to know exactly how Israeli and Egyptian delegates would have distributed their points had they actually used AW. However, although different point allocations could produce different issue resolutions, none of the properties that AW guarantees—envy-freeness, efficiency, and equitability—would be altered. Thus, we emphasize the *methodology* of reaching a fair settlement rather our particular distribution of points, which we believe to be plausible but certainly not the only plausible allocation.

Table 8.1
Hypothetical Israeli and Egyptian Point Allocation

Issue	Israel	Egypt
1. Sinai	35	55
2. Diplomatic Recognition	10	5
3. West Bank/Gaza Strip	20	10
4. Linkage	10	5
5. Palestinian Rights	5	20
6. Jerusalem	20	5
Total	100	100

The allocation of points in Table 1 is based on our preceding analysis of each side's interests in the six issues. Briefly, it reflects Egypt's overwhelming interest in the Sinai, Sadat's insistence on at least a vague statement of Israeli recognition of Palestinian rights to protect him from other Arab nations, the Israelis' more limited interests in the Sinai, and Begin's strong views on Eretz Israel—that is, retention of the West Bank–Gaza Strip and control over Jerusalem. Note that each side has a four-tier ranking of the issues: most important (55 points for Egypt, 35 for Israel), second most important (20 points), third most important (10 points), and least important (5 points).

Our hypothetical allocation represents what we believe would be a truthful, rather than a strategic, point distribution by each side. Although in theory it is possible to benefit from deliberately misrepresenting one's valuation of issues, in practice this would be difficult and might only hurt one's cause (Brams and Taylor 1996).

Initially under AW, Egypt and Israel each win on the issues for which they have allocated more points than the other party. Thus, Egypt would be awarded issues 1 and 5, for a total of 75 of its points. Israel would be awarded issues 2, 3, 4, and 6, for a total of 60 of its points.

Because Egypt has more of its points than Israel has of its points, some issue or issues must be transferred, in whole or in part, from Egypt to Israel in order to achieve equitability. Because the Sinai (issue 1) has a lower ratio ($\frac{55}{35} \approx 1.57$) of Egyptian to Israeli points than the issue of Palestinian rights (issue 5) does ($\frac{20}{5} = 4.0$), the former must be divided, with some of Egypt's points on issue 1 transferred to Israel to create equitability. This transfer on the lowest-ratio issue ensures that AW is efficient—there is no settlement that is better for both sides.

In this instance, the adjustment is determined as follows:

$$20 + 55x = 60 + 35(1-x),$$

which yields $x = \frac{75}{90} = \frac{5}{6} \approx 0.83$. As a result, Egypt "wins" 83 percent of issue 1, along with all of issue 5, for a total of 66 of its points. Israel is given 17 percent of issue 1, plus all of issues 2, 3, 4, and 6, for the same total of 66 of its points. This final distribution is envy-free, equitable, and efficient.

It should be noted that AW, using the hypothetical point allocations of Table 1, produces an outcome that mirrors quite closely the actual agreement reached by Egypt and Israel. From Israel's perspective, it essentially won on issue 2, because Egypt granted it diplomatic recognition, including the exchange of ambassadors. Israel also had its way on issue 3, when Egypt "openly acknowledged Israel's right to claim in the future its sovereign rights over the West Bank and Gaza" (Kacowicz 1994, 139). Additionally, Israel won on issue 4, because there was no formal linkage between the Camp David Accords—or the peace treaty later—and the question of a Palestinian state or the idea of Palestinian self-determination. And, finally, Jerusalem was not part of the eventual agreement, which can be seen as Israel's prevailing on issue 6.

Egypt prevailed on issue 5: Israel did agree to the Aswan formulation of recognizing the "legitimate rights" of Palestinians. That leaves issue 1, on which Egypt wins 83 percent, according to our hypothetical division.

As we previously noted, AW requires that goods of issues be divisible in order for the equitability-adjustment mechanism to work. In fact, the Sinai issue was multifaceted and thus lent itself to division. In addition to possible territorial divisions, there were also questions about Israeli military bases and airfields, as well as Israeli civilian settlements and the positioning of Egyptian military forces.

Egypt won on most of these issues. All of the Sinai was turned over, and the Israelis evacuated their airfields, military bases, and civilians settlements. However, Egypt did agree to demilitarize the Sinai and to the stationing of U.S. forces to monitor the agreement, which represented a concession to Israel's security concerns. Viewing this concession as representing roughly one-sixth (17 percent) of the total issue seems to us a plausible interpretation of the outcome.

One problem that arises for our hypothetical case is the additivity that AW requires. In the case of Camp David, it can be argued, the recognition of Palestinian rights was not independent of territorial issues. For Sadat, in particular, recognition may have been more important because of his failure to win Israeli concessions on the West Bank, the Gaza Strip, and Jerusalem.

Although finding tolerably separable issues—whose points can be summed—is never an easy task, skillful negotiators can attenuate this problem. They seem to have done so in reaching a consensus on the various issues that split the two sides in the Panama Canal Treaty negotiations in the 1970s (Raiffa 1982). An additional lesson to be drawn from the Panama Canal case is that lumping issues invariably results in each side's receiving fewer of its points (Brams and Taylor 1996).

At Camp David, we believe, the two sides might have come up with a different division of issues than we proposed, which might have facilitated the application of AW. Nevertheless, we think our list works well, at least to illustrate the potential of AW, with both sides obtaining nearly two-thirds of their points.

CONCLUSIONS

Was the Camp David agreement fair? Many Egyptians were disappointed with the results of the Camp David talks. A former foreign minister of Egypt, Ismail Fahmy, wrote, "The treaty gives all the advantages to Israel while Egypt pays the price. As a result, peace cannot last unless the treaty undergoes radical revision" (Fahmy 1983, 292).

Quandt (1986, 255) also takes the view that Israel did better in the negotiations, but our reconstruction of the negotiations using AW suggests that the settlement was probably as fair as it could be. If Fahmy were correct in his belief that an unfair peace could not last, then the last two decades of peaceful relations—albeit a "cold" peace—between Israel and Egypt is testimony to the contrary.

Reinforcing this view is the fact that the negotiators, though they undoubtedly desired to "win," realized that they could not because they were not in a zero-sum situation. Abetted by Jimmy Carter, they were driven to seek a settlement that, because it benefitted both sides more or less equally, could be considered fair.

The biggest surprise, we think, is that *any* agreement was reached at Camp David. In political disputes in general, and in international disputes in particular, players often spend much time and energy on procedural matters before they ever address substantive questions. The Egyptian-Israeli negotiations were no exception: the two sides fought vigorously over procedural issues at several points in the negotiations (Quandt 1986, 108).

Disputants have a strong incentive to do this because procedures can be manipulated to bring about different outcomes (Riker 1986; Brams 1990). By guaranteeing a resolution that is fair according to several important criteria, AW, by contrast, affords disputants the opportunity to focus on substantive issues.

Another problem that plagues international disputes is that one side may fear that it will come out looking worse than the other, inducing it to abandon talks altogether rather than settle for a one-sided resolution—and explaining it back home. At Camp David, Sadat at one point expressed such a fear and packed his bags with the intent of returning to Egypt. Only a strong personal appeal from Jimmy Carter, coupled with certain threats, kept Sadat from breaking off the negotiations (Brzezinski 1983, 272).

By guaranteeing an outcome that is envy-free, equitable, and efficient, AW can reduce such fears and help keep negotiations on track. We believe it would have worked well at Camp David, producing a less crisis-driven settlement, even if the outcome would not have differed much from that which actually was achieved.

This is not to say that fair-division procedures such as AW are without shortcomings. For one thing, formal algorithms do not have the flexibility of informal procedures. Furthermore, as we have already mentioned, the synergies that various combinations of issues can create could pose difficulties for the additivity requirement of AW.

Nonetheless, the benefits of a straightforward procedure that guarantees important properties of fairness are considerable. The failure of negotiations has caused great human misery throughout history. To the extent that it can help resolve some of these conflicts, AW, we believe, offers substantial promise for the future.

REFERENCES

Brams, Steven J. 1990. *Negotiation Games: Applying Game Theory to Bargaining and Arbitration.* New York: Routledge.

Brams, Steven J., and Alan D. Taylor. 1996. *Fair Division: From Cake-Cutting to Dispute Resolution.* Cambridge, U.K.: Cambridge University Press.

Brams, Steven J., and Jeffrey M. Togman. 1998. "Camp David: Was the Agreement Fair?" In *New Directions in the Study of Conflict, Crisis, and War,* edited by Frank P. Harvey and Ben D. Mar. London: Macmillan.

Brzezinski, Zbigniew. 1983. *Power and Principle: Memoirs of the National Security Adviser, 1977–1981.* New York: Farrar Straus Giroux.

Carter, Jimmy. 1982. *Keeping Faith: Memoirs of a President.* New York: Bantam Books.

Dayan, Moshe. 1981. *Breakthrough: A Personal Account of the Egypt-Israel Peace Negotiations.* New York: Alfred A. Knopf.

Fahmy, Ismail. 1983. *Negotiating for Peace in the Middle East.* Baltimore, Md.: Johns Hopkins University Press.

Kacowicz, Arie Marcelo. 1994. *Peaceful Territorial Change.* Columbia: University of South Carolina Press.

Kolm, Serge-Christophe. 1996. *Modern Theories of Justice.* Cambridge, Mass.: MIT Press.

Quandt, William B. 1986. *Camp David: Peacemaking and Politics.* Washington, D.C.: Brookings Institution.

Raiffa, Howard. 1982. *The Art and Science of Negotiation.* Cambridge, Mass.: Harvard University Press.

Riker, William H. 1986. *The Art of Political Manipulation.* New Haven, Conn.: Yale University Press.

Stein, Janice Gross. 1993. "The Political Economy of Security Agreements: The Linked Costs of Failure at Camp David." In *Double-Edged Diplomacy: International Bargaining and Domestic Politics,* edited by Peter B. Evans, Harold Jacobson, and Robert Putnam. Berkeley, Calif.: University of California Press.

Telhami, Shibley. 1990. *Power and Leadership in International Bargaining: The Path to the Camp David Accords.* New York: Columbia University Press.

Young, H. Peyton. 1994. *Equity in Theory and Practice.* Princeton, N.J.: Princeton University Press.

———, ed. 1991. *Negotiation Analysis.* Ann Arbor: University of Michigan Press.

Zajac, Edward E. 1995. *Political Economy of Fairness.* Cambridge, Mass.: MIT Press.

PART V

The Future of Territorial Conflict

9
Love Thy Neighbor?:
Economic Integration and Political Friction in a
Period of Globalization

Andrew Kirby

INTRODUCTION

In this chapter I address the globalization thesis that has become influential in cultural studies, history, political geography, sociology, and some parts of political science (Harvey 1995; Jusdanis 1996; Brenner 1997; Castells 1997; Duara 1997). By emphasizing the transformations that have occurred within capitalism—most obviously, the creation of a truly global economy—various commentators have sought to undermine the analytical importance of the nation-state system. In large measure, their argument stems from the fact that the collapse of state socialism, in its various forms, has created vast new investment opportunities. These, coupled with a dramatic increase in the capacity of information technologies, have served to diminish the economic and political importance of many territorial states. Mingione, for example, points to the "internationalization of economic and sociocultural operations, the consolidation of large multinational conglomerates, the globalization of financial sectors, and the formation of supranational bodies such as the UN, the EEC, the FAO [and] the World Bank" (Mingione 1991, 433).

Furthermore, as threats of so-called traditional nuclear war recede and various interstate alliances have collapsed, nations that have existed for decades have sprung apart, as regional tensions, subdued by force and ideology over decades, reappear. The world map of the late twentieth century is being continually redrawn, as new republics emerge in Europe, the Middle East, Africa, and the former Soviet Union. Smaller—and weaker—territorial states are being created. At the same time, other agglomerations are also appearing: an expanded NATO, an enlarged Association of South East Asian Nations (ASEAN), NAFTA, and, with the European Monetary Union, a more closely integrated European Community.

For some, this "transnational moment" constitutes nothing less than "a rejection of both the system and the *Weltanschauung* inaugurated by the Peace of Westphalia in 1648 . . . [that] recognized the reality of . . . dynastic states" (Jusdanis 1996, 142–143). Yet this is a massive misreading of the manner in which the development of a global capitalist system has wormed its way into the fabric of the state system. As I shall argue, there are indeed threats to the short-run stability of individual states, but that is indicative of a political-economic ecology, extant at the world scale, that has always witnessed winners and losers. Such a perspective should not serve to trivialize the territorial state; nor should it be taken as a hint that the power of the individual state apparatus is also at an end. The United States, to take one example, has maintained its armed forces and has entered an era of organization designed to facilitate new forms of intervention in multiple theaters of war. Many smaller—and weaker—states are nonetheless still capable of armed adventures, especially if new neighbors are also small and weak. Much of the hardware produced during the cold war is still in existence and, since the advent of easy and invisible interstate money transfer, available for purchase by any entity (Castells 1997).

In short, although the globalization thesis points to various economic restructurings and concomitant political agglomerations, it cannot be used to predict relations between states during a period of rapid social and economic change. In the next section, I explore the concept in greater detail, in order to develop insights that address these relations.

GLOBALIZATION, SOVEREIGNTY AND STATE POWER

The term *globalization* has been defined as "the process whereby the population of the world is increasingly bonded into a single society"

(Albrow 1993, 248). This can be seen to occur in a number of ways. First, there are the electronic media of communication, the speed of which was first identified as contributing to a "global village" almost forty years ago (McLuhan 1962). Second, we can identify the ways in which popular culture and capitalism have blended to generate a veritable McDonaldization of the planet, such that food, entertainment, and even mores have, to some extent, been homogenized (Ritzer 1996). Third, as McDonaldization proceeds, it generates cultural and social resistance, and this is turn has broadened the applications of global thought, notably in the environmental context, where issues like pollution are no longer seen as local or national in compass (see, for example, Taylor 1997). There are those who describe great things emerging from—or perhaps within—the Internet, seen as a new space that transcends traditional territories and powers; those who dwell on the Net view themselves not as citizens but as Netizens, with new allegiances and transcendent communal responsibilities (Rushkoff 1994; Castells 1997).

Yet the novelty of this global era can be overstated. First, despite protestations to the contrary, it is no new phenomenon. Braudel (1984, 14) reminds us that the "perspective of the world" was at the core of mercantilism and has been in existence for centuries: as he observes, "there have always been world- economies." Marx and Engels wrote of "the bourgeoisie chasing over the whole surface of the globe" (1965, 377). Of course, that physical labor has been replaced by instantaneous interaction, and the Internet may indeed be the ultimate expression of time-space compression (Giddens 1991; Harvey 1995). Nonetheless, we should not overlook the fact that the Internet is excessively driven by United States corporations, that its lingua franca is English, and that there are increasing efforts to police it as if it were simply another space controlled by the nation-state, like a territorial ocean or a sector of outer space.

Globalization—as the term is used in such contexts—is really a misnomer, insofar as corporations are so explicitly of a place. Accumulation does occur everywhere, and these transactions have become subliminal, but the story is much more complex. The locus of investment depends heavily on the perceived stability of recipient regimes, and the returning flows of capital are remarkably predictable: investment returns to specific sites, where it is guarded by national monetary policies and other forms of protection. Put simply, prosperity still depends on "flagship" corporations—Coca-Cola, BMW, Sony—winning trade wars with rivals from other countries, a process that is, in turn, bound up with currency exchange rates. These are traditional accumulations accruing to territorial states, and these patterns of winners and losers remain in a contested economic system.

In reality, globalization may be better cast as "Americanization" (Sassen 1996). Viewed this way, we can argue that projects of global reach may actually reinforce the importance of the conceptual fabric of the state system. Because corporations become much more vulnerable when they operate in so many different contexts, the extension of legal understanding between states becomes more pressing. Consequently, legal supports and complicated financial filters are being imposed on markets around the world. Indeed, one way to interpret the recent concern for the investments of Holocaust victims is to remind ourselves that this is part of a process whereby the Swiss banking system, long an independent entity, is coming under the control of American norms (Hyndman 1997). Similarly, this is how we should interpret efforts to control the development of aggressive forms of capitalism that are branded as piratical. The manufacture of unlicenced software in factories operated by the People's Liberation Army in China or the production of compact discs in Bulgaria is really competition between corporations that rapidly becomes recast as struggles between territories, using levers such as Most Favored Nation status.

Sassen (1996, 27–28) summarizes these concerns as follows: "It is clear that defining the nation-state and the global economy as mutually exclusive operations is highly problematic. The strategic spaces where many global processes take place are often national: the mechanisms through which the new legal forms necessary for globalization are implemented are often part of state institutions; the infrastructure that makes possible the hypermobility of financial capital at the global scale is situated in various national territories." In short, it is by no means obvious that the system of territorial states is doomed to extinction in an era of global economic interaction, as is frequently claimed. Moreover, we can see that if the territorial state remains the key to understanding the unfolding of society at any scale, it is in large part because the state apparatus remains astonishingly powerful.

THE STATE APPARATUS

Much is made of the rapid progress that has been achieved in "the information age" (Castells 1997). Now it is easier for me to read, say, the Internet version of the *Sydney Morning Herald* than walk to the store for a local newspaper. Yet, although these technologies make global finance possible and can be seen to increase the independence of the individual—via access to a superfluity of data about the world—they also add significantly to the arsenals of state organizations. The case against bomber Timothy McVeigh in the United States shows the length to which the state apparatus can and will go to assemble information on a single individual. From the analysis of telephone records, credit-card slips, and videotapes taken in private establishments, the state's organizations can now mount highly detailed surveillance, even after the fact. The implications of this for personal liberties have been extensively rehearsed (Kirby 1997).

Of course, these powers are deployed only in specific contexts, and it is probably easier for the U.S. Department of Justice to bring a case of murder against McVeigh than it is for it to bring a case of price rigging against Archer Daniels Midland. Although Sassen (1996, 38) concludes that "the fact of being global gives these [global economic] actors power over individual governments," this is true only if we assume that the interests of corporations and of governments are fundamentally opposed. If we accept the more obvious reality, that capitalism is a growth machine and that it is the responsibility of the state to manage it, the question of "who has power over whom?" fades significantly. Certainly, there is evidence that a specific form of liberal welfare statism—the "Rhine model"—is in retreat in parts of Europe, but these are complex cultural questions rather than definitive reflections on the evolution of the political economy or the future of the state (Saunders 1995, 102–120).

This brief analysis of globalization thus suggests that a revised interpretation is needed. It is too simple to suggest that territorial states are unimportant from here on, although there *are* complex changes at work. The state apparatus is actually more powerful, notably with respect to surveillance. However, individual states are placed increasingly in contexts in which they are in competition, one with another, especially over trade policy and the like. In such situations, predictable things begin to happen: the integrity of the territorial state is brought into question, and this leads often enough to conflict.

Friction of this type is visible between the larger trading nations, as already noted, but is also prevalent between neighbors. Economic development may promote cooperation, but it can simultaneously generate externalities that can spread readily across national boundaries. For instance, the fires that were set in Indonesia during 1997 to clear land for plantations resulted in disastrous levels of air pollution that, in turn, harmed both tourism and rates of external investment throughout Southeast Asia. Unusually, neighboring countries used the forum of the ASEAN alliance to bring pressure to bear on Indonesia to put its house in order, a severe transgression of the cultural and political norms of the region. Nonetheless, such infringements are inevitable and will be more frequent as economies become more deeply implicated, one with another.

Relations between the United States and Mexico are instructive in this regard. While the two countries have become figuratively closer over trade, as symbolized by the signing of NAFTA, a heightened tension with respect to immigration and drug trafficking has also emerged. This dissonance is relatively easy to read. As countries appear to surrender themselves to their neighbors and rivals, so it becomes politically imperative to assume a heightened stature over symbolic issues, especially the integrity of the national boundary. The following case study indicates the complexities of this kind of situation, in which increased economic interaction coexists with tension, suspicion, and greater displays of force.

THE MEXICAN-AMERICAN BORDERLANDS

The border zone that connects Mexico and the United States stretches for more than 2,000 miles. For years, it was a unique example of a developed nation abutting an economy based on subsistence agriculture and a state-controlled economy. More recently, it became an experiment in which a new expression of core capitalism, namely the *maquiladora* system, was installed from Matamoros to Tijuana. The *maquilas* are American assembly plants that enjoy the benefits of cheap labor in a historically stable neighbor. More than 400,000 jobs were created during the 1980s alone, and, to the satisfaction of nationalist politicians, this was initially achieved without full-scale penetration by foreign companies.

The explicit interlocking of the Mexican and American economies in this region has initiated social transformation. For example, as American television programs have become popular via satellite dishes and as more workers have learned English as a precursor to migrant labor, so different ideas of family structure, sexuality, and nationality have begun to diffuse. Spanish-language stations in Arizona, Texas, and California have also built up their audiences, via a new and distinct style that is neither explicitly American or solely Mexican. This economic and cultural reconstruction has affected many facets of life: for instance, the large numbers of women who have moved into the formal and informal economies on both sides of the border constitute an important social change. The state socialist party, the Partido Revolucionario Institucional, has lost its monopoly on political power in Mexico and has been eclipsed along the border, where the free-trade party, the Partido de Acción Nacional, boasted a gubernatorial incumbent as early as 1990.

The growth of the *maquilas* has been characterized by problems such as poor workplace safety, air pollution caused by the burning of both garbage and wood for fuel, and water pollution that results from inadequate sewage treatment and the dumping of toxic and other wastes in unmonitored sites on both sides of the border. Although economic expansion has occurred in all border towns, it has frequently been in marginal locations that lacked basic infrastructure such as water, power, and sewage hookups. Newer residences have been built by the corporations and restricted to long-term employees. Politicization has been limited but is inevitable with regard to quality-of-life issues—the need for potable water, the regularization of landholding, and the provision of education.

BORDERS IN A GLOBAL ECONOMY

A border zone is the farthest outpost of the nation-state's sovereignty. This control may be cartographic at best, as is the case with the oceans or space, and as a result, a border zone can also be a place of independence. Precisely because the nation-state is so closely bound up with its territorial existence, visible expressions of sovereignty are common, with the Berlin Wall being perhaps the most poignant symbol of the cold war. The boundary that separated the two Germanys was less a military construction than an ideological and panoptic one. Of course, concrete is never enough to exclude all external influences. Electronic messages—via television, radio, fax machines, and the Internet—can all cross borders, as do most manifestations of commerce, both legal and illegal.

In the case of MexAmerica, the border plays a "mediating role" (de Certeau 1984). Core and semiperiphery are separated by wire, steel fences, and ditches so that people and things can be channeled through official checkpoints. In years past, those without documents could stroll through a break in the wire, which added to the creation of a complex ecology of border residents, including migrant workers, bicultural residents, and the binational *fronterizos* (Martinez 1990). It is important to emphasize that these social developments have not been restricted to one or other side of the border. Unionization in the maquilas is Mexican labor versus American corporations, for example. Similarly, demands for public services in the *colonias populares* are directed to state government in Mexico but also implicate the economic system that revolves around the maquiladoras (see Peña 1997).

In MexAmerica, ties between state governments and the national government are weak; much stronger connections exist between state governments that can interact over issues (such as the environment) in the annual Border Governors' Conference. Local officials in both countries can also pursue their own agendas: for example, some city officials have ordered police officers not to cooperate with officials of the U.S. Immigration and Naturalization Service (INS) who are searching for undocumented workers and refugees seeking sanctuary in the United States.

In addition, many unofficial grids connect individuals and institutions. Such networks often involve government personnel who interact outside the restrictions of formal channels. Because they are formless, I have described them as recombinative networks, but it should be emphasized that their impacts can be large (Kirby 1993). The following examples are taken from the two cities of Nogales that together constitute the single metropolitan entity known as Ambos Nogales. Recent economic development there has generated a population of approximately 250,000, of which 20,000 are in Nogales, Arizona, and the remainder are in Nogales, in the Mexican state of Sonora. The changes are leading to various forms of rapprochement, on both formal and informal levels.

On one hand, the imperative of maintaining levels of economic development is legitimated by proactive organizations such as the Border Trade Alliance, the Arizona-Mexico Commission, and the Organization for Free Trade and Development. On the other hand, separate institutional entities on each side of the border have relatively close links in matters of resource distribution. These include El Proyecto Arizona-Sonora, a transnational educational program dealing with persons with AIDS on both sides of the border, and Hands across the Border Foundation, an educational program funded by the Kellogg Foundation to facilitate student exchanges. In addition, various medical agreements between hospitals allow Mexican residents to cross into Arizona to obtain free medical care and have diverted some resources back into Sonora. There is also more aid between city governments: firefighters in Ambos Nogales have a mutual-assistance agreement, and water is frequently pumped from the United States to Mexico when water pressure is low or water is in short supply.

BORDER CONFLICTS

As the integrated economic and social base of the border zone expands, so it seems that the symbolic divide has necessarily increased. The state apparatus is increasing its presence via a process of "militarization" of the borderlands. There are political calls for greater vigilance with regard to illegal entry, crime, and smuggling, which is bound up with attacks on immigration, affirmative action, and the like (Smith and Tarallo 1995). These efforts appear to preserve the integrity of the nation-state but send contradictory signals in the process. Even as NAFTA was being constructed, the deployment of U.S. National Guard units along the border in 1988, plus the invasion of Panama in December 1989 for drug-related reasons, generated a fear in Mexico that U.S. forces were about to cross the border—and little has occurred to diminish this apprehension. Armed U.S. officers routinely chase suspects into Mexico, although Mexican law-enforcement personnel are expressly forbidden to carry weapons in the United States.

The symbolic dimensions of the border are manifested, then, in terms of the presence of police forces of various types, and in recent years these have been coordinated under the aegis of the so-called War on Drugs. In addition to local law-enforcement units and traditional federal departments, such as the Drug Enforcement Administration, the U.S. Customs Service, the U.S. Border Patrol, and the Federal Bureau of Investigation, new organizations have been created to maintain the sanctity of the border. Joint Task Forces coordinate the activities of federal, state, and local units and amalgamate active service units from the Navy, the Army, the Marine Corps, and the Air Force.

The extent of the drug trade should not be dismissed: for example, U.S.$250 million worth of cocaine was seized in Arizona in one raid alone in 1997. Economic activity—running drugs or undocumented workers—has now spawned a reactive institutional apparatus, designed to protect the ideology of the nation-state that is upheld by the integrity of the border. In just one U.S. state, the list of agencies involved is almost infinite: the sheriff's departments in several counties, the Arizona Department of Public Safety, the Tucson Metropolitan Area Narcotics Trafficking Interdiction Squad, the U.S. Border Patrol, and units of the U.S. National Guard. The armed forces also employ the kinds of hardware that are more usually associated with warfare, including spotter aircraft, helicopters, and tethered balloons.

The costs of these operations are astronomical—the INS alone costs U.S.$3 billion annually. Yet the biggest burden is inevitably borne by the populations that flow through the border zone. As the peso has devalued, so the imperatives to undertake migrant labor in the United States have increased. As the border has become militarized, so those crossing have been forced to find more isolated, and more dangerous, crossing points. The numbers who die while attempting to cross the border have increased dramatically: 1,185 persons died between 1993 and 1996, from causes that include drowning, exposure, and gunshot wounds.

SUMMARY

MexAmerica reveals the complex relations that can now exist between neighbors, even those who ostensibly share relatively similar outlooks. Nor does this complexity depend solely on the existence of a large prosperity gradient between them. Hyndman (1997), for example, has written persuasively about the relations between Kenya, Ethiopia, and Somalia during recent years. The Horn of Africa has witnessed prolonged ethnic strife throughout much of this century, although Western refugee organizations have done much to bring the countries to some level of quiescence, one with another, via famine-relief funds. Even so, Hyndman shows that the flows of aid are not at all matched by the free passage of refugees fleeing from drought or warfare: as she notes, "borders are more porous to humanitarian aid flowing from Europe to Africa than to the displaced people for whom such aid is intended" (p. 173).

In short, the realities of a world in which elements of economic integration is perceptibly occurring are to be found in spaces where different political economies touch. The necessity for food aid is not producing rapprochement but is actually generating more conflict—albeit it mostly vocal—between North Korea and South Korea than has existed for some time. The sovereignty of North Korea is clearly deemed to be tarnished by this charity, with the result that levels of verbal aggression rise correspondingly. Something analogous is also visible in Israel, where relations between Jews and Palestinians have reached a new low point. Historic ethnic conflicts have been both challenged and sharpened during this decade as the Israeli economy has expanded rapidly. Palestinians have been incorporated into the national economy, a reality that has both immediately challenged the long-standing economic superiority of Israeli Jews and brought larger numbers of Jews and Palestinians into daily contact. One way in which this tension becomes marked is by periodic closings of the Green Line, the internal frontier that separates the two groups; again, we see the need to segregate and control, even within a single territory (Kirby and Abu-Rass 1999).

CONCLUSIONS

I have shown some of the complexities of relations between states in an era of global capital movement. One by one, traditional antagonists have entered into trade agreements, so that the world is now bound by complex dyadic interactions. At the same time, movements of people have accelerated, as both migrants and refugees have redoubled their efforts to flee poverty and regional insecurity and to seek safety and prosperity in the core nations.

This globalization of capital, labor, and politics has led some commentators to announce the diminution of the territorial state. Marginalized by corporations with budgets larger than their own, subordinated by new alliances, and undermined by regional separatist movements, the familiar territorial state that was in many places ushered in by the twentieth century might seem in danger of departing by the end of millennium. Yet, as I have shown in this synopsis, the globalization thesis is frequently unexamined, and too many inferences are drawn from scant evidence. In particular, we are contrasting a contemporary economic reality with one that existed during a half-century of imperial struggle between East and West. It is not nostalgic to suggest that during that period, a very explicit form of statist political economy existed across the planet. It was remarkable for its stability, and in large measure that stability was a result of a self-conscious coalition between capital and labor; this stability occurred both in the East and in the West, albeit in rather different ways. It does not seem so surprising that the collapse of the ideological struggle that underlay this world order has provoked a riot of investment and labor mobility, but that is based on a comparison with the second half of the century: a comparison with the first half of the century reminds us of a prior moment of global capital formation, new forms of industrialization, and labor hypermobility. In sum, it would be a mistake to try to project the globalization thesis too far. The territorial state is not doomed; indeed, much can be made of its increasing importance as trade becomes more and more complex and more competitive.

This is not to argue that all is without incident. As I have indicated, frictions between states—over trade, over migrants, over debts, and over issues of belief—remain highly visible. This is especially true in regional settings and between neighbors. As I have shown with the MexAmerican example, the very act of coming together in terms of trade and culture produces crises of sovereignty and confidence. This is occasioned not merely by the flows from one nation to another but also by the ways in which complex social and political ecologies develop in the interstices between countries.

What we see are changes in everyday life that are structured most visibly by local organizations and local governments. Places and their populations reveal their independence from their national bureaucracies, and in doing so they threaten the integrity of the territorial state.

Witness the evolution of the littoral in the People's Republic of China, where mercantile capitalism sits uneasily alongside dirigiste state control. The return of Hong Kong in 1997 provided yet another example of this evolution, and the warnings concerning freedom of speech emanating from Beijing reflect its need to maintain sovereignty.

This is not to argue, of course, that all countries are facing border conflicts as a result of global integration. Every example of tension within regions and between neighbors—Italy and Albania; India and Pakistan—is balanced by new rapprochements, such as the inclusion of former Warsaw Pact republics in NATO. Rather, the message is that globalization makes the system of territorial states neither obsolete nor irrelevant.

Part of this chapter was presented to a conference sponsored by the International Sociological Association in Berlin in July 1997; another part is a revision of portion of a chapter in my book, *Power/Resistance*, dealing with MexAmerica. My thanks go to Bob Jessop, Paul Diehl, and Julia Patterson for their comments on some or all of the contents.

REFERENCES

Albrow, M. 1993. "Globalization." In *Twentieth Century Social Thought*, edited by W. Outhwaite and T. Bottomore. Oxford: Blackwell.

Braudel, Fernand. 1984. *The Perspective of the World*. New York: Harper and Row.

Brenner, Neil. 1997. "Global, Fragmented, Hierarchical: Henri Lefebvre's Geographies of Globalization." *Public Culture* 10, no. 1: 135–168.

Castells, Manuel. 1997. *The Power of Identity*. Oxford: Blackwell.

De Certeau, Michel. 1984. *The Practice of Everyday Life*. Berkeley: University of California Press.

Duara, P. 1997. "Transnationalism and the Predicament of Sovereignty." *American Historical Review* 102: 1030–1051.

Giddens, Anthony. 1991. *The Consequences of Modernity*. Stanford, Calif.: Stanford University Press.

Harvey, David. 1995. "Globalization in Question." *Rethinking Marxism* 8, no. 4: 1–17.

Hyndman, Jennifer. 1997. "Border Crossings." *Antipode* 29: 149–176.

Jusdanis, G. 1996. "Culture, Culture Everywhere: The Swell of Globalization Theory." *Diaspora* 5: 141–161.

Kearney, M. 1995. "The Local and the Global." *Annual Review of Anthropology* 25: 547–565.

Kirby, Andrew. 1993. *Power/Resistance*. Bloomington: Indiana University Press.

———. 1997. "Is the State Our Enemy?" *Political Geography* 16: 1–13.

Kirby, Andrew, and Thabit Abu-Rass. 1999. "Employing the Growth Machine Heuristic in a Different Political Economic Context. In *The Urban Growth Machine,* edited by A. Jonas and D. Wilson. Albany: State University of New York Press.

Martinez, O. 1990. "Transnational Fronterizos." *Journal of Borderland Studies* 5: 79–94.

Marx, K., and F. Engels. 1965 [1848]. *The Communist Manifesto.* Peking: Foreign Language Press.

McLuhan, M. 1962. *The Gutenberg Galaxy.* Toronto: University of Toronto Press.

Mingione, E. 1991. *Fragmented Societies.* Oxford: Blackwell.

Peña, Devon G. 1997. *The Terror Machine: Technology, Work, Gender and Ecology on the US-Mexico Border.* Austin, Tex.: CMAS Books.

Ritzer, G. 1996. *The McDonaldization of Society.* Thousand Oaks, Calif.: Pine Forge.

Rushkoff, Douglas. 1994. *Cyberia: Life in the Trenches of Hyperspace.* London, Flamingo.

Sassen, S. 1996. *Losing Control? Sovereignty in an Age of Globalization.* New York: Columbia University Press.

Saunders, Peter R. 1995. *Capitalism: A Social Audit.* Buckingham, U.K.: Open University Press.

Smith, M. P., and A. Tarallo. 1995. "Proposition 187: Global Trend or Local Narrative?" *International Journal of Urban and Regional Research* 19: 664–676.

Taylor, P. J. 1997. "Modernities and Movements: Anti-Systemic Reactions to World-Hegemonies." *Review* 20: 1–17.

10

The Geopolitics of an Evolving World System: From Conflict to Accommodation

Saul B. Cohen

INTRODUCTION

The purpose of this chapter is to investigate the role of geopolitics in promoting war and peace in the light of geopolitical changes brought about by the end of the cold war. For those who heralded the collapse of the Soviet Union as the harbinger of a so-called New World Order under a Pax Americana, the current world turbulence must surely be disappointing. Instead of the predicted stable international system, "wars against the people" have been replaced by "wars among the people." All too often, the lifting of ruthless repression has made possible unrestrained ethnic-religious conflicts based on age-old animosities.

Is conflict the inevitable price of newly gained freedom and the opening up of political systems? What role does geopolitics play under conditions whereby international wars perform a subsidiary role to internal conflict and international terrorism? Is current conflict part of a dialectic process that will ultimately lead to a more peaceful and stable world system? These are questions that loom in any assessment of the new geopolitics.

To be sure, the savage conflicts that broke out in Bosnia, Chechnya, Nagorno-Karabakh, Georgia, and Afghanistan after the toppling of communist regimes and the tribal and religious conflict elsewhere reflect widespread turbulence. But headlines of war tend to push into

the background many peaceful transitions of rule, or territorial re-
configurations. The secessions of Slovenia, Ukraine, Moldova, Mace-
donia, the Baltic states, and Kazakhstan all occurred peacefully or
with only minor turmoil. So did the division of former Czechoslovakia and the reunification of Germany. Moreover, the changeover of
regimes was relatively smooth in Poland, Romania, Bulgaria, and
Mongolia.

Where conflict has broken out as the aftermath of the cold war, its
scale has generally been limited: examples include Albania, Cambodia, Tajikistan, and the Democratic Republic of the Congo (formerly
Zaire). Even in Afghanistan, the fighting between the Taliban and its
tribal opponents has not caused the deaths of tens of thousands or the
displacement of millions of refugees that occurred during the cold war
when the Soviet Union and the United States took sides in the struggle in that country.

We need to be mindful that the collapse of the Soviet Union has
opened the doors to far greater international intervention to halt or
limit warfare where the eruption of conflict cannot be prevented. The
Gulf War was contained because Russia collaborated with the West.
Russia's influence also helped moderate Serbia's behavior in its fighting with Croatia and in the latter stages of the war in Bosnia. Most recently, Russia took the lead to mediate the crisis in the standoff between the United States and Iraq over the U.N. weapons-inspections
program.

Of course, intervention has its limitations and, indeed, it may
fail, as it did Somalia and as it may, eventually, in Bosnia or the Middle East. But the international system is now much more open to outside mediation. Such issues as human rights and war crimes, rarely
raised to any effect during the cold war, have become high on national agendas.

Thus even though wars continue to rage, the end of the superpower struggle has surely moderated their impact. No longer is world
and regional stability threatened by conflict involving massive
armies, and no longer do major powers have the excuse to use the
"falling domino" theory to intervene in other nations' affairs in ways
that reinforce internal and interstate strife.

Although the current geographical focus of conflict has shifted,
the creation and persistence of geopolitical fault lines that attend con-

flict continue to characterize the international system. These fault lines are the boundaries between global, regional, and national forces, as well as the new ones within countries that were buried by repressive regimes.

GEOPOLITICS AND GEOGRAPHY

Because geopolitics has different meanings for historians and international relations specialists than it does for most geographers, a "geographical" definition is in order. My definition of geopolitics is "the role played by geographical space in influencing the political organization of the world system and in formulating political and military strategy." Such a definition provides a spatial conceptual framework for the international system.

The dynamism of places and movement and their interconnections are the underpinning of geopolitical analysis. It is the key to understanding the changing geopolitical contours of the power relationships between and among various political entities and the other aspects of human organization that affect the operations of these entities, such as the economic, cultural, racial or religious framework. Flows of ideas, migrations, trade, capital, communications, arms, and drugs all have a spatial impact on the world system in which scale, hierarchy, and areal complexity undergird its geopolitical frameworks. Many of the theories that deal with the relationship between geography and politics are flawed because they do not take into account this spatial complexity and dynamism.

Oversimplification, based on distortion or misreading of Halford Mackinder's theories (1919, 1943), characterized the old geopolitics of German *Geopolitik* and the cold-war theories of containment. It has more recently produced such optimistic scenarios of a new world order as: Fukuyama's theory that modern science and the struggle of man for recognition has led to the collapse of tyranny, establishing capitalist liberal democracies as the end state of the historical process (1992); a view of a world in perpetual turmoil (Brzezinski 1993); and a prediction that the international system is destined to be ruled by intransigent nationalism (Lukács 1993). Huntington (1996) is correct in rejecting the concept of a single global and essentially western culture. However, his gloomy thesis that the future will be one of bloody global wars between great world civilizations or cultures is debatable because it, too, glosses over complexity while all but ignoring the deep religious, political, national, and ethnic rivalries within these civilizations, as well as other causes for war such as thirst for personal power, corruption, and social unrest. Such a view also ignores the geographical overlap of some of the regions.

Definitions acquire fuller meaning when they are expressed in paradigmatic terms. The paradigm I used in this analysis is that of a world organized within a system of nested geopolitical frameworks—from global to regional to national to subnational (Cohen 1963, 1982, 1984, 1990, 1991, 1993). The highest-order framework is geostrategic, for what occurs within that framework can have an impact on all parts of the world. The other frameworks are geopolitical, or tactical, in the sense that they are geographically limited: because the geopolitical frameworks lie within geostrategic realms, they can, of course, play a strategic role as well.

The paradigm also assumes that the spatial structure is in dynamic, not static, equilibrium. Such a structure is hierarchical but flexible, and the power that flows is shared by the different parts at different levels. It is further hypothesized that this structure evolves according to organismic developmental principles (Werner 1948; Bertalanffy 1968). The process is from a system of atomized, feudal states to undifferentiated, loosely organized empires, to the differentiated national state system initiated at Westphalia, to today's emerging specialized and integrated multinodal world network.

In a dynamic system the world cannot be in perfect order, but it is not in chaos. Turbulence and conflicts are part of the developmental process, propelling the participants from lower and higher levels. Progress comes from perturbations, as long as they are limited in time and space. In effect, conflict and accommodation are in dialectic relationship with one another. Failure to recognize this state of dynamic equilibrium is what leads to the world-policeman syndrome. For those who would rush to involve the United States and the international community in efforts to prevent conflict at a wide number of points along the earth's surface (Brzezinski 1997), the understanding of dynamic equilibrium and its role in the evolution of the world political system is sadly and dangerously limited.

DYNAMIC EQUILIBRIUM

Geopolitical developmental theory posits a world in dynamic equilibrium in which change is necessary to maintain the equilibrium. Moves to higher stages of development are often accompanied by considerable turmoil, as exemplified currently in Afghanistan, Algeria, and Congo. But this means short-term localized and regional instability, not world structural chaos.

Proponents of chaos theory tend to forget that the cold-war period was just as unstable as the present period, if not more so, when measured by wars and the loss of life. During the cold war conflicts took place in Korea, Vietnam, Cambodia, the Taiwan Strait, Indonesia, Sri Lanka, Afghanistan, Lebanon, Yemen, Algeria, the Western Sahara, Chad, the Sudan, the Ogaden, Ethiopia, Mozambique, Angola, South Africa, Nigeria, Namibia, Congo, the Falkland Islands–Malvinas, Nicaragua, and Guatemala and between India and Pakistan, India and China, Iraq and Iran, and Israel and the Arab states. All told, approximately 150 external and internal conflicts erupted during this period, with up to 20 million deaths and massive dislocations of people. Neither the military balance between the United States and the Soviet Union nor the nuclear stalemate succeeded in limiting conflict at a time when containment policy was pursued by the West as a means of maintaining a form of static global equilibrium.

Admittedly, savage conflicts and international terror continue to rage: more than two dozen conflicts were waged in 1996 alone. We should be mindful, however, that most, save for those attributable to the breakup of the Soviet empire, had their origins in the cold-war period. Moreover, many long-standing conflicts have recently been resolved—even if sometimes uneasily, as in Cambodia, the Philippines, Mozambique, Angola, Liberia, Sierra Leone, El Salvador, Nicaragua, Guatemala, Lebanon, and Israel-Jordan, Northern Ireland, and the unilateral cease-fire recently announced by the Basque ETA in Spain. Also, hot wars in Chechnya, Georgia, Azerbaijan-Armenia, Tajikistan, and Bosnia have been ended.

In addition, China and India have agreed to partial demilitarization of their disputed border. Russia and China have agreed to demarcate the border over which they had such bloody conflicts in the 1960s and to thinning military forces there. India and Pakistan have agreed to try to negotiate a nonaggression pact. In South America, the boundary disputes between Venezuela and Guyana, Chile and Argentina, and Argentina and the United Kingdom (over the Falkland Islands–Malvinas) have been muted. The Peru-Ecuador border, over which the two countries fought in 1995, is still an open issue, but they are pledged to resolve the dispute along their 50 miles of undemarcated boundary.

THE NATIONAL STATE

Can the national state continue to be the mainstay of the international system? Many analysts forecast its demise in the face of the rising strength of regional and world governmental organizations, the increased influence of nongovernmental organizations, and the globalization of information and economic forces. I firmly believe that the state will not merely survive the changes that are being imposed on it but will thrive because of them.

Predictions about the demise of the state are hardly novel. Marx held that with the victory of the workers over the bourgeoisie and the emergence of a classless society, the state as an instrument of centralized control would wither away. If Marxism was a rational economic response to the conditions of the nineteenth century, it did not fit those of the twentieth, and it certainly has no relevance for the coming century. Many new proponents of the redundance of the national state now rest their case on broader international currents. For example, Drucker (1993) speaks of the "new knowledge society" that transcends national borders. For him, internationalism, regionalism, and tribalism will shape this society, and the state's role will be relegated to that of a mere administrative instrument.

Although the case for the national state is far broader than an economic one, arguments based on economics lend support to its continued viability. Thus Taylor (1989) posits: "Without the territorial state, there would be no capitalist system. . . . In world systems analysis the inter-state system is integral to the operation of the world-economy" (169). Kennedy (1993) also holds that a nationalist-based, mercantile world order will persist.

This modern era is quite unlike the economic-imperialist era, when colonies sold low-cost extractive products and had to buy high-cost goods. As capital accumulates locally from the value added, it becomes reinvested in advancing the economy of smaller states as well as larger ones.

However, economics is not the only or major reason for the national state—the sense of belonging to something socially and territorially is even more important. The state fulfills the cultural and psychological yearnings of particular people. Even though economic and political interdependence poses a threat to national cultures, it also provides people with the strength to hold on more tightly to what they value most. For countries that have recently emerged from colonialism or in which the economy was dominated by the West, this issue is especially prominent. Edward Said (1994) cogently observed that there is need for a reconquest of space through a new, decolonized identity. Today, political control of their own territory permits the nations of the former colonial world to be selective in what they accept of western culture and in what they reject.

That national state sovereignty varies in its functions and powers within the international system reflects the strength of decentralization forces as well as the power of globalism and world regionalism. There is no question that what transpires within a national state is increasingly influenced by international ideological movements, such as environmental and human rights, by global economic institutions and multinational corporations, by the internationalization of politics through foreign moneys and other forms of pressure by the world financial markets, and by the media. But the state can turn these forces to its advantage in achieving its own goals. In the last analysis, the national state remains the glue of the international system, the major mechanism that enables a people to achieve a self-realization inextricably bound to with its sense of territoriality.

GEOPOLITICAL STRUCTURE

The *geo* in geopolitics starts with spatial structure. This structure is a complex of spatially overlapping units: geostrategic realms, geopolitical regions, nation-states, and subnational areas such as provinces, metropolitan areas, cities, and their subdivisions. These differing political territorial components are filters for the increasingly important transnational forces, the movement of which helps to knit together the world system, sometimes increasingly at the expense of preexisting connections. As specific levels of the system develop, such as the "global city" or the geopolitical region, they can derive strength through interaction with one another or with other levels, or they can drain strength from them. Map 1 depicts the current world structure of realms and regions that is organized around such a shared-power system.

Geostrategic Realms

The highest level of the global structure comprises its two geostrategic realms: the Trade-Dependent Maritime Realm and the Eurasian Continental Realm. A realm is a part of the world large enough to possess globally influential characteristics and functions that serve the strategic needs of the major powers and states with which they are politically and economically linked. It is a framework shaped by circulation patterns linking people, goods, and ideas. Control of strategically located land and sea passageways holds the framework together.

In broad historic terms, the character of the Maritime Realm has been shaped by exchange. Such forces as mercantilism, capitalism, and industrialization gave rise to the modern national state and to economic and political colonialism. Access to the sea facilitates circulation, and moderate coastal climates have made for relative ease of living conditions that aid economic development. The open systems of this realm facilitate the struggle for democracy, and immigration spawns pluralistic societies.

The Eurasian Continental Realm, in contrast, is inward oriented and less dependent on outside economic forces or cultural contacts. Until the mid–twentieth century, land and inland river travel were the major modes of transportation. The self-sufficient nature of the economy, belated entrance into the industrial age, and lack of sea access to world resources all contributed to politically closed systems and societies. Highly centralized and generally despotic forms of government through the ages became breeding grounds for the emergence of communism in the cores of the realm.

Dependence on international trade also differentiates the states of the Continental and Maritime Realms. The continentality that pervades the Eurasian Realm is both a physical and a psychological condition. Russia and North and most of Central China have been hemmed in historically. Even when technology alters the previous reality (as in the Soviet space conquests), the earlier mentality persists. The breakup of the Soviet Union and the United States–led plans to expand NATO into Central and possibly Eastern Europe surely now reinforce this feeling of isolation among the Russians. One should not underestimate the ambivalence of China over Hong Kong as its most important opening to the world. Even though it serves as China's major vehicle for investment capital for its industries and for expanding international trade, it also represents the threat of political and cultural penetration by the Maritime Realm via Southeast China, the only portion of China that historically and culturally has been characterized by a maritime outlook.

The rift between the two Continental powers, China and the Soviet Union, that took place during the late 1950s and early 1960s was caused by more than differences of ideology and strategy; it was also based on China's resentment at being treated as a subordinate by the Soviet Union. Today, however, the two nations are clearly equals; indeed, until Russia regroups, China is in many ways the more dominant. Ultimately the differences will narrow, given Russia's nuclear arsenal and large pool of scientific and technological personnel, its higher resource-to-population ratio, its more advanced economy, and its exposure to western innovations. Now that the two powers are approaching each other from a position of parity, western cold-war policies based on splitting China from Russia need to be reconsidered. The two share the split-personality, amity-enmity relationship of intimate neighbors. As great as their differences may be, both are mutually vulnerable along their lengthy frontier and feel the need to prevent containment by the Maritime world. V. P. Lukin, chair of the Foreign Affairs Committee of the Russian Parliament, put it succinctly (1997, A3): "We are simply doomed to develop strategic relations with China. We are close neighbors and would like to survive." Expanding trade and the 1997 agreement between the two countries to settle border disputes is recognition of their mutual interests.

This reflects the perception that the Eurasian Continental Realm is in danger of being penetrated from all sides because of its vulnerability to U.S.–led strategic pressures. For Russians, the penetration is now being spearheaded by NATO's political-military intrusion into its western borderlands. For China, the military threat is exacerbated by

the economic muscle of its Offshore Asia neighbors and by the growing dependence of its industrial base on western capital and trade.

The Soviet victory in World War II once again pushed the boundary of the Continental Realm westward to the Elbe River as Germany
was divided. Now, with the rollback of the Iron Curtain and the dismantling of the Warsaw Pact, the boundary is being moved eastward
by Maritime world pressures. Russia is in no position militarily or
economically to stop NATO's expansion. There are limits to how far
the boundary can be pushed, however. Despite U.S. pledges of support
for the aspirations of the three Baltic states to join NATO (as expressed in the U.S.–Baltic States Charter of Partnership), the caution
with which NATO is treating membership applications from these
states, as well as from Romania and Bulgaria, is based on recognition
of the primacy of Russian strategic interests in the Eastern Baltic and
Black Seas.

Although the former Soviet republics in the Caucasus and Central
Asia have gained their independence, they are not free of Heartlandic
Russia's strategic oversight. Western, Iranian, Afghan, are South Asian
pressures are not likely to shake Russian control of the region. Resolving disputes in the Crimea and Transnistria and mediating the
conflicts in Georgia, Armenia, Azerbaijan, and Tajikistan remain
Russian responsibilities into which the West has not intruded. Moreover, western investors in the oil and gas industries of Azerbaijan,
Turkmenistan, and Kazakhstan need Russia's cooperation to maintain
access these resources.

The scramble among U.S., European, and Japanese oil companies
to gain positions in the wealthy oil areas of the Caspian Sea has drawn
the West into Central Asian geopolitics. Former American foreign policymakers like Henry Kissinger, James Baker, and Zbigniew Brzezinski, as well as prominent Europeans, constitute an increasingly powerful lobby for challenging Russian geopolitical dominance over
Azerbaijan, Kazakhstan, and Turkmenistan. The major foci of that
challenge are proposed pipelines to bypass Russian territory. Baku, the
Caucasus Mountains, Turkey and the Gulf of Iskenderun, and even
Afghanistan-Pakistan have all been suggested as routes to break Russia's spatial monopoly. So has Iran, although the United States is
strongly opposed to such a route. This is a dangerous political game.

Penetration of the Central Asian portion of the Heartland by the West may succeed as a short-term strategy, but in the long run it is likely to boomerang and lead to Russian countermeasures, not only in Central Asia but also in the Middle East and Eastern Europe.

At the southeastern end of the Continental Realm, the withdrawal of American and Soviet power from the Indochinese arena has given China the opportunity to extend its East Asian sphere of influence southward. China has major differences with Vietnam, especially over territorial waters that hold gas and oil reserves, but it is unlikely to plunge into conflict with its battle-hardened neighbor. On the other hand, Vietnam, as well as Laos and Cambodia, are scarcely in a position to challenge their northern neighbor's strategic pressures.

In the northeast, a reunified Korea allied to the United States would be viewed by both China and Russia as a serious Maritime strategic intrusion into the Continental Realm. If the two Koreas were to merge, it is likely that the two realms would come to a strategic accommodation through the withdrawal of American forces from the peninsula and the drastic reduction of the Korean armed forces. The recent Russo-Japanese agreement to settle the issue of the southern Kuril Islands and to sign a peace agreement strengthens the prospects for overall regional accommodation.

Geopolitical Regions

Geopolitical regions are the second-highest level of the world geopolitical structure (see Map 1 and Table 1). Most regions are subdivisions of realms, although some may be caught between or are independent of them. Regions are united not only by geographical contiguity and close political, cultural, and military interactions but also by the historical migration and intermixture of peoples and by shared histories of national emergence. The regions of the Maritime Realm currently are Anglo-America and the Caribbean, Maritime Europe and the Maghreb, Offshore Asia, South America, and Sub-Saharan Africa. Within the Eurasian Continental Realm are the Russian Heartland and East Asia. The independent geopolitical region of South Asia, the Middle East shatterbelt, and a potential East European Gateway Region complete this geopolitical level.

Map 1. **Geostrategic Realms and Geopolitical Regions —**
End of the Twentieth Century

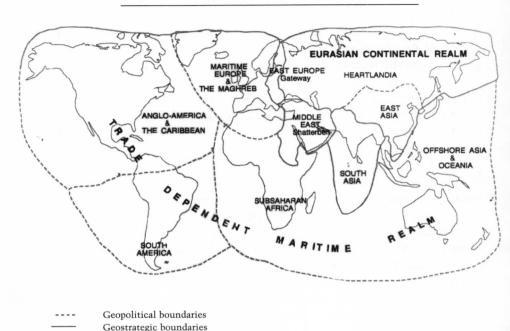

---- Geopolitical boundaries
—— Geostrategic boundaries

Distinctions between realm and region are distinctions between the strategic and the tactical. States can operate at both levels of the hierarchy and thus maintain dual levels of orientation. For example, Australia is part of both the Maritime Realm and the Offshore Asia Region. By belonging to both realm and region, it is able to benefit from the two settings. Strategically Australia is a crucial link within the Maritime Realm's global network. Culturally, politically, and ethnically it retains its historic British roots as well as its World War II–born ties to the United States. Economically, its trade with Offshore Asia—60 percent of its exports are so oriented—is a source of considerable strength.

The world geopolitical map is continuously evolving. In a dynamic world, the geopolitical framework is subject to both prominent and subtle changes. Sub-Saharan Africa was a shatterbelt during the

1970s and 1980s, that is, a region highly fragmented by its internal divisions whose divisions are exacerbated by the competing pressures from outside great powers. In southern Africa, the fragmentation was compounded by the intrusive actons of South Africa. With the collapse of the Soviet Union and the pullback of China from its ambitious efforts in East Africa, Sub-Saharan Africa has been returned to the strategic sphere of the Maritime Realm. Although the subregional differences currently have little overall significance, it is possible that southern Africa—under the leadership of a strong South Africa—and West Africa—under a stable and revitalized Nigeria—will become separate geopolitical regions that also embrace Central Africa.

The ephemeral nature of shatterbelts is demonstrated by what has happened in Southeast Asia, a shatterbelt that emerged after World War II. It is disappearing as a separate geopolitical unit, as its island and southern peninsular portions merge into Offshore Asia economically and politically. On the other hand, former Indochina, no longer under Soviet influence, is being pulled strategically toward East Asia. The geopolitical future of Myanmar is less predictable. When it emerges from its current isolation, it could join either Southeast Asia or South Asia.

The development of geopolitical regions, coupled with the disappearance of Shatterbelts, is making a substantial contribution to the stability of the global system. Within Continental Eurasia, when China broke away from Soviet domination to assert its East Asian independence, the Soviets' refusal to back China's threats against Taiwan and to support its 1959 border war with India were important in limiting these conflicts, as well as in acting as a restraint on Soviet African ambitions.

The emergence of Maritime Europe was of similar importance in limiting American hegemonic control over the Maritime Realm. In reaction to its loss of global power and its economic and military dependence on the United States, postwar Europe began to build a series of economic and political institutions with an eye to regaining its strength through regional unity. As a renewed center of geopolitical power, Europe was able to reestablish its influence in strategically important areas (Parker 1983). Although its involvement in the Middle East remained limited, its postcolonial relations with Africa (the Yaounde Convention of 1963 and the Lome Convention of 1973)

Heartland	Russia	Ukraine	—	Russian Far East	—	Chechnya, Crimea, Tuva, Yakutia (Sakha Rep.), N.-NE. Siberia	Slavonic Antata (Russia, Belarus, Ukraine, Kazakhstan); Great Turkestan (Uzbekistan, Tajikistan, Kyrgyzstan, Turkmenistan)
East Asia	China	Vietnam	—	Hong Kong-Shenzhen (new city)-Coastal Guangdong-Fujian	—	Tibet, Xinjiang	China-Taiwan
South Asia	—	India, Pakistan	—	Pashtutnistan, Punjab, Tamil Eelam-Nadu	—	Baluchistan, Kashmir, Kerala, Nagaland, Northern Myanmar	Pakistan-Afghanistan
Middle East	—	Egypt, Israel, Iran, Iraq, Turkey	Bahrain, Cyprus	Mount Lebanon, Palestine (West Bank-Gaza Strip)	—	Khuzistan-Southern Iraq, Kurdistan	Southern Arabia-Persian Gulf, Syria-Lebanon-Iraq
Central and East European Gateway	—	Poland	Estonia, Latvia, Finland, Slovenia	—	—	Transylvania, Transnistria	Baltic nations, Bosnia-Croatia-Serbia
Sub-Saharan Africa	—	Nigeria, South Africa	Djibouti	Eritrea, Zanzibar	Mayotte, Réunion	Cabinda, Cape Provinces, Northern Somalia, Shaba, Southern Sudan	

Table 10.1
The World Geopolitical System in the Twenty-First Century

Region	Major Powers	Second-Order Powers [22]	Existing Gateways [17]	New Gateways [25]	New Postcolonial [12]	New Rejectionists-Separatists [31]	New Confederations [11]
Anglo-America	United States	Canada	—	Alaska, Bermuda, British Columbia, Hawaii, Quebec,	—	—	—
and the Caribbean		Mexico, Venezuela	Bahamas, Trinidad	Aruba-Netherlands Antilles, North Mexico, Puerto Rico	Cayman Islands, Fr. Guiana, Guadeloupe, Martinique, St. Martin	Eastern Nicaragua	Colombia-Venexzuela, Westindia
South America	—	Argentina, Brazil	—	—	—	Southern Brazil	—
Maritime Europe-Maghreb	European Union	Algeria	Andorra, Luxembourg, Malta, Monaco, Finland Madeira Islands,	Azores, Catalonia, Northern Ireland, Vascongadas (Basque country), Gibraltar	Canary Islands	Brittany, Crete, Greenland, Scotland, Sicily	—
Offshore Asia	Japan	Australia, Indonesia, South Korea, Thailand	Hong Kong, Taiwan, Singapore	Guam, Southwestern Australia	American Samoa, French Polynesia, Northern Caledonia, Northern Mariana Islands	East Timor, Ryukyu Islands, Sulu Islands-Southwestern Mindanao, West Irian	China-Taiwan

marked the return of Maritime Europe as an influential power there. Moreover, Willy Brandt's 1970 *Ostpolitik,* which normalized West Germany's relationships with the German Democratic Republic, Poland, and the Soviet Union and increased Western European trade with the eastern bloc, put a damper on American capacities to dictate cold-war policies. Europe also acted as a restraint on U.S. arms policies that would have expanded the war in Bosnia, has taken independent positions on trade with Iran and Cuba, and is taking an active petroleum-development role in Iraq and Iran over U.S. objections.

The emergence of South Asia as an independent geopolitical region began with the role that India played in mediating the Korean War. India then openly rejected pressures by both the United States and the Soviet Union to join their respective blocs. Its domination of South Asia was affirmed by its war victories over Pakistan, its support of Bangladesh's independence, and its influence over Nepal and Sri Lanka.

Offshore Asia developed its geopolitical unity out of regional material and human-resource complementarity, the search for capital markets, the capacity for economic growth, and mutual defense needs. The region was initially defined—in 1963—as extending from South Korea to Japan, Taiwan, the Philippines, Australia, and New Zealand. Since then it has expanded to include Indonesia, Singapore, Malaysia, and Thailand. Granted that Offshore Asia still depends on the American military shield, nevertheless, led by Japanese capital investments and aid, the region has developed its own identity as an economic powerhouse and has taken political initiatives in Vietnam and Cambodia independent of American actions. Japan and Singapore took the initiative to organize a supplementary fund in conjunction with the bailout by the International Monetary Fund of the Indonesian economy during the financial crisis of 1997. Japan's resistance to U.S. pressures to open its markets wide is another example. Offshore Asia's emergence has clearly affected the balance within the Maritime Realm, increasing the pressure on the United States to seek consensus with the other two regional power centers. Despite the region's present financial difficulties, the inherent strength of Japan, whose economic policies have been so instrumental in undermining the region's economies, will ultimately be the leading factor in the restoring offshore Asia to health.

A legitimate question is whether the enhanced role of geopolitical regions may become a factor that will divide, not help unite, the world system. For example, fears have been expressed that a united Europe, especially if it establishes a common currency and an independent military mechanism, may raise barriers against the rest of the world. Although there is some basis for such concern, there are powerful off-setting forces. The special relationships that individual Western European powers have historically enjoyed with such areas as the Maghreb, Central and Eastern Europe, Latin America, and the Middle East mitigate against the notion of a "Fortress Europa." So do the historical, cultural, and political-military bonds that link Europe to the North Atlantic world. Indeed, pressure is growing in the European Union to expand world trade in order to cope with the unemployment that accompanies the downsizing of inefficient industries.

Second-Order Powers

Second-order powers are a relatively new element in the geopolitical structure. Since I first discussed them in 1976, some of them have clearly established their capacities to influence events within their regions.

The emergence of such states has had an important impact on the global system (see Map 2). However, these states are still evolving, and their status remains fluid. To be a second-order power, a country must not only possess military and economic capacities and ease of access to the rest of the region but also have the will to exercise regional influence. Moreover, its neighbors must be willing to engage with it. For example, South Africa was a regional power in a negative sense while it was ruled by whites. It supported rebel forces trying to overthrow the governments of its newly independent neighbors. Now that it is governed by native Africans, its influence is welcomed by them. It has taken the lead in training a small, all-African peacekeeping force, and President Nelson Mandela has played a major role in seeking to mediate the Congo rebellion that led to Mobutu Sese Seko's overthrow (although he failed to stop the fighting in the 1998 uprising against President Kabila). In addition, its investments are becoming dominant in southern African country economies. Until Israel achieves peace with its neighbors, it too will not be received by its neighbors as a full-fledged regional power.

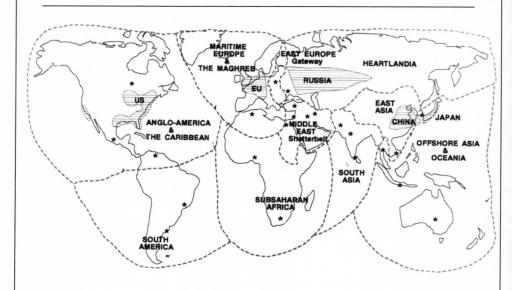

Map 2. **National Sovereignty and Geopolitical Regions in the Twenty-First Century**

- - - -   Geopolitical boundaries
★   Second order powers

▦   Major power cores

	Major Powers (5)	2nd Order Powers (22)
Anglo-America & the Caribbean	US	Canada, Mexico, Venezuela
South America	——	Argentina, Brazil
Maritime Europe / Maghreb	EU	Algeria
Offshore Asia	Japan	Australia, Indonesia, South Korea, Thailand
Heartland	Russia	Ukraine
East Asia	China	Vietnam
South Asia	——	India, Pakistan
Middle East	——	Egypt, Israel, Iran, Iraq,
Central & East Europe Gateway	——	Turkey, Poland
SubSaharan Africa	——	Nigeria, South Africa

Some second-order states, like Canada, Mexico, Brazil, Sweden, India, Australia, Turkey, Iran, Egypt, Vietnam, and Indonesia, have proved their mettle. Nigeria, despite its current turmoil, is part of the group. As a regional leader, it has contributed large peacekeeping forces in Liberia and Sierra Leone. Although the possibility remains that Nigeria may break up, the haunting memory of the War of Secession between Biafra and Nigeria from 1967 to 1970 is likely to forestall another territory-based civil war.

However, Argentina, Algeria, Poland, Iraq, South Korea, Thailand, Ukraine, and Pakistan remain marginal regional players because of their current economic or military circumstances. States like former Yugoslavia, Morocco, Saudi Arabia, Cuba, and Congo (Democratic Republic of the Congo) have, as previously noted, lost their opportunity to become second-order powers because internal ethnic or religious divisiveness sapped their strength or because conflicts with their neighbors undermined their potential influence.

STATE PROLIFERATION

Geopolitical developmental theory hypothesizes that the world system moves toward ever-increasing specialization and integration of these specialized parts. The trend toward specialization is demonstrated by the proliferation of new states and by the prospects for new regional groupings. In 1970 there were 140 national states; in 1990 the number was 175; and in 1997, 193, of which 185 were members of the United Nations.

This multiplicity of states represents a quadrupling since 1939. The number should continue to increase, reaching between 250 and 275 within the next quarter-century. Paradoxically, devolution of existing states also provides long-range opportunities for new kinds of loose confederations to emerge on a basis of mutual benefit.

Proliferation of states comes from the independence of territories or the division of existing sovereign states. It often has been and will continue to be accomplished by war. Although more than 100 territories and former colonies have already achieved independence and nearly all have joined the United Nations, 43 are still dependencies. Many have very small populations and/or provide their administering powers with strategic military bases. Others are in a state of complete economic dependence and cannot afford the luxury of national independence. Those most likely to opt for independence are areas that are sufficiently rich in resources, have favorable tourist bases, and/or are financial havens. As the world becomes a more open system, the advantage that such territories currently enjoy from retaining colonial ties will decrease.

Included in Table 1 are the dozen colonial areas that are most likely to attain independence soon. Caribbean colonies can take better advantage of their location as gateways between South America and Anglo-America should they become independent, or Postcolonial entities. In the Pacific some American territories and European colonies may find independence a desirable vehicle for bridging the Pacific Rim and the West. Indeed, Guam, which has received special economic concessions from the United States, is poised to become a gateway.

Even more new states are likely to come from existing national entities. They fall into the rejectionist-separatist category. Civil and guerilla wars and active or latent political struggles for independence punctuate the map of the world—a state of turbulence likely to persist in many postindependence countries until regional integration takes hold. Table 1 and Map 3 depict those Rejectionist-Separatist areas that have the greatest chances for success. They contain peoples who operate from historic core areas in which they have maintained their cultural, linguistic, religious, or tribal distinctiveness. Many of those listed in both the rejectionist-separatist and gateway columns of Table 1 may achieve only qualified forms of independence, becoming in effect, pseudostates or stateless, because they lack the military capacity to gain their full objectives. However, far-reaching autonomy that permits independent economic and social policies and provides for separate political structural links, including membership in the United Nations, is attainable for some.

The independence-autonomy negotiations between Russia and Chechnya may provide a model for other pseudostates, as could Northern Ireland or an ultimate Israel–Palestinian Authority agreement. Similar states may also emerge from the devolution of large and ethnically religiously or linguistically diverse states such as China, Canada, Indonesia, India and Congo.

Map 3. **National Sovereignty and Geopolitical Regions in the Twenty-First Century**

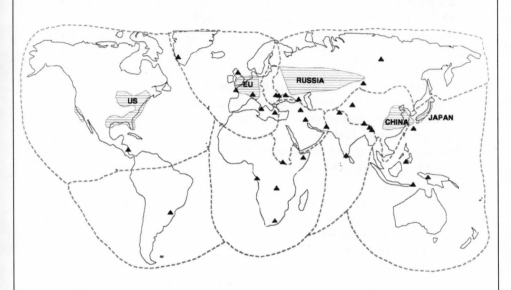

 - - - -   Geopolitical boundaries
▲   Rejectionists / separatists

           Major power cores

	Rejectionists / Separatists (31)
Anglo-America & the Caribbean	East Nicaragua
South America	S Brazil
Maritime Europe / Maghreb	Brittany, Crete, Greenland, Scotland, Sicily
Offshore Asia	E Timor, Ryukyu Is, Sulu Is / SW Mindanao, W Irlan
Heartland	Chechnya, Crimea, Tuva, Yakutla
East Asia	Tibet, Xinjiang
South Asia	Baluch, Kashmir, Kerala, Nagaland, N Myanmar
Middle East	Khuzistan, S Iraq / Kurdistan
Central & East Europe Gateway	Transylvania, Trans-Dniestria
SubSaharan Africa	Cabinda, Cape Provinces, N Somalia, Shaba, S Sudan

GATEWAY STATES

Gateways are the third category of potential new states. They play novel roles as nodes in integrating regional and world systems. Seventeen countries already serve as gateways, and prospects exist for the establishment of an additional twenty-five (see Map 4 and Table 1). The distinguishing characteristics of the modern gateway are strategic locations to promote economic exchange and the unhampered political capacity to do so by having sovereign status.

Examples of gateways can be found in both history and the present era. Sheba, Tyre, Nabatea, and Palmyra were gateways, as were the Hanseatic League and the Lombard city- states. Today Andorra, the Bahamas, Bahrain, Djibouti, Finland, Luxembourg, Malta, Monaco, Singapore, Slovenia, Trinidad, and, in its special political status, Hong Kong are examples of gateway or exchange sovereignties. A common characteristic of gateways is that all are endowed with strong, entrepreneurial traditions with links to different parts of their regions, and often the globe. These links are often strengthened by ties to overseas communities.

Gateways have the further advantage of starting from bases of relative prosperity. Small in area and population, gateways can aspire to sovereignty because they are not military threats to their present hosts, although the latter are likely to require security guarantees that they not become bases for threats from foreign countries. In addition to gateway states, gateway cities such as Rotterdam (Europort) and gateway regions such as the eastern Baltic also contribute to integration of the global system.

Proposed gateways within the European Union can attain a sovereignty somewhere between home rule, or the right to run local affairs in the sense of the European concept of "subsidiarity," and an independence free of host-state restraints. For example, in claiming nationhood, the Catalans and the Basques aspire to a Europe of regions that are parallel mechanisms to the states in which they are located. Both demand control of language, labor, social security, pensions, local taxation, and a higher proportion of the taxes levied by Spain as they strive to achieve a nationhood that would go well beyond Spain's 1979 Statute of Autonomy.

Map 4. **Gateways and Geopolitical Regions in the Twenty-First Century**

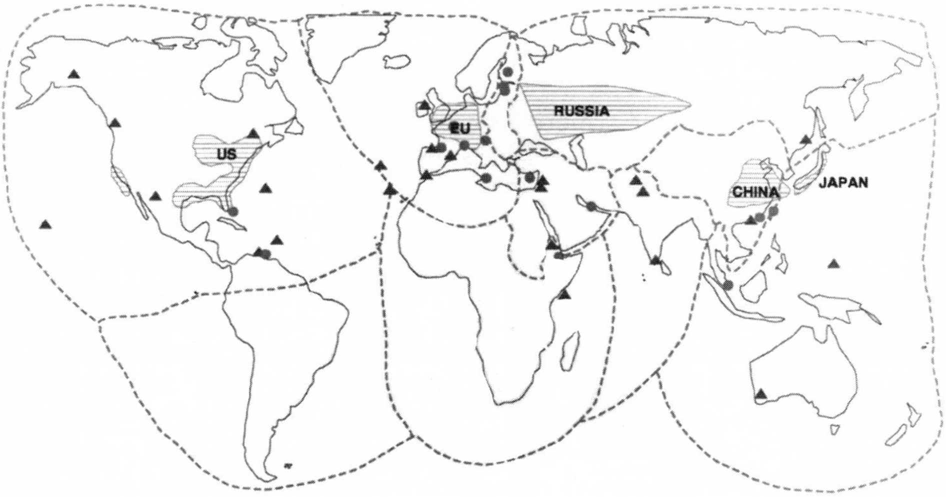

---- Geopolitical boundaries
▲ New Gateways
● New postcolonial

Major power cores

	New Gateways (25)	Existing Gateways (17)
Anglo-America & The Caribbean	Alaska, Bemuda, British Columbia, Hawaii, Quebec Aruba / Neth Antilles, N Mexico, Puerto Rico	Bahamas / Trinidad
South America	——	——
Maritime Europe / Maghreb	Azores, Catalonia, N Ireland, Madeira Is, Vascongadas, Gibraltar	Andorra, Luxembourg, Malta, Monaco, Finland
Offshore Asia	Guam, SW Australia	Hong Kong, Singapore, Taiwan
Heartland	Russian Far East	——
East Asia	Hong Kong / Guangdong / Fujian	——
South Asia	Pashtunistan / Punjab, Tamil Eelam / Nadu	——
Middle East	Mt. Lebanon, Palestine (W Bank / Gaza)	Bahrain, Cyprus
Central & East Europe Gateway	——	Estonia, Finland, Latvia, Slovenia
SubSaharan Africa	Eritrea, Zanzibar	Djibouti

PROSPECTS FOR GEOPOLITICAL RESTRUCTURING

Prospects for substantial changes in the world geopolitical structure hinge on the course of events in the Middle East, Turkey, Central and Eastern Europe, China, and the Caribbean. The end of the Cold war signaled the possible beginning of the geopolitical transformation of the Middle East from a shatterbelt to two separate regions. Its western half may become affixed to Maritime Europe, creating a new "Euro-Mediterranea," while its eastern half operates as a small, independent unit or is merged with lands to its north or east. Now that Russia has retreated from its role as a regional intervener, the West is free to seek solutions that will bring a measure of unity to the Mediterranean and Arabian parts of the region.

The prospective geopolitical region of Ero-Mediterranea would be a reincarnation of the Roman Mediterranean-Atlantic world, with boundaries extended into Central Europe (see Map 5). Harbinger of such a region is the Euro-Mediterranean Partnership established at Barcelona between members of the European Union and countries of the Eastern and Western Mediterranean. Euro-Mediterranea would coalesce around two sprawling industrial–postindustrial cores—the English Channel–Rhine axis and the Gulf of Valencia–Gulf of Genoa axis. Creation of such a region depends, however, on Turkey's remaining oriented to the West and NATO and on resolution of the Arab-Israeli conflict. At present the peace process has been markedly slowed down, though not derailed.

If the Middle East were to divide geopolitically, the states from the Tigris-Euphrates through The Iranian Plateau might join with western and northern Afghanistan and Tajikistan to form a separate Islamic Bloc under Iranian hegemony. Iran's role as a strong regional power would be pivotal if it could resolve the religious differences with its Sunni neighbors. Were such an Islamic bloc to emerge, the Arabian peninsula and particularly Saudi Arabia's Eastern Province, would become a small shatterzone, and the new Islamic region would seek geopolitical status independent of both the maritime and the Eurasian continental realms. Possibilities for other significant restructuring are raised in the form of the following questions, although space does not permit them to be discussed here.

Map 5. Prospective Geopolitical and Gateway Regions in the Twenty-First Century

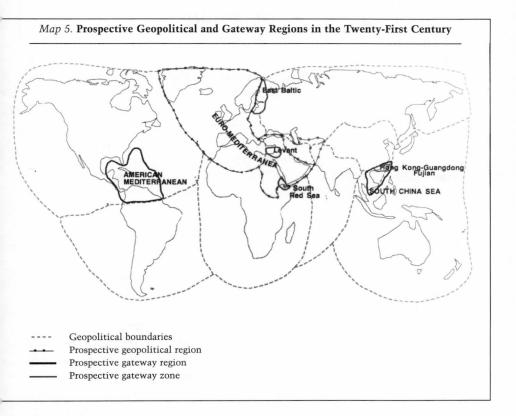

- - - - Geopolitical boundaries
—•—•— Prospective geopolitical region
▬▬▬▬ Prospective gateway region
———— Prospective gateway zone

1. Turkey—if rejected by the European Union (EU), will it become oriented to the Eurasian Continental realm-either in alliance with Russia, or as part of a new Western Asian Islamic geopolitical region?
2. Central and Eastern Europe—will it realize its potential to become a Gateway region, or become geostrategically redivided between the Maritime European and Russian Heartland regions?
3. China: Will it remain intact as a Eurasian Continental region with a strong Maritime component, or will it split, with its south and central coastlands joining Offshore Asia?
4. Central America and the Caribbean: Can it become a gateway, bridging Anglo-America, South America, and Maritime Europe?

CONCLUSION

The developing international geopolitical system is in equilibrium because of its dynamism, and because of the openness of its diverse parts to the flows of people, goods, and ideas—be these parts national states and their subsections, geopolitical regions, or geostrategic realms. It works because it has ever-increasing numbers of units and optional channels of movement that permit the network to bypass chokeholds.

The nodes of the systems vary in scale and importance. They include the major and second-order powers and the gateways that are, in effect, the routers that tie the layering of distributed networks into a seamless web. The regional powers and the gateways play increasingly critical roles in stabilizing the system.

As states specialize, reaching out for more markets and sources of capital and raw materials, they become increasingly free of dependence on one major or regional power, and the number of political and economic links that radiate from a single node increases. Today's approximately 200 sovereign states probably have an average of eight substantial international links, and the world's system has 1,600 links. By the end of the next quarter-century, as many as 250 to 275 sovereign states may exist, each with an average of ten links, making for a system total of from 2,500 to 2,750. Clearly, disruptions in flows of the earlier international network had a greater destabilizing effect on the system as a whole than they do in today's world, where greater options are available for redirecting links. The denser and more complex the network, the greater the stability.

The aftermath of the cold war does not mean a world free of tension and, sometimes, intense conflict. However, it does mean a world of turbulence in which conflict is geographically contained and of shorter duration and the complex geopolitical framework of which serves as a facilitator of, not a barrier to, international accommodation.

The first half of the twentieth century was the era of great powers, and the second half was dominated by the two superpowers. The twenty-first century, in contrast, will be an era of power sharing among a wide variety of states of different sizes and functions. The hierarchy of states that binds the system will be flexible, not rigid. Although the major powers of the world will continue to dominate the international system, their leadership will be measured by ability to initiate and then find consensus, not by dominance. To recognize that the coming century will be the era of power sharing is to understand geopolitical realities and to build on these realities to craft a stronger, more integrated international system.

REFERENCES

Bertalanffy, Von L. 1968. *General Systems Theory*. New York: Brazillier.

Brzezinski, Z. 1993. *Out of Control: Global Turmoil on the Eve of the 21st Century*. New York: Scribner's / Robert Stewart.

———. 1997. *The Grand Chessboard: American Primacy and Its Geopolitical Imperatives*. New York: Basic Books.

Cohen, S. B. 1963. *Geography and Politics in a World Divided*. New York: Random House; repr. London: Methuen, 1964; 2d ed. repr. New :York: Oxford University Press, 1973.

———. 1982. "A New Map of Global Geopolitical Equilibrium: A Development Approach." *Political Geography Quarterly* 1: 223–241.

———. 1984. "Asymmetrical States and Global Geopolitical Equilibrium." *SAIS Review* 4: 193–212.

———. 1990. "The World Geopolitical System, in Retrospect and Prospect." *Journal of Geography* 89, no. 1: 1–12.

———. 1991. "Global Geopolitical Change in the Post–Cold War Era." *Annals of the Association of American Geographers* 81: 551–580.

———. 1994. "Geopolitics in the New World Era: A New Perspective on an Old Discipline." In *Reordering the World: Geopolitical Perspectives on the 21st Century*, edited by George J. Demko and William B. Wood. Rev. ed. 1998, in press. Boulder, Colo.: Westview Press.

Drucker, P. 1993. *Post Capitalist Society*. New York: Harper Business.

Fukuyama, F. 1992. *The End of History and the Last Man*. New York: Free Press.

Heslin, S. 1997. "The New Pipeline Politics." *New York Times*, November 10, A31.

Huntington, S. 1996. *The Clash of Civilizations and the Remaking of World Order*. New York: Simon and Schuster.

Kennedy, P. 1987. *The Rise and Fall of the Great Powers*. New York: Random House.

———. 1993. *Preparing for the Twenty-First Century*. New York: Random House

Lukács, J. 1993. *The End of the Twentieth Century and the End of the Modern Age*. New York: Ticknor and Fields.

Lukin, V. P. 1997. Quoted in the *New York Times*, April 24, A3.

Mackinder, Halford. 1919. *Democratic Ideals and Reality*. New York: Henry Holt; repr. New York: W. W. Norton.

———. 1943. "The Round World and the Winning of the Peace." *Foreign Afairs* 21: 595–605.

Parker, G. 1983. *A Political Geography of Community Europe*. London: Butterworths.

Said, Edward. 1994. *Culture and Imperialism*. New York: Vintage Books.

Taylor, P. J. 1989. *Political Geography, World-Economy, Nation- State and Locality*. 2d ed. New York: Longman Scientific and Technical.

Werner, H. 1948. *Comparative Psychology of Mental Development*. Rev. ed. New York: International University Press.

Whittlesey, D. 1939. *The Earth and the State*. New York: Henry Holt.

SELECTED BIBLIOGRAPHY

Agnew, John, and Stuart Corbridge. 1995. *Mastering Space: Hegemony, Territory, and International Political Economy*. London: Rutledge.

Allcock, J., G. Arnold, A. Day, D. S. Lewis, L. Poultney, R. Rance, and D. J. Sagar. 1992. *Border and Territorial Disputes*. Rev. 3rd ed. London: Longman.

Bremer, Stuart. 1992. "Dangerous Dyads: Conditions Affecting the Likelihood of Interstate War, 1816–1965." *Journal of Conflict Resolution* 36: 309–41.

Cohen, Saul. 1973. *Geography and Politics in a World Divided*. 2nd ed. New York: Random House.

Cohen, Saul, 1982. "A New Map of Global Geopolitical Equilibrium: A Developmental Approach." *Political Geography Quarterly* 1: 223–41.

Diehl, Paul F., ed. 1996. "Territorial Dimensions of International Conflict." *Conflict Management and Peace Science* 15 (special issue): 1–112.

———. 1991. "Geography and War: A Review and Assessment of the Empirical Literature." *International Interactions* 17: 121–37.

———. 1985. "Contiguity and Military Escalation in Major Power Rivalries, 1816–1980." *Journal of Politics* 47: 1203–11.

Duchacek, Ivo. 1986. *The Territorial Dimension of Politics: Within, among, and across Nations*. Boulder: Westview.

Gleditsch, Nils Petter, and J. David Singer. 1975. "Distance and International War, 1816–1965." In *Proceedings of the International Peace Research Association, Fifth General Conference*, ed. M. R. Kahn. Oslo: International Peace Research Association.

Goertz, Gary, and Paul F. Diehl. 1992. *Territorial Changes and International Conflict*. London: Routledge.

Huth, Paul. 1996. *Standing Your Ground: Territorial Disputes and International Conflict*. Ann Arbor: University of Michigan Press.

Kacowicz, Arie. 1994. *Peaceful Territorial Change*. Columbia: University of South Carolina Press.

Kelly, Philip. 1986. "Escalation of Regional Conflict: Testing the Shatterbelt Concept." *Political Geography Quarterly* 5: 161–80.

Kirby, Andrew, and Michael Ward. 1987. "The Spatial Analysis of War and Peace." *Comparative Political Studies* 20: 293–313.

Koch, Howard, Robert North, and Dina Zinnes. 1960. "Some Theoretical Notes on Geography and International Conflict." *Journal of Conflict Resolution* 4: 4–14.

Kocs, Stephen. 1995. "Territorial Disputes and Interstate War, 1945–1987." *Journal of Politics* 57: 159–75.

Kratochwil, Friedrich. 1986. "Of Systems, Boundaries, and Territoriality: An Inquiry into the Formation of the State System." *World Politics* 39: 27–52.

Kratochwil, Friedrich, P. Rohrlich, and H. Mahajan. 1985. *Peace and Disputed Sovereignty: Reflections on Conflict Over Territory.* Lanham, Md: University Press of America.

Lemke, Douglas. 1995. "The Tyranny of Distance: Redefining Relevant Dyads." *International Interactions* 21: 23–38.

Mandel, Robert. 1980. "Roots of Modern Interstate Border Disputes." *Journal of Conflict Resolution* 24: 427–54.

O'Loughlin, John, and Luc Anselin. 1991. "Bringing Geography Back to the Study of International Relations: Spatial Dependence and Regional Context in Africa, 1966–1978." *International Interactions* 17: 29–61.

Roy, A. Bikash. 1998. *Blood and Soil.* Columbia: University of South Carolina Press.

Starr, Harvey, and Benjamin Most. 1976. "The Substance and Study of Borders in International Relations Research." *International Studies Quarterly* 20: 581–620.

Starr, Harvey, and Benjamin Most. 1978. "A Return Journey: Richardson, 'Frontiers,' and Wars in the 1946–1965 Era." *Journal of Conflict Resolution* 22: 441–117.

Starr, Harvey, and Benjamin Most. 1983. "Contagion and Border Effects on Contemporary African Conflicts." *Comparative Political Studies* 16: 92–117.

Starr, Harvey, and Benjamin Most. 1985. "The Forms and Processes of War Diffusion: Research Update on Contagion in African Conflict." *Comparative Political Studies* 18: 206–229.

Tir, Jaroslav, Philip Schafer, Paul F. Diehl, and Gary Goertz. 1998. "Territorial Changes, 1816–1996: Procedures and Data." *Conflict Management and Peace Science* 16: 89–97.

Vasquez, John. 1995. "Why Do Neighbors Fight?: Proximity, Interaction, or Territoriality." *Journal of Peace Research* 32: 277–93.

Ward, Michael, ed. 1992. *The New Geopolitics.* Philadelphia: Gordon and Breach.

Weede, Erich. 1973. "Nation-Environment Relations as Determinants of Hostilities Among Nations." *Peace Science Society (International) Papers* 20: 67–90.

CONTRIBUTORS

STEVEN J. BRAMS is a professor of politics at New York University. He is the author or coauthor of twelve books that involve applications of game theory and social-choice theory to voting and elections, international relations, and the Bible and theology. His two most recent books are *Theory of Moves* (Cambridge University Press, 1994) and, with Alan D. Taylor, *Fair Division: From Cake-Cutting to Dispute Resolution* (Cambridge University Press, 1996). He is a fellow of the American Association for the Advancement of Science, a Guggenheim fellow, and a past president of the Peace Science Society (International).

SAUL B. COHEN is professor emeritus of geography at Hunter College and the City University of New York. He is a past director of the Graduate School of Geography at Clark University, has served as president of Queens College, and is past president of the Association of American Geographers. He has held visiting professorships with the U.S. Naval War College and Hebrew University. He is the author or editor of eleven books and more than one hundred scholarly articles, including the three-volume *Columbia Gazetteer of the World* (Columbia University Press, 1988). His major writings are in geopolitical theory and political geography, including Jerusalem and Israel. In addition, he has helped initiate national educational curriculum reform and reorganized teacher training through the Association of American Geographers and the U.S. Department of Education. He is a member of the New York State Board of Regents, chairing the Elementary, Middle Secondary, and Continuing Education Committee.

PAUL F. DIEHL is a professor of political science at the University of Illinois, Urbana-Champaign, and has held faculty positions at the University of Georgia and the State University of New York at Albany. His recent books include *International Peacekeeping* (Johns Hopkins University Press, 1994) and, with Gary Goertz, *Territorial Changes and International Conflict* (Routledge, 1992), as well as two edited volumes, *The Dynamics of Enduring Rivalries* (University of Illinois Press, 1998) and *The Politics of Global Governance: International Organizations in an Interdependent World* (Lynne Rienner, 1997). He is the editor of seven other books and the author or more than eighty articles on international-security matters. He is the recipient of numerous grants and awards from such organizations as the National Science Foundation, the United States Institute of Peace, and the Lilly Foundation. His areas of expertise include the causes of war, U.N. peacekeeping, and international law.

DOUGLAS M. GIBLER received his doctorate in 1997 from Vanderbilt University where he also served as visiting assistant professor of political science. He is currently a lecturer in international policy studies at Stanford University. In the past three years he has published several articles related to both alliances and territorial issues in such journals as *International Studies Quarterly*, *International Interactions*, and *Conflict Management and Peace Science*.

PAUL R. HENSEL is an assistant professor of political science at Florida State University. His articles have appeared in the *Journal of Conflict Resolution*, the *Journal of Peace Research*, *International Organization*, *Conflict Management and Peace Science*, and *Political Geography*. His current research interests include territorial disputes and the evolution of militarized interstate rivalry.

PAUL K. HUTH is an associate professor of political science and senior associate research scientist at the Institute for Social Research, University of Michigan. He is the author of *Standing Your Ground: Territorial Disputes and International Conflict* (University of Michigan Press, 1996) and *Extended Deterrence and the Prevention of War* (Yale University Press, 1988). In addition, he has published articles in such journals as the *American Political Science Review*, *World Politics*, the *Journal of Conflict Resolution*, and the *International Studies Quarterly*. In 1996 he received the Karl W. Deutsch Award, and in the same year *Standing Your Ground* was co-winner of the Quincy Wright Award.

ANDREW KIRBY is a professor and the chair of social sciences at Arizona State University West, in Phoenix; he has also taught at the Universities of Arizona, Colorado, and Reading. His articles on international relations (coauthored with Michael Ward) have appeared in *Comparative Political Studies* and *International Interactions*. His most recent books are *Power/Resistance: Local Politics and the Chaotic State* (Indiana University Press, 1993) and the edited collection *The Pentagon and the Cities* (Sage Publications, 1992). He is currently serving as the editor of the international journal *Cities*. In 1996 he gave the second Elsevier Lecture on Political Geography to the Association of

American Geographers, entitled "Is the State our Enemy?" and he gave the 1997 Wilkinson Annual Lecture to the Department of Geography at the University of Reading, U.K.

DAVID NEWMAN is a professor of political geography and the founding chair of the Department of Politics and Government at Ben Gurion University of the Negev in Israel. He holds a bachelor's degree from the University of London and a doctorate from the University of Durham, U.K. He has published widely on territorial issues relating to the Arab-Israeli conflict and on theoretical issues concerning boundaries and the changing notions of territorialism. His latest book is *The Dynamics of Territorial Change: A Political Geography of the Arab-Israel Conflict* (Westview, in press). He is editor of the international journal *Geopolitics*.

PAUL D. SENESE is an assistant professor of political science at the State University of New York at Buffalo. His research on international conflict and escalation have appeared in the *Journal of Politics, Conflict Management, and Peace Science*, the *Journal of Conflict Resolution*, and *International Studies Quarterly*.

BETH SIMMONS is an associate professor of political science at the University of California, Berkeley. She is author of *Who Adjusts? Domestic Sources of Foreign Economic Policy During the Interwar Years* (Princeton University Press, 1994), which won the American Political Science Association's Woodrow Wilson Award in 1995. Recently a senior fellow at the United States Institute of Peace, her current research interests include the role of law in international relations and state compliance with international legal obligations.

JEFFREY M. TOGMAN is an assistant professor of political science at Seton Hall University and a visiting scholar at the Center for European Studies, New York University. His current research focuses on immigration policies in advanced industrialized societies.

JOHN P. VANZO is a doctoral candidate in international relations at Florida State University. He has served as a defense analyst during the Carter administration. His research interests include geopolitics and military history.

INDEX